Seduced by Science

Seduced
by Science

*How American Religion
Has Lost Its Way*

Steven Goldberg

NEW YORK UNIVERSITY PRESS
New York and London

NEW YORK UNIVERSITY PRESS
New York and London

Library of Congress Cataloging-in-Publication Data
Goldberg, Steven, 1947–
Seduced by science : how American religion has lost its way /
Steven Goldberg.
p.   cm.
Includes bibliographical references and index.
ISBN 0-8147-3104-X (alk. paper)
1. Religion and science—United States. 2. Bible and science.
I. Title.
BL240.2 .G65 1999
291.1'75—dc21   98-40190
                              CIP

New York University Press books are printed on acid-free paper,
and their binding materials are chosen for strength and durability.

Manufactured in the United States of America

10 9 8 7 6 5 4 3 2 1

In memory of my mother, Helen Goldberg

Contents

Acknowledgments

I am grateful to many colleagues for their comments on this book. I would particularly like to thank Richard Chused, Lisa Heinzerling, Jeffrie Murphy, Louis Michael Seidman, Girardeau Spann, and Mark Tushnet. I also benefited from the help of my research assistants Anne Lockner and Matthew Gardner.

The Georgetown University Law Center provided a wonderful environment for research and writing, as well as financial support in the form of writers' grants. The students in my classes kept me thinking, and the staff helped greatly every step of the way.

I received helpful suggestions during presentations of my ideas at the Center for the Study of Law, Science, and Technology at the Arizona State University College of Law; the Greenwall Fellowship Program; and the Georgetown University Law Center. An earlier version of chapter 2 of this book appeared in volume 5 of the *Southern California Interdisciplinary Law Journal*.

Finally, words cannot express my debt to Missy, Joe, and Becky.

1

Introduction

American religion has fallen into a trap. Just at the moment when it has the political strength and the legal right to participate effectively in public debate, it has lost its distinctive voice. Instead of speaking of human values, goals, and limits, it speaks the language of science.

Religious leaders claim, for example, that the science of genetics teaches us about our fundamental nature because genes are the essence of our being. Thus patenting human gene sequences must be prevented in order to stop private ownership of mankind, God's creation. And cloning must be resisted because clones share the same genes, the most important aspect of our humanity.

Some of these leaders also claim that whereas genetics explains our essential human nature, other branches of science validate the Bible. The scientific establishment will not admit it, they say, but empirical evidence supports the biblical account of creation, since a proper understanding of the Flood explains the fossil evidence we see around us. The Flood itself can be explained with modern meteorology and geology.

Furthermore, many clergy preach that scientific studies demonstrate that prayer is powerful medicine. Doctors should use it the way they use aspirin or antibiotics. Some doctors resist the use of prayer, but that is no different from their resistance to other alternative therapies such as homeopathy and acupuncture.

Religious leaders of many faiths and perspectives are making claims like these. The problem is not that these claims might be wrong from a scientific point of view. Right or wrong, they are the wrong claims to make.

The most important teachings religion offers our times—teachings about the meaning and purpose of finite human life—are not susceptible to scientific proof. When religion gives in to temptation and steps into the world of empirically testable hypotheses, it becomes just a subset of science. Some phenomena are caused by viruses, some by comets, some by God. When ministers, priests, and rabbis expound on double-blind studies and the genetic causes of behavior, they do not elevate religion. They trivialize it. Religious leaders should instead use the legal freedom they enjoy under modern interpretations of the Constitution to speak to the timeless concerns of the great faiths.

Many scientists will dispute the idea that the examples I have given, as well as those that will come later, are all drawn from the world of modern science. To most mainstream scientists, genetics is certainly scientific, but prayer as medicine may be less so, whereas the science used to validate the book of Genesis is pseudoscience at best. But from our point of view, what these fields have in common is more important than what separates them. All of them present mechanistic explanations for human behavior and the world around us. All of them crowd out spiritual concerns. Many Americans do not distinguish between mainstream scientists and other users of scientific terminology. When people of faith today are seduced by science, they are as likely to be won over by a New Age practitioner as by a Nobel Laureate. But in either case, religion loses its distinctive voice.

I realize that clergymen and people of faith do not spend all day thinking about everything from a scientific perspective. My concern in this book is those situations where religion confronts new developments in science. I believe the tendency is to read too much into those developments, to forget that fundamental matters are often unchanged by the latest results from the laboratory, and to miss the chance to add an important voice from a faith-based perspective to the public debate that follows scientific advances.

To some extent, when religious leaders respond from a scientific perspective to the latest headlines about astronomy or medicine, they are simply being faddish. They want to appear up-to-date rather than behind the times. But to a considerable degree there is a greater problem, a problem that stems from being swallowed up by the materialistic perspective that pervades our culture.

It is hardly surprising that religion is tempted by science. In the United States the scientific perspective has extraordinary influence. The Enlightenment roots of our Constitution and the progressive, optimistic nature of our national culture make America the most hospitable nation on earth for science.[1] Rightly or wrongly, we look to science not only to provide energy and medicine, but also to illuminate our understanding of economics and education and to improve our psyches with self-help movements too numerous to list. People seeking prestige for their point of view are eager to label it "scientific."

But science is powerful precisely because it is narrow. It has never claimed to be the sole judge of all that is important or sensible. In particular, science has limited utility in the field of morality. Science can tell us a lot about what *is* but precious little about what *ought to be*. Thus, religion forfeits a vital role—the exploration of values—when it speaks the language of science. Moreover, within its narrow field, science tends to be optimistic, confident that people can find definite answers to hard questions. When science oozes into other fields, that optimism can become hubris. Traditional religion, if it manages to avoid adopting the mechanistic perspective, can teach us something about humility and faith.

It is the fundamental nature of science that prevents it from teaching us about humility, values, and faith. Scientists gain knowledge about the natural world by framing and testing hypotheses. To use the terminology of Karl Popper, a philosopher regarded as having had the "largest methodological influence on actual scientists in this century,"[2] scientists are primarily concerned with those hypotheses that can be falsified by a negative result. The statement "Small objects fall toward the earth" is a scientific hypothesis because it can be tested. With each favorable result we become more confident of its truth. Most importantly, however, we are willing to reject the hypothesis if our tests show that objects fall away from the earth. Thus, the statement "The moon is made entirely of green cheese" is also a scientific hypothesis, since it can be (and has been) falsified.

By contrast, the statement "God exists" is not scientific, because it is not subject to empirical testing. But that does not mean, either logically, historically, or in any other sense, that the statement "God exists" is wrong or nonsensical. As Popper himself wrote, falsifiability is

> *a criterion of demarcation between empirical science on the one hand and pure mathematics, logic, metaphysics, and pseudo-science on the other.* . . . The broad line of demarcation between empirical science . . . and . . . metaphysics . . . has to be drawn right through the very heart of the region of sense—with meaningful theories on both sides of the dividing line—rather than between the region of sense and nonsense.[3]

Quite a few interesting and important statements are not scientific—statements about what is good and right and moral, for example, as well as statements about what we cannot know. It is here that religion can add the most to American public discourse. But at present, too many religious leaders are too busy working in the vineyards of science.

In the second half of the nineteenth century, many religious leaders made a similar mistake. Faced with the spread of science, industrialization, and capitalism, they dealt with those forces by embracing them.[4] As James Turner has argued, church leaders actually made it easier for people to drop their belief in God because the leaders "too often forgot the transcendence essential to any worthwhile God. . . . [I]n trying to meet the challenges of modernity, they virtually surrendered to it."[5] Today, with a hunger for spiritual meaning reasserting itself throughout our society, there is a danger that instead of satisfying that hunger with teachings about faith and values, clergy will feed it with ultimately unsatisfying mechanistic models.

This book describes the unfortunate tilt of the Judeo-Christian perspective toward science and calls for a redirection back to the central moral concerns where that perspective has the most to offer.

We begin with three dramatic instances of religion's flirtation with science. Chapter 2 concerns the involvement of religious leaders in the debates over the patenting of the human genome. Leaders of all of the major denominations have denounced the idea that patents should be available for those who discover important sequences of human genetic material. Opposition to patenting may or may not be well founded in terms of the traditional goals of intellectual property law—this area abounds with difficult questions about how we can create the best incentives for medical breakthroughs. But the religious opposition is troubling not because of legal questions but because of the basis of that opposition: patenting should be banned because genes define who we are. One might expect unsophisticated agnostics to make that assumption, not the leaders of faiths that have long believed that humans are more than the sum of their physical parts. The same confusion marks some of the religious response to the possibility of cloning a human being. There are many good reasons to oppose such cloning, but when religious leaders tell us that a cloned human would be identical to another or that he would lack a soul, they are again buying into a shockingly materialistic view of human nature.

Chapter 3 explores the incursions of science into religious understandings of the Bible. Here it tends to be more fundamentalist religions that have taken the bait. Modern creation scientists try to provide a scientific basis for Genesis and thus, among other things, to discredit the theory of evolution. The science they use is problematic, but their bigger mistake is in how they use it. There is a remarkable contrast here with William Jennings Bryan and other early fundamentalists. For Bryan the central questions raised by evolution concerned human morality, and his disputes with science were correspondingly narrow. Modern creation scientists are so taken with the scientific model that they deflect attention away from fundamental moral issues and into matters concerning carbon dating and plate tectonics. For some creation scientists the Bible becomes a science text. From that perspective, it is just another book. It is a strange notion indeed that the Bible needs to be elevated by association with science.

Chapter 4 analyzes the new obsession with the medical power of prayer, an obsession that has spread far into mainstream religion. Ministers have praised scientific studies designed to measure whether prayer can cure disease. The results to date are controversial, but the prospects for success cannot be dismissed out of hand. We still have a great deal to learn about the mind-body connection, and science may someday reach a consensus that prayer is one of those things that can improve our health. But there is real danger here if religion is to be anything more than just another therapy like meditation or biofeedback—useful for arthritis, not indicated for pancreatic cancer. There is another, far more distinctive, far more powerful set of ideas behind prayer—ideas about acceptance and peace and inner understanding—that are threatened by the medical model. Those ideas will be quickly forgotten if people of faith come to treat prayer only as medicine.

The next set of chapters explores the legal framework in which religion can participate in American public discourse. This exploration is vital because some of the impetus behind religion's seduction by science appears to be the unfounded belief that unless religion is garbed in secular clothing it cannot enter the public square.

Chapter 5 explains how the free speech and due process protections in the Constitution protect the right of religious Americans to speak out and preach their faith, as well as the right to educate their children in private, religious schools. Religious leaders sometimes employ the currently fashionable rhetoric of victimization, acting as though religion is threatened in America, even comparing the status of believers with the status of slaves before the Civil War. No one benefits from this sort of misunderstanding of American law.

Chapter 6 explores the Constitution's protection of the free exercise of religion. The Supreme Court has made clear that the content of traditional religious belief—in particular, the nonscientific articles of faith that underlie religion—are beyond the power of the government to regulate. Moreover the Court has emphasized that religious practices cannot be suppressed simply because people in power disagree with them or find them offensive. Difficult questions arise concerning whether the government can apply neutral laws, such as those that criminalize drug use, against religious practices that violate those laws. Under present law, government can restrict religion that way, and Congress's attempt to change that approach through the Religious Freedom Restoration Act has been struck down. But the government is free to accommodate religious practices that would otherwise violate the law, and it has often done so.

Chapter 7 concerns the constitutional requirement that religion not be established by the state. Here the legal situation is admittedly complex. There are substantial limits on the ability of religion to play a role in public school curricula or to introduce prayer into the public school day. But those limits may well serve the best interests of religion in the long run, since religion in the public schools would be religion subject to public control. The voucher issue illustrates the problem. Similarly, religious displays supported by the government often create more risks than benefits. Recent judicial decisions suggest that public observance of Good Friday comes at a substantial cost—if the warm embrace of government is not resisted, Good Friday may become as secularized as Christmas.

Chapter 8 addresses a widespread misunderstanding about the role of religious arguments in political debate. There is no legal restriction on the use of such arguments, as American history from the slavery controversy through the civil rights movement demonstrates. Modern judicial decisions concerning abortion reaffirm this point. The issue is not whether religion has the right to be heard; the issue is what it will say. Abortion again provides an example, since on some occasions people of faith on both sides of that issue have fallen into the trap of believing that a scientific discovery can resolve what, in the end, is a moral question.

Having completed a survey of the legal terrain, we will be able to turn to where religion should be headed. Chapter 9 sets forth a positive vision of the contribution religion can make to American discourse. There is, of course, no single religious point of view. This book focuses only on the Judeo-Christian tradition, and even within that tradition there are many perspectives. But it is safe to say that some concerns are underrepresented in American debate because religious leaders too often play the role of ersatz scientist. Religion can introduce a sense of humility, faith, and values to our public discussions. In particular, religion can serve as a counterweight to those scientists who act as though physics can give us a general Theory of Everything or as though sociobiology can explain all of human behavior. On matters of current concern such as the legal status of homosexuals and physician-assisted suicide, religion can provide a focus on the value choices at hand rather than on the mistaken view that these matters can be resolved by science.

Chapter 10 surveys alternative perspectives on the relationship between science and religion. That relationship has varied throughout history, although one common theme has been efforts to reconcile science and faith. It is perhaps not surprising that some modern variations on that theme—efforts to find scientific evidence for God—run the risk of playing too much into the hands of science. Chapter 11, the conclusion, tries to right the balance by suggesting how religious leaders can react to science without losing their way.

2

Gene Patents and the Soul

A few years ago I read a front-page story in the *New York Times* reporting that leaders from more than eighty religious denominations had issued a statement opposing the patenting of human genes.[1] Because I teach both law and religion and law and science, I was eager to learn more. I wondered what religious perspectives were being brought to bear on this developing area of science and law. But when I obtained the statement and its underlying documentation, I was shocked. It turned out that the history and substance of the church leaders' statement revealed an abandonment of any distinctive religious perspective in favor of precisely the materialistic point of view characteristic of science. By treating genes as the core of our humanity, the religious leaders had joined modern scientists and philosophers in rejecting any spiritual account of our nature.

More recently, when Dolly the sheep was cloned, a debate began over the cloning of humans. Some clergy in the debate repeated the mistake of treating people as nothing more than their genes. As the debate over human cloning continues in the decades to come, it will be particularly important for religious leaders to provide a broad perspective on human identity lest this debate be dominated by the narrow conception of humanity characteristic of modern science.

Let us begin with the statement of opposition to gene patenting to see where and why the religious leaders went astray.

Setting the Stage: Religion Enters the Public Square

The church leaders' 1995 statement came at a propitious time. From Richard John Neuhaus's *The Naked Public Square* in 1984 to Stephen L. Carter's *The Culture of Disbelief* in 1993, there had been repeated calls for wider religious participation in public discourse.[2] For decades American religion had seemed limited to two public voices. First, there was America's famous (or notorious) "civil religion," the vague set of platitudes with which we Americans reassure ourselves that we are a religious people and pretty much leave it at that.[3] A famous example came when President Eisenhower was quoted as saying, "Our government makes no sense unless it is founded in a deeply felt religious faith—and I don't care what it is."[4]

The second voice for religion was heard in the political demands of the Moral Majority.[5] Although religion had played a role in American political debate throughout our nation's history, it seemed by the 1980s that on many political issues only conservatives were using religious discourse and then only in reference to rather narrow concerns.[6] Neuhaus sought a broader and deeper role for religion:

> Our quarrel with politicized fundamentalism is not that it has broken the rules of the game by "going public" with Christian truth claims. Christian truth, if it is true, is public truth. It is accessible to public reason. It impinges upon public space. At some critical points of morality and ethics it speaks to public policy. Our quarrel with politicized fundamentalism is not so much over the form of religion's role in society but over the substance of the claims made. To put it differently, our quarrel is primarily theological.[7]

Carter crystallized the discontent with these two limited roles for religion by urging opinion leaders to drop the distinction between "religious matters and important matters," treat religion as something more than a hobby, and use theological considerations across the political spectrum.[8] In 1994 President Clinton praised Carter's book.[9]

Thus the May 1995 statement against gene patenting enjoyed perfect timing. Covered on the front page of the *New York Times* a week before it was formally issued[10] and unveiled at a major press conference in Washington, D.C.,[11] the statement drew worldwide respectful attention.[12] Nor could those who issued the statement be characterized as representing a narrow slice of the political spectrum. The signers were leaders from more than eighty denominations, including Protestant, Catholic, Jewish, Buddhist, Muslim, and Hindu groups.[13] The statement itself was brief:

> We, the undersigned religious leaders, oppose the patenting of human and animal life forms. We are disturbed by the U.S. Patent Office's recent decision to patent human body parts and several genetically engineered animals. We believe that humans and animals are creations of God, not humans, and as such should not be patented as human inventions.[14]

Clearly this statement was more an expression of a mood than a detailed analysis of either patent law or theology. On the patent law front, the reference to a "recent decision" was odd, since the Patent Office had approved patents of the type described for many years.[15] From a theological perspective, the equating of humans and animals as creations of God ran counter to many traditions represented by the signatories,[16] whereas the implication that plants, which are also patentable,[17] are not creations of God was puzzling. What we were left with was the notion that there is something morally troubling about patenting certain living material.

To understand the statement and the way in which it partakes of the very scientific tradition it seeks to criticize, we have to look first at the underlying patent controversy and then at the origins of the statement itself.

Patenting Life: The Legal Background

Pursuant to the power granted in Article 1, Sec. 8 of the Constitution,[18] Congress has created a patent system that confers on inventors a monopoly on their invention for a set term of years.[19] The monopoly is good even against others who come up with the same invention completely on their own.[20] In return, the invention is made public.[21] This blend of incentives for private research coupled with public disclosure to help other researchers is a major form of protection for intellectual property under American law.

By statute, there are four basic requirements to receive a patent. First, under 35 U.S.C. § 101, the invention must concern patentable subject matter, which is defined as any "process, machine, manufacture, or composition of matter."[22] These are broad categories— a "process," for example, can be a way of doing something, rather than a physical object.[23] In addition, patents can issue only if three other requirements—utility, novelty, and nonobviousness—are met.[24]

Before turning to the patenting of living material, we must note two basic limitations on patent law. First, inventors have alternatives to the patent system. They can, for example, use trade secret law for a new product. Trade secret protection is more easily obtained, and it does not result in disclosing the invention to the world. On the other hand, it does not protect against others who come up with the same idea on their own.[25]

The second limitation is that patent protection along with alternatives such as trade secret do not exhaust the government's ability to regulate a product or process. A drug might be patented, for example, but it still must pass Food and Drug Administration scrutiny before it can be marketed.[26] With these limitations in mind, we can begin to understand the development of patent law in the area covered by the religious leaders' statement.

Prior to 1980 it was clear, thanks to specific federal legislation, that plants could be patented,[27] but otherwise the patenting of living material was an open question. In that year the U.S. Supreme Court directly confronted the question of whether a living thing could be patentable subject matter in *Diamond v. Chakrabarty*,[28] which concerned a patent application for a genetically engineered bacterium capable of breaking down crude oil and thus believed to be useful for treating oil spills.[29] The Court in *Chakrabarty* found that living things could indeed constitute "manufacture" or "composition of matter" and thus could be patented.[30] The Court rejected the argument that Congress had to expressly authorize patent protection for living things, quoting language from congressional reports suggesting that Congress wanted patentable subject matter to "include anything under the sun that is made by man."[31] And the Court maintained that the policy issues raised by genetic engineering ought to be addressed directly by Congress, not by the Court.[32]

Of course, any patent application involving living material still had to meet the statutory requirements of utility, novelty, and nonobviousness. But the rush to patent living things was under way. A genetically engineered mouse used in breast cancer research was the first animal to be patented;[33] cell lines derived from human organs also received patent protection.[34]

All of these developments engendered considerable debate and controversy for years before the church leaders issued their 1995 statement. Legal, policy, and moral objections were raised to *Diamond v. Chakrabarty* and its progeny, while defenders vigorously supported the decision. A host of questions were debated. Is patent protection the best route to scientific progress?[35] In the absence of patents would trade secret law dominate?[36] Does the potential for misusing these powerful technologies mean that they should be banned?[37] Congress rejected proposals to forbid the patenting of living material or to otherwise severely restrict research,[38] and a biotechnology industry based in part on patent rights came into being.[39] But the policy debates over biotechnology continued, and the ultimate size and nature of the industry remains uncertain.[40]

All of these factors were in place before the church leaders spoke out. The more immediate cause of their statement was the early 1990s dispute over the patenting of human gene sequences. Spurred by the massive government undertaking known as the Human Genome Initiative, researchers had begun to uncover in human genetic material specific DNA sequences that code for particular proteins with specific functions.[41] It therefore became possible to know, for example, what part of the human genome might be associated with a given disease.[42]

Patent applications were quickly filed by inventors who discovered a gene with an important function, cloned that gene, and then had it carry out its function by expressing a certain protein outside of the human body.[43] Of course, applications in this field, as in any other, have to meet the standards of utility, novelty, and nonobviousness. But here there is a more fundamental problem. Patents are not available for laws of nature or physical phenomena that exist apart from human intervention.[44] Such items are not considered patentable subject matter because no one person invents them and thus no one should have a monopoly on them. As the U.S. Supreme Court held in a 1948 patent case involving naturally occurring bacteria:

> [P]atents cannot issue for the discovery of the phenomena of nature.
> . . . The qualities of these bacteria, like the heat of the sun, electricity, or the qualities of metals, are part of the storehouse of knowledge of all men. They are manifestations of laws of nature, free to all men and reserved exclusively to none.[45]

The Court in *Diamond v. Chakrabarty* had not rejected this doctrine: it had stressed that the oil-eating microorganism involved in that case was a genetically engineered bacterium not found anywhere in nature.[46]

The argument that DNA sequences and the proteins for which they code are not human inventions is not a trivial one. But there is a powerful counterargument. Going back to 1911, the courts have upheld patents for isolated and purified forms of a product that exists in nature only in an impure state.[47] Learned Hand, for example, upheld a patent for a purified form of adrenaline that had been isolated from the natural adrenal gland:

> But, even if it were merely an extracted product without change, there is no rule that such products are not patentable. Takamine [the inventor] was the first to make [adrenaline] available for any use by removing it from the other gland-tissue in which it was found, and, while it is of course possible logically to call this a purification of the principle, it became for every practical purpose a new thing commercially and therapeutically. That was a good ground for a patent.[48]

Today the area of gene patenting remains an open one. Most observers believe that the modern courts are not likely to bar such patents on the product-of-nature theory since isolating and purifying a natural substance is a reasonably well-established basis for patents.[49] But even if that is true, the hurdles of novelty, utility, and nonobviousness remain substantial. An early attempt by the National Institutes of Health to patent thousands of gene fragments was found by the Patent and Trademark Office to fail all three tests.[50] More narrow gene patent requests by private parties have succeeded with the office, but their fate in the courts remains unclear.[51] Others have proposed that process patents for the methods used in obtaining gene sequences would be appropriate; but nonobviousness seems a problem under current law, and this approach remains controversial.[52]

Moreover, here, as with the earlier controversy over genetically engineered organisms and animals, policy arguments are still being pursued on both sides.[53] Some fear, for example, that research into new medicines will move more slowly if patents have been granted on gene sequences, while others contend that the opposite is true.[54] There continue to be calls for congressional action against gene patents.[55] It was against this backdrop that the church leaders spoke out.

Religion, Genes, and the Death of Dualism

Why did the religious leaders subscribe to a statement opposing the patenting of human material and genetically engineered animals? On one account, they were simply being enlisted in the decades-old controversy over whether the risks of a new technology outweigh the benefits. Support for this view comes from the fact that the statement was organized in part by Jeremy Rifkin's Foundation on Economic Trends.[56] Rifkin is a long-time opponent of genetic engineering who has raised a host of health, safety, environmental, and other objections to the technology.[57] To some observers, the statement by the religious leaders reflected nothing more than Rifkin's talents as a lobbyist. Thus, Ted Peters, acting director of the Center for Theology and the Natural Sciences, said the statement served "only the cause of Jeremy Rifkin."[58]

But there is more to it than that. The Joint Appeal Against Human and Animal Patenting, as it was formally called, was organized by two groups: Rifkin's foundation and the General Board of Church and Society of the United Methodist Church.[59] For the Methodist Church this statement grew out of a long enterprise. A close look at that enterprise reveals how scientific perspectives came to swamp traditional religious concerns.

In 1988 the General Conference of the Methodist Church created a task force to study the moral implications of genetics research.[60] The task force produced a set of recommendations that formed the basis of a report that was approved by the General Conference in 1992.[61] That report sets forth the rationale that lies behind the Joint Appeal approved by the religious leaders in 1995.[62]

The Methodist report does not oppose genetics research. It recognizes the potential benefits from such research in areas such as agriculture and medicine, it notes that incentives are needed if this research is going to be undertaken, and it even proposes public funding in areas where private funding is likely to be inadequate.[63] On the other hand, the report condemns the use of genetics "for eugenic purposes or genetic enhancements designed merely for cosmetic purposes or social advantage."[64]

These are rather typical observations about genetics. They echo earlier debates about research in this field. The interesting feature of the Methodist report arises precisely in the area of patenting, the area that later formed the basis of the 1995 Joint Appeal.

The report squarely opposes patents on gene sequences. Patents constitute a form of exclusive ownership, and such ownership of genetic information is said to be inconsistent with "the sanctity of God's creation and God's ownership of life."[65] Now as we have seen, the Methodists support financial incentives to assure that valuable genetics research is done. What is more, the Methodist report itself, immediately after opposing "patents on organisms themselves," supports process patents "wherein the method for engineering a new organism is patented, provid[ing] a means of economic return on investment while avoiding exclusive ownership of the organism."[66]

If the government can fund genetics research, if it can even give you a patent on a process for discovering valuable human genetic information, the opposition to patenting the genetic sequence itself requires some explanation. A process patent, after all, would exclude everyone but a sole inventor from using what might be the most efficient way to learn about genes and disease, thus raising all the questions about whether patents support or retard scientific progress. Moreover, as we have seen, the question of regulating the arguably dangerous consequences of genetic research is independent of patent law—the government could regulate the biotechnology industry directly, as it does the drug industry. In fact, the Methodist opposition to gene patents does not turn on the progress or side effects of science. It is based wholly on the idea that the genes themselves are vital to "the sanctity of God's creation."[67] The report stresses that genetics has a profound impact on the very nature of humanity. Genetic science, we are told, "explores the essence of life."[68] It forces us "to examine, as never before, the meaning of life";[69] it even promises "to alter . . . human nature."[70] In sum:

> Developments in genetic science compel our reevaluation of accepted theological/ethical issues including determinism versus free will, the nature of sin, just distribution of resources, the status of human beings in relation to other forms of life, and the meaning of personhood.[71]

These are extraordinary sentiments. First of all, the most ardent scientist is far more careful than the Methodist report is to note that human behavior involves a complex interaction of genetic and environmental influences. As one group of scientists and policy makers put it, "[t]he number of combinations that 100,000 genes can form interacting with one another and with the environment is essentially infinite, so we do not now foresee [the Human Genome Initiative], at any rate, leading to fundamental changes in what we regard as the nature of the self."[72] The Methodist report simply overestimates the impact of genetics research and underestimates the complexity of human behavior.

More importantly, no matter how much we can learn about human nature from genetics, even when we factor in the environment, we still have learned only about the material side of human beings. There may be more to being human, and the modern science of genetics adds nothing to the ancient philosophical question of whether humans are utterly material.[73] Descartes himself, in his *Discourse on Method*, imagined a creature physically identical in every respect to a human being, a creature that could wake, sleep, dream, smell, taste, and speak, before concluding that such a being would not be human because it would lack a soul.[74] Methodists as well have traditionally believed that humans have nonmaterial souls.[75]

Modern science certainly does not claim that it can prove the nonexistence of the soul. On the contrary, the dominant philosophical assumption of most twentieth-century scientists has been precisely the opposite: science deals with falsifiable propositions, that is, propositions that can be demonstrated wrong in an empirical test.[76] As we noted in chapter 1, science simply does not speak to the validity of other systems, such as metaphysics, pure mathematics, or logic.[77] Stepping back for a moment, we can best understand the Methodist statement in light of the modern trend among elites away from any hint that people have a spiritual side as well as a material one, that is, any hint of dualism. The idea that human beings might have a nonmaterial side has an ancient and respectable history among religious and secular thinkers.[78] Modern science has advanced not by attacking dualism, but by setting it aside, that is, by defining as nonscientific inquiries into the spiritual. Nonetheless, in recent years, dualism has retreated, indeed nearly disappeared, as elite discussions of human nature have increasingly assumed that people are just matter and energy.

The modern debate over the nature of consciousness is illustrative. This is an area of enormous ferment, with rival theories galore and a general consensus that we do not have a full understanding of the subject.[79] There have been, for example, theories that binary computers could attain consciousness, with vigorous rebuttals from numerous quarters.[80] Yet, even those who attack computer consciousness go out of their way to assert that human consciousness is a purely physical phenomenon.[81] Whether they seek the origins of consciousness in evolutionary biology or quantum physics, the opponents of computer consciousness fall over themselves in pledging allegiance to physical explanations.[82]

It is understandable that scientists who study the human brain believe that they will someday explain the human mind. But even when one moves from laboratory and theoretical studies of the brain to clinical observations of the whole person, the elite rejection of dualism continues. Oliver Sacks publishes sensitive studies of the complex and paradoxical behavior of his patients, yet Sacks stresses that he utterly rejects "mystical" and "dualistic" explanations of human behavior.[83] He argues that his approach has been "to exempt nothing from the domain of natural science"[84]; indeed, he maintains that clinical neurologists like himself are less prey to spiritual ideas than are laboratory scientists:

> Clinical neurologists . . . have a somewhat better record here, for they have daily to face the richness of human life, the complexity of the phenomenal world; whereas a physiologist can spend a life with spinal preparations and decerebrate animals, in a world of nerve potentials, synapses, and reflexes—such a life may fail to be a corrective to dualism, may even foster its mystical development.[85]

Sacks need not worry that dualism will rear its head. Materialistic science has extended so far in our world that even traditionally religious topics are swallowed up. Not only is there a technical *Journal of Near-Death Studies,* but that very journal has published analyses of the death of a computer program.[86]

It is, of course, understandable, even definitional, that scientific work would stress the material. But the scientific worldview has begun to absorb modern philosophy as well. As Thomas Nagel has written:

> Philosophy is also infected by a broader tendency of contemporary intellectual life: scientism. Scientism is actually a special form of

idealism, for it puts one type of human understanding in charge of the universe and what can be said about it. At its most myopic it assumes that everything there is must be understandable by the employment of scientific theories like those we have developed to date—physics and evolutionary biology are the current paradigms—as if the present age were not just another in the series.[87]

To get a sense of the extent of this phenomenon, consider the prominent group of modern philosophers, dubbed "the new mysterians," who question whether any materialist theory will ever be able to explain the subjective human experience of consciousness.[88] One would think that here at least there is room for the nonmaterial perspectives that have played such a role in the history of Western philosophy and religion. Yet one would be wrong. None of these philosophers support dualism.[89] They leave no role for the spiritual. Consciousness in their view is utterly physical. They simply believe that humans are incapable of discovering the relevant physical laws, just as rats are incapable of discovering quantum mechanics.[90] As the most prominent among them, Colin McGinn, has written:

> Resolutely shunning the supernatural, I think it is undeniable that it must be in virtue of *some* natural property of the brain that organisms are conscious. There just *has* to be some explanation for how brains [interact with] minds.[91]

This statement reflects a touching faith in science. It does not represent any opening to the spiritual.

So in an era when the mechanical view of human life is sweeping through science, medicine, and philosophy, there is a tremendous opportunity for religious speakers to fill the gap, to remind us that there may be more than molecules in a human being. Yet the Methodist report fits right into these modern trends in science, medicine, and philosophy. It assumes that genes are the key to what we are. Of course, not all religious leaders fell into this trap.[92] But as Mark Hanson has pointed out, the problem goes beyond the Methodist report itself—many of the statements made on gene patenting by leaders of various denominations have included the theologically problematic idea that "genes are sacred" in some special way.[93]

Consider the public comments made when the statement on gene patenting was released in 1995. Rabbi David Saperstein, director of the Religious Action Center of Reform Judaism, opposed gene patents on the ground that "life and its building blocks belong in the hands of God, not in the hands of corporations seeking financial fortune,"[94] whereas Dr. Richard Land, executive director of the Southern Baptist Christian Life Commission, argued that to grant patents for human genetic information "represents the usurpation of the ownership rights of the Sovereign of the universe."[95] Neither Rabbi Saperstein nor Dr. Land believes that granting ownership of a physical device usurps God's rights. They are talking as though it is our DNA that makes us special in the eyes of God. Whether you call it the soul or the spirit or use some other term, the real uniqueness of people is missing from this argument. I am convinced that despite the contrary view of many scientists and philosophers, the majority of ordinary people continue to believe that humans have a nonmaterial side.[96] Religious leaders would be well advised to catch up with their troops and to provide leadership on an issue that simply does not turn on laboratory results.

It remains true that the mapping of the human gene and the concomitant debates about intellectual property are vital. And there is no reason that religious leaders cannot play a role in those debates. They can raise concerns, as many have, about the misuse of science, the consequences for human dignity, and the ramifications of new technologies for the poorest among us.

But if that is all that religion does, it is missing its most distinctive role. It is precisely during this era—when deterministic models, from evolutionary biology to artificial intelligence, are dominant—that the claim that humans have a nonmaterial side most needs to be heard in elite debate. The endpoint of determinism applied to people is a world without choice or responsibility. Determinism robs us not only of the ability to blame wrongdoing, but of the ability to praise virtue. Most religious leaders in the Judeo-Christian tradition know this, but it is easy to forget in the blare of publicity over the latest scientific breakthrough. Sometimes the desire to be trendy may outweigh the desire to be reflective.

But perhaps the situation is worse than I think. Perhaps some of the clergy who signed the Joint Appeal do in fact believe that humans are simply the sum of their genes. If that is the case, the question of whether the essence of a human can be patented is hardly of great importance. After all, even if a machine cannot be patented, it is still a machine.

Cloning Dolly and Cloning Humans

Early in 1997, the relationship of our genes to our humanity again entered the public spotlight. When Ian Wilmut cloned a sheep and upset the assumption that cloning an adult mammal was impossible, the reaction was immediate—the cloning of humans suddenly became a subject of raging debate.[97]

It is important to keep straight what cloning means in this context. Wilmut's approach—which might be applicable to humans, although this remains uncertain[98]—began by fusing cells from an adult sheep, known as the donor, with another sheep's egg cell from which the nucleus had been removed. The donor is the mammal being cloned. Only its genetic material was in the new embryo, which was ultimately implanted in a third sheep, which gave birth to a lamb, Dolly. Dolly is thus a genetic match—a clone—of the donor sheep.[99] Dolly is like an identical twin to the donor sheep, except that, whereas identical twins are the same age, Dolly is years younger than her "twin."

The possibility of human cloning, which has never been achieved, first excited interest in the 1970s.[100] When Dolly showed that the possibility of human cloning was real, there was a tremendous reaction. Conferences were held, commissions were formed, legislation was proposed. The most widespread view was that, although research on cloned human embryos might lead to beneficial medical advances, it would be wrong to allow such an embryo to go to full term—that is, human cloning, the creation of delayed identical twins, should not be permitted.[101]

It is easy to understand the uneasiness virtually everyone feels about human cloning. You could, in principle, make multiple clones of the same person, flooding the world with thousands of little babies who look like the infant Tiger Woods or like Madonna. Even if you make only one clone of an adult, the baby would not only be the delayed twin of the adult; it would be a child without the usual complement of two genetic parents. We do not know a lot about what it would be like to grow up under those circumstances. For all of these reasons, many strong arguments have been lodged against human cloning,[102] including arguments from a religious perspective that stress the role of the family.[103]

Although human cloning undoubtedly presents important risks of misuse and important threats to accepted patterns of childbirth and child-rearing, it is important to keep in mind some undisputed truths. The clone would not, in fact, be identical to its donor. It would, after all, grow up in a different environment, indeed in a different era. Just as identical twins end up being very separate people, the clone of Tiger Woods would be very separate from his "father." He might not play golf at all.[104]

And for those of us who take the traditional religious perspective, the clone would be his own person in spiritual terms as well. He would have a soul and a personality of his own in every respect. When Dolly hit the news, most religious leaders, to their credit, recognized this point.[105] But some, swept up in the excitement of a new scientific development in a society that venerates science, lost their bearings. Rabbi Bernard King of Congregation Shir Ha-Ma'alot in Irvine, California, asked of cloning, "Will we be creating intellectuals and artistic geniuses without a soul? That could be very dangerous."[106] The Reverend Gregory Wingenbach, executive director of the Kentuckiana Interfaith Community, argued that cloning destroys "the individuality of the human being."[107] John M. Haas, president of the Pope John Center for the Study of Ethics in Health Care, said that cloning would "jeopardize the personal and unique identity of the clone."[108] Henry Greely, a bioethicist at Stanford University, answered comments of this type—comments that suggest that traditional identical twins lack individual personal and spiritual qualities—with remarkable precision:

> The problem is, we sanctify DNA. People seem to want to be eager to view their genome as their essence, instead of just molecules that pass on certain traits. In our secular culture, it's almost taken the place of the soul. That's way overblown.[109]

As cloning and related issues posed by the new genetics are debated in the years ahead, religious leaders should take the lead in showing the limits of the scientific model, rather than in racing to keep up with the latest trends. It is precisely because humans are unique, spiritual individuals that we are empowered to make choices about what types of genetic manipulation should serve us and what types we should set aside. In the end, I am convinced that many of the religious leaders who unwittingly adopted the scientific model when they commented on the patenting of genes or the cloning of Dolly would, on reflection, reject the strictly materialistic view. These leaders could then make a unique contribution to American debate, the kind of contribution Stephen Carter envisioned when he called for religion to be "an independent moral force" in American society.[110] Imagine if religious leaders joined together in a statement covered by the *New York Times* asserting that in many important respects the precise nature of the human genetic code is beside the point. That would open an area of discussion we rarely hear.

3

Using the Bible as a
Science Text

The theory of evolution has challenged the faith of millions since its emergence in the nineteenth century. Though large numbers of Protestants, Catholics, and Jews have had no difficulty accepting the theory while retaining their religious beliefs, others have struggled with what they see as a difficult conflict.

From the nineteenth century until the 1960s, this struggle took a variety of forms. Most often, religious people troubled by evolution interpreted the book of Genesis to accommodate some aspects of the theory while arguing for the special creation of human beings and for a moral code embedded in traditional biblical teachings.

In the 1960s, however, the focus shifted dramatically. A new group, the "scientific creationists," moved to the forefront. They maintain that every detail in Genesis is scientifically correct. Going far beyond most earlier opponents of evolution, they argue that the earth is only ten thousand years old, that the days described in the creation account in Genesis lasted exactly twenty-four hours, and, most importantly, that these and other features of the Bible are correct by the standards of modern science. Today, creation scientists of this stripe dominate the antievolution movement.

Scientific creationists have not won over mainstream scientists, and they have been remarkably unsuccessful in high profile legal battles. But the greatest flaw with scientific creationism from the perspective of traditional religion is its focus. By buying into the scientific approach, scientific creationists have shifted attention from faith and values and have reduced the Bible to the level of a science text. When the leader of scientific creationism remarks that Lot's wife became a pillar of salt by chemical replacement,[1] you can be pretty sure that someone is missing the point.

To understand how scientific creationism represents a new and unwarranted immersion of religion in science, let's begin by looking at earlier reactions to evolution. We will see a more nuanced approach—one that has been lost in the modern infatuation with science.

Early Religious Reactions to Evolution

Darwin, like most scientists, stood on many shoulders. A central assumption of his work was the vast age of the earth. Although the book of Genesis does not state when creation occurred, most biblical interpretations prior to the nineteenth century placed creation only a few thousand years in the past.[2] But geologists had begun to challenge this idea long before Darwin. James Hutton argued in 1788 that the earth developed over millions of years from uniform geological processes; thus, hills have eroded into sediment and sediment has compacted into rock for eons.[3] By the 1830s, long before modern dating techniques using radioactive isotopes, Charles Lyell's *Principles of Geology* had fully convinced the scientific world that the geologic features and fossils we find around us can best be explained by seeing the earth as enormously old.[4]

By the time Darwin wrote *The Origin of the Species* in 1859 he was able to draw on these ideas as well as related notions of how life might have emerged.[5] Darwin argued that all of the living beings on earth, from plants to humans, evolved by a process of natural selection through which a struggle for existence determines which random variations survive to be inherited.[6] This theory challenged the prevalent religious assumptions of the time on several fronts: not only did it assume a process taking millions of years, but it also removed God's design as the source of the variety around us, it denied the separate creation of the various species, and, most importantly, it denied any special status to humans as compared to animals. In short, to many religious leaders Darwin's work tended "to efface every impression of an acting Deity."[7]

As Darwin's ideas gained support throughout the scientific community, nineteenth-century religious leaders responded in a number of ways. A small number, following the British preacher and scientist Philip Henry Gosse, simply took the view that God had created the earth with the appearance of age. Just as Adam, although never attached to a mother, had a navel, so too the earth had various fossils and other geologic records.[8] Gosse titled his book *Omphalos,* which means navel.[9] This view can certainly be supported as a matter of pure faith. At some point, whether we are scientists or not, we have to take some things on faith—the evidence of our senses, for example. An individual who firmly believes that the earth was created five minutes ago can be hard to dissuade.

But this attitude toward evolution was not a major feature of nineteenth-century thinking any more than it is today. Indeed, when we look at religious reactions to Darwin in that era, it is remarkable how much reconciliation took place, right from the start.

Even if we begin with those who opposed Darwin's ideas, we find less conflict with the scientific community than you would expect from the perspective of modern creationism. The primary reason is that so many religious people accepted the view that the earth was very old. The Princeton Seminary's Charles Hodge, whose 1874 book *What Is Darwinism?* attacked evolution as atheism, accepted the earth's great age because he believed the days described in Genesis were geologic epochs.[10] The Presbyterian evangelist Alexander Patterson, author of the influential 1903 anti-Darwin tract *The Other Side of Evolution,* believed that an enormous historical gap occurred between the first and second verses of Genesis.[11] According to Patterson, the Bible was silent about this period, during which much of the geologic record accumulated.[12]

These day/age and gap theories were widely held by opponents of Darwin. Ronald Numbers, in his classic history of the creationist movement, concludes a survey of early opponents of Darwin by saying he had failed to find a single cleric "who rejected the antiquity of the earth, denied the progressive nature of the fossil record, or attached geological significance to [Noah's] flood."[13] Opponents of Darwin focused their attacks on the idea that man descended from apes. And even these attacks were not directed at the scientific community as such. Nineteenth-century clerical opponents of Darwin embraced a "populist conception of validation," believing that the issues involved should be judged not by scientists alone but by "the whole intelligent part of mankind."[14] As Alexander Patterson put it, Darwin's theories must appear "before the judgment seat of Christian Common Sense," where "the best juryman will be the intelligent non-scientific mind."[15] These critics of Darwin were concerned about his theory precisely because of its impact on ordinary people, that is, because it had the potential to undermine traditional morality.[16] This is why the "central point" for these religious leaders was the connection between humans and brutes.[17] Even *The Fundamentals,* the essays published between 1910 and 1915 that gave fundamentalism its name, tended to downplay criticism of Darwin, accept an ancient earth, and emphasize key matters of faith—the early fundamentalists saw no need to drive evolution as a whole out of American culture.[18]

It should not surprise us that devout Christians, living in the shadow of Darwin and opposed to the view that humans descended from apes, could still see the Bible as consistent with broad areas of evolutionary theory. Even believers in biblical inerrancy recognized that Scripture sometimes speaks through metaphors and parables.[19] Inerrancy is the view that the Bible is without error, but that humans may misinterpret it—it is a long way from biblical literalism.[20] By the first half of the nineteenth century—in other words, even before Darwin—the vast majority of America's religious leaders had rejected literalism, including a literal interpretation of Genesis. Virtually none of them believed, for example, that the sun revolved around the earth.[21] The dominant view was that the Bible spoke the truth, but in popular rather than scientific language. As the leading theologian Moses Stuart of Andover Seminary put it in 1829, God fit the words of the Mosaic narrative "to the feelings, views, and methods of expression, existing in the time of Moses. . . . *[T]he Bible was not designed to teach the Hebrews astronomy or geol-*

ogy."[22] From this vantage point, it made perfect sense to dispute that man descended from apes precisely because of its moral implications, while muting or dropping entirely objections to other features of geology and evolution where the biblical language could accommodate the new developments and central ethical teachings were not at stake.

We have been discussing those religious leaders who opposed Darwin. It should also be noted that by 1900 even these relatively mild critics were in the minority—the bulk of America's religious thinkers had followed the bulk of America's scientists in accepting Darwinian evolution as an accurate scientific theory.[23] This hardly meant that they had abandoned traditional morality. They argued powerfully that just as the Bible is not a science text, evolutionary theory is not a moral guide.[24] They insisted on a sharp distinction between humans and other animals and on a normative role for religion that science could not supply.[25] People with this set of views are sometimes called theistic evolutionists, since they accept Darwinian theory but they believe it does not—indeed it cannot—contradict their belief that God's creativity began and sustains the universe and endows individuals with moral responsibility.[26]

If it seems to you that theistic evolutionists are not so different from early critics of Darwin, you are right. When you keep in mind that those critics tended to accept an ancient earth, were not inclined to challenge the findings of geology on the basis of Noah's flood, and even accepted a limited role for the evolution of some living beings, the differences became fairly narrow. The critics of Darwin maintained that God created humans separately from apes and endowed those humans with a soul. The theistic evolutionists maintained that God created humans through the process of evolution and endowed those humans with a soul. As Ronald Numbers put it, "[c]reationists of the Victorian era generally assimilated the findings of historical geology to such an extent that today they seem intellectually closer to the theistic evolutionists of their time than to the scientific creationists of the late twentieth century."[27]

Remarkable as it may seem, even the antievolutionism that blossomed during the 1920s under the leadership of William Jennings

Bryan had little in common with the modern variety of creationism. Bryan's movement led to laws, later struck down, against the teaching of evolution[28] and to textbook restrictions, later largely removed, on the same subject.[29] It also led to the Scopes trial, which resulted in a conviction (later reversed) for teaching evolution and a public reaction that hurt the antievolution cause.[30] Throughout all of this, Bryan adhered to a set of beliefs that are a far cry from his image as a biblical literalist.[31] Indeed, at the height of the antievolution movement of the 1920s, most opponents of evolution, utilizing the familiar day/age and gap interpretations of Genesis, accepted many of the teachings of modern geology.[32]

The anti-Darwin movement of the 1920s grew out of an increasing concern that evolutionary thinking had undermined traditional values.[33] It was a fundamentalist movement with populist overtones centered largely in the South.[34] Bryan, the Great Commoner and thrice-defeated Democratic candidate for president, became through his involvement in the Scopes trial the most prominent opponent of Darwin in America. And an opponent he surely was—he called Darwinism "guesses strung together," and he never accepted that man had evolved from other creatures.[35] But Bryan, like other creationists of his day, focused narrowly on human origins.[36] He did not care whether plants and animals had evolved,[37] and he believed that the days described in Genesis had lasted eons.[38] His objections to evolution were based on the belief that it led to moral decay, and he emphasized that the truth or falsity of evolution should be decided by the common people, not by the scientific elites.[39] Bryan's attitude was best summed up in his famous statement that he was "more interested in the Rock of Ages than the age of rocks."[40] He never could have imagined that decades later religious opposition to Darwin would indeed focus on the age of rocks.

Modern Creation Science

The March 1961 publication of *The Genesis Flood* by John C. Whitcomb, Jr., and Henry M. Morris launched the modern creation science movement. Reversing mainstream religious beliefs, creation scientists argued that the earth was only a few thousand years old, that the days of creation lasted twenty-four hours, and that Noah's flood created the modern fossil record. They supported their position with a literal interpretation of the Bible and with an unrelenting use of scientific argumentation. This effort was successful among many devout Protestants precisely because *The Genesis Flood* looked like legitimate science, complete with scholarly citations.[41] As Christopher P. Toumey put it, "[b]y adducing technical authority in support of biblical narrative, [Whitcomb and Morris] wove together conservative Protestant values and the American faith in science, creating one fabric of belief out of two."[42] Today, among antievolutionists, creation science "floods the world";[43] the very word creationism has come to mean belief in the very recent appearance of life on earth and a geologically significant flood.[44] Opponents of Darwin who reject these beliefs often find, to their chagrin, that people lump them with modern creation scientists.[45] These moderate opponents of Darwin are in good company— today's creation scientists openly attack William Jennings Bryan because Bryan, like other fundamentalists of his era, did not believe in a literal reading of Scripture.[46]

Henry M. Morris, a Ph.D. engineer, and John C. Whitcomb, Jr., a theologian, met in 1953 and discovered a mutual interest in rejecting any inconsistency between the literal words of Genesis and the findings of geology.[47] Drawing on earlier theories, they concluded that a proper understanding of Noah's flood paved the way to reconciling science and religion; to them the flood became more central even than the question of human origins, which had concerned Bryan and his predecessors.[48] The result of their collaboration was *The Genesis Flood*.

To get a sense of modern creation science, there is no substitute for reading *The Genesis Flood* itself.[49] It begins with the authors candidly stating that they write "from the perspective of full belief in the complete divine inspiration and perspicuity of Scripture. . . . Our conclusions must unavoidably be colored by our Biblical presuppositions, and this we plainly acknowledge."[50] But, they argue, evolutionists also start with presuppositions—in particular, a belief in the essential continuity and uniformity of geological processes over time.[51]

The introduction and the first several chapters of *The Genesis Flood* are devoted to establishing that "a worldwide flood actually destroyed the entire antediluvian human population, as well as all land animals, except those preserved in a special Ark constructed by Noah."[52] A portion of this argument is devoted to attempting to refute the biblical interpretations of "many Christian scholars"[53] and "[c]onservative Christians,"[54] who have maintained, for over one hundred years, that the Bible describes a local flood and that Noah's Ark did not have a representative of every living creature on the entire earth.[55] This endeavor requires the authors of *The Genesis Flood* to engage in some difficult matters of interpretation, since the biblical references to the Flood do not compel the reading that it covered the whole earth.[56]

But the vast bulk of *The Genesis Flood* is given over to a review of the scientific evidence that the authors believe supports the idea that a universal flood created the fossil record and that the earth is only about ten thousand years old. The arguments involve a mixture of attacks on standard geology along with positive arguments in favor of the biblical account. A central argument is that mainstream dating methods that show a very old earth, such as radioactive decay techniques, are unacceptable because they assume that physical processes have been uniform over time and the Bible tells us of great discontinuities, such as the Flood, that render that assumption unacceptable.[57]

Throughout all of the arguments in favor of a young earth, *The Genesis Flood* utilizes the terminology and trappings of modern science. Findings from throughout the mainstream scientific world, including the findings of evolutionists, are used when they support the authors' thesis. Research on ancient land bridges and the dispersion of animal populations is used to explain how kangaroos made it onto the Ark.[58] The greenhouse effect is used to support the possibility of a universally warm climate in the biblical era.[59] The Van Allen radiation belt is invoked to explain how radioactive processes might have changed over time.[60] The Flood itself is attributed to "a combination of meteorologic and tectonic phenomena."[61] Throughout the book there are numerous charts, equations, and photographs lending a scientific air to the enterprise. The displacement tonnage of the Ark, for example, is calculated (using the Hebrew rather than the Babylonian cubit) at about 19,940 tons.[62]

The Genesis Flood launched the creation science movement. Building on its arguments, later creationists have invoked principles from thermodynamics, quantum mechanics, and modern analyses of protein structure to support belief in the creation account in the Bible.[63] A host of organizations, most notably the Institute for Creation Research and the Creation Research Society, have emerged to carry forth the creation science effort.[64]

The Legacy of Creation Science

Creation science has not succeeded in shaping mainstream science or in winning a place in the nation's public school classrooms for the book of Genesis. What it has done instead is to further the troubling notion that American religion must adorn itself in the trappings of science in order to be taken seriously.

Mainstream scientific organizations, including the National Academy of Sciences, have utterly rejected the creationist approach.[65] Scientists have emphasized that because creationists are not open to evidence that contradicts Genesis, they are not operating in a truly scientific fashion. Moreover, scientists and scholars who have studied the scientific method have criticized the creationists for picking and choosing data and for misunderstanding basic scientific concepts. The only real dispute from the traditional scientific perspective has been over how harshly to state the negative verdict on creationists—typical formulations range from "Their understanding of scientific method is limited"[66] to "[T]hey present [a] caricature of science [based on] no evidence"[67] to "Creationists have constructed a glorious fake, which we can use to illustrate the differences between science and pseudoscience."[68] In the final analysis, mainstream researchers in fields ranging from biology to physics to geology and on to anthropology have found that creationism is completely inconsistent with their understanding of science and with their work.[69]

Nor has creation science improved the legal claims of antievolution activists. In fairness, it was not created to achieve that end. Disputes over the teaching of evolution in the public schools began before the Scopes trial of 1925 and continue to the present day.[70] Modern creation science did not arise because of those disputes. Indeed, its origin in the early 1960s came during a lull in public antievolution activity and reflected an inward-looking desire by conservative evangelicals to revive literal Bible interpretation with scientific evidence.[71]

Creationism's forays into the courtroom began after the U.S. Supreme Court's 1968 decision in *Epperson v. Arkansas.*[72] In *Epperson* the Court struck down an Arkansas statute that prohibited the teaching of evolution in the public schools. The Court found the statute was an unconstitutional establishment of religion because it was passed for a religious purpose, that is, to further the belief that Darwin is inconsistent with Genesis.[73] At the time of this decision, only Arkansas and Mississippi had antievolution statutes on the books, and the Mississippi statute was struck down soon after *Epperson.*[74]

Creationists developed a legal strategy in reaction to these decisions. Beginning in the 1970s, antievolutionists brought about the passage of various statutes requiring that whenever evolution was taught in the public school, the rival science of creationism must be taught as well.[75] The proponents of these statutes maintained that they were not establishing religion—they were simply requiring that the teaching of evolution, which they regarded as a controversial scientific theory, be balanced by an alternative view, creation science. But the courts, in the legal challenges that followed, did not see it that way. Indeed, creation science statutes suffered an "unbroken string of courtroom defeats."[76] After a major trial of Arkansas's 1981 Balanced Treatment for Creation-Science and Evolution-Science Act, federal judge William Ray Overton found that creation science "is simply not science. . . . [Creationists] do not take data, weigh it against the opposing scientific data, and thereafter reach . . . conclusions. . . . Instead, they take the literal wording of the Book of Genesis and attempt to find scientific support for it."[77] Judge Overton concluded that the statute unconstitutionally established religion.[78] The U.S. Supreme Court reached the same conclusion when it assessed the Louisiana Creationism Act in 1987.[79] The opinion of Justice William J. Brennan, Jr., for the Court found that the act was not really about science education but was designed "to restructure the science curriculum to conform with a particular religious viewpoint."[80] Although battles over the teaching of evolution continue before various local school boards, creation science has not proven to be the ticket to success in the courts.

It is harder to assess the impact of creation science on public opinion. It is true that surveys taken in the 1980s and 1990s show that Americans are about equally divided between those who believe that God created man in his present form in the past ten thousand years and those who believe that humans developed over millions of years with God guiding the process.[81] Creation science supports the former proposition and may be somewhat responsible for its popularity, although it is hard to tell how many hold this belief apart from the influence of creation science. In any event, there is no evidence that belief in God or in the importance of religion or in its relevance to human problems has increased since the appearance of creation science in the early 1960s; those beliefs were very widely held in the United States before that time.[82]

In the end, creation science should be assessed on its own terms. Creationists are unmoved by the argument that they are not open to the possibility that the Bible is wrong. Creationism, even to its proponents, is not a science in the sense of being a set of testable hypotheses that must be rejected if the evidence so requires. They freely admit that their belief in the Bible is "dogmatic";[83] indeed they often argue that the theory of evolution is similarly untestable.[84] To creationists, science is a limited inductive enterprise in which the Book of Nature must fit into the picture provided by the Book of Scripture.[85] Henry M. Morris, coauthor of *The Genesis Flood,* has written:

> If man wishes to know anything about Creation (the time of Creation, the duration of Creation, the order of Creation, the methods of Creation, or anything else) his sole source of true information is that of divine revelation. . . . Therefore, we are completely limited to what God has seen fit to tell us, and this information is in His written Word. This is our textbook on the science of Creation![86]

And Morris does indeed treat the Bible as a science text, as his writings on the construction of the Ark[87] and his casual comment that Lot's wife became a pillar of salt through chemical replacement indicate.[88]

If creationists are untroubled by taking an approach to science that differs from modern norms, they are equally untroubled by their lack of success in winning over mainstream scientists. Although creationists often have technical degrees, their primary audience is not the scientific community. They rarely submit their articles to peer-reviewed journals. Their target audience is religious members of the lay public.[89] And creationists can expect some success with that audience precisely because they are outside of the scientific establishment. By the 1960s the mainstream scientific community was beginning to be seen by many as part of a remote elite that deserved suspicion rather than respect.[90]

So what are we left with? Modern creation science is described by even sympathetic outside observers as "bad science"[91] or "folk science."[92] If its own proponents regard the Bible as infallibly true, why do they enlist scientific evidence to support it?

The reason is that creationists are swept up in the worldview that places science at the heart of everything. If mainstream science does not support your beliefs, then perhaps New Age science or unorthodox science or fringe science will fill the bill. Modern Americans cling to scientific rhetoric no matter what the issue and no matter how controversial the spokesman.[93] As Christopher P. Toumey put it, "[i]n an age obsessed with scientific sanctification, the creationist movement provides great comfort to many conservative

Christians by attributing scientific credibility to biblical beliefs."[94] In today's climate, there is no substitute for using science to confer legitimacy, even on the Bible.[95]

Alternative Approaches to Evolution

What a strange notion it is that religious belief is strengthened by draping it with whatever bits of scientific evidence one can find. Traditional faith does not work that way. If you believe, in faith, that during communion the wine becomes the blood of Jesus, no scientific evidence can shake that faith and no scientific evidence is needed to bolster it.

This is important not because of philosophical questions about the limits of empiricism. It is important because modern creationists are lending support to the idea that science is central to everything. By treating the Bible as a science text, they move its spiritual and moral teachings to the sidelines.[96]

Look at what has happened in the precise area of evolution. From the mid–nineteenth century up until the modern creation science movement began in 1961, the claims of antievolutionists centered almost entirely on the idea that man had descended from monkeys. This focus stemmed from the fact that the question of descent was seen as bearing on human nature and human morality. But modern creation scientists are obsessed with geology and hydrology, with only occasional mentions of human descent.[97] This process does not elevate the Bible; it diminishes it.

Creation science has diminished religion in another way as well. One of its spinoffs has been the text *Of Pandas and People: The Central Question of Biological Origins*.[98] Written by two biologists, both veterans of the creation science movement, the text presents scientific attacks on Darwinism.[99] There is no mystery as to why it was written—as one of the authors, Percival Davis, put it, "[o]f course my motives were religious. There's no question about it."[100] Thus, in terms of its methodology, *Pandas* is identical to *The Genesis Flood:* it seeks scientific support for religion. The only difference is that *Pandas* is designed to avoid the legal problems that have kept creation science out of the public school classroom.[101] It does not argue for the biblical account of creation but limits itself to supporting the idea of intelligent design; that is, because evolution cannot account for the diversity of life we see around us, some intelligent agent must have been involved.[102] Although *Pandas* does not openly identify the "intelligent agent" with God, the connection is obvious enough that some Christian conservatives have fought to get this book into the classrooms.[103]

The "intelligent design" attack on evolution may not succeed in the courts, since judges may well see it as just another effort to inject religion into the public schools. But the more important problem with this movement is what it makes of religion. The notion that religious belief must simultaneously be watered down by vague references to "an intelligent agent" and propped up by citations to scientific papers is insulting to religion.

It is vital here to keep matters straight. A scientific attack on Darwinism is appropriately addressed to the scientific community. Of course, any challenge to a widely accepted theory will be met with resistance, but the history of science suggests that some challenges succeed and some fail; over time the very human and imperfect process of scientific development does yield consensus.[104] But if you believe as a matter of religious faith that the Bible is literally true, you can put science to one side in your understanding of Scripture. Human reason is limited, and there is no reason to assume that God always operates by the laws we understand. There are devout Christians and Orthodox Jews who take this view, and they have no use for the creationist agenda—indeed they believe it is "impious and just plain stupid to try to prove from science that the Word of God is true."[105]

Of course, for countless devout Christians and Jews, modern creation science is not an issue because they do not believe that the Bible and evolution are inconsistent. This has been traditional Catholic teaching since at least 1950,[106] and it is the view of many Protestants and Reform and Conservative Jews.[107] For these believers the Bible is not written to be read like a high school text, and

God is not incapable of operating through evolution. Freed of the desire to bow at the altar of science and of the need to reduce God to "an intelligent agent," these people can get on with the task of developing and imparting morally robust religious teachings.

Whether they believe in the theory of evolution or not, those religious leaders who avoid being swallowed up by the scientific worldview are in the best position to carry out the most important tasks of religion. They know that science cannot answer the moral questions that are of the greatest importance, that science cannot tell us how to live our lives. As the theologian Paul Holmer has written, "it is not true that a specific kind of continuity in the natural order affects the life of the human spirit. . . . Sin is not found in the brutes, and anyone who professes to find it there misunderstands the concept 'sin.'"[108]

So for those with traditional religious faith, Darwinism cannot deflect their focus. Whether rejected or accepted, evolution cannot speak to the vital issues of right and wrong. Even committed evolutionists concede that "science simply cannot (by its legitimate methods) adjudicate the issue of God's possible superintendence of nature."[109] It is only the bizarre focus of the creation scientists that obscures this truth.

4

The Medical Power
of Prayer

From 1991 to 1993, seven hundred coronary patients at
the Brockton/West Roxbury Veterans Affairs Center in Massachusetts were randomly assigned to two groups. Each patient in the first
group was visited by a chaplain for prayer and conversation for an
hour a day both before and after surgery. In particular, a chaplain
often came by to join the patient in prayer right before surgery. In
the second group, by contrast, there was much more limited contact
with the chaplains, typically just a minute or two a day.

These patients were undergoing some of the most invasive procedures in modern medicine, including bypass operations, valve re-
placements, and open-heart surgery. Yet the study, directed by Dr.
Elisabeth McSherry, found that members of the group who had
more extensive contact with the chaplains had fewer complications
after surgery and were released, on average, two days sooner than
the patients in the other group.[1]

Scientific Studies of Prayer

This study hardly stands alone. Researchers have found that those
who pray and go to church suffer from fewer physical and psycho-
logical ailments, have lower blood pressure, and are more likely to
recover quickly from hip fractures.[2] In many of these studies, control groups were used to assure that the effects were not based on
income levels, smoking habits, or other factors.[3]

There are modern studies that go even farther; studies that follow classic double-blind procedures and find medical benefits from prayer even when the patient does not know that prayers are being offered on his behalf. Consider the famous research done by the cardiologist Randolph Byrd at the San Francisco General Hospital in 1984. Over a ten-month period almost four hundred coronary care patients were randomly assigned to two groups, just as in the VA study. But here there was no way for the patient or his doctors or nurses to know which group he was in, because the patient did not spend more or less time praying with a chaplain. Instead, in the San Francisco study, devout Christians prayed for the members of one group but not the other. Those doing the praying were given the names of the patients and a description of their ailments, but they never met the patients. When the study was completed, the prayed-for patients were less likely to have suffered from congestive heart failure during recovery, had less need for antibiotics, had fewer cases of pneumonia, and generally fared better in a variety of ways.[4]

The medical power of prayer has generated a cottage industry of scientific work. A survey by research psychiatrist Dr. David Larson has found nearly three hundred studies on the topic, with about 80 percent showing that religion is good for your health.[5] Dr. Dale Matthews of Georgetown University, a major researcher in the field, has concluded; "I can say, as a physician and scientist—not just as a Christian—that, scientifically, prayer is good for you. The medical effects of faith on health are not a matter of faith but of science."[6] And the impact of these studies has spread far beyond the medical community. Consider Dr. Larry Dossey's best seller *Healing Words: The Power of Prayer and the Practice of Medicine,* or Dr. Herbert Benson's equally popular book *Timeless Healing: The Power and Biology of Belief.*[7] It is hardly surprising that *Newsweek* magazine offered a cover story on prayer and health that described ongoing research work in the field.[8] And the ultimate stamps of scientific legitimacy are being bestowed: Congress has created the Office of Alternative Medicine in the National Institutes of Health to scientifically study, among other phenomena, the power of prayer,[9] while private institutions such as the Johns Hopkins School of Medicine have accepted foundation grants to study "faith and medicine."[10]

There certainly are dissenters from the view that prayer is good medicine. A number of scientists are more than a little skeptical about the entire field. And there are some serious difficulties with many of the studies in this area. When an individual prays for his own improvement, it is difficult to separate the power of prayer from the placebo effect, that is, from the benefits that flow simply from the belief that one is doing something useful. Moreover, some of the studies purporting to show that praying can improve your condition have been criticized for a lack of adequate controls and for results that are not statistically significant.[11] Particularly sharp criticism has been directed at the alleged effect of intercessory prayer, that is, at those few studies, like those of Dr. Byrd, that claim that one person's prayer can help another without the recipient's even knowing that the prayer is taking place. Later studies have failed to replicate this effect,[12] and Dr. Byrd's own work has come under sharp criticism.[13] Even the most fervent believer in intercessory prayer has to concede that there are difficult conceptual problems with a controlled study of the type Dr. Byrd attempted. It is hard to show that the people supposedly praying for the sick are actually doing so, and it is even harder to be sure that no one is praying for the control group. Relatives unaware of the study (or unsympathetic to it) may be praying in great numbers, and others around the world may be praying for everyone who is sick.

But from the point of view of traditional science, there is no reason to rule out in advance the medical power of prayer. It is hardly implausible that an individual can improve his own health through prayer. As early as 1902, William James wrote that "in certain environments prayer may contribute to recovery, and should be encouraged as a therapeutic measure."[14] Even a harsh critic of modern studies on the power of prayer has written that, "[i]t is undeniable that the mind affects the body in many ways. Therein lies a fertile field for rigorous science; also a fertile field for exaggerated claims."[15] It is the job of science to weed out the exaggerations and to find out whether there is a core of truth. Even the more controversial area of intercessory prayer, as implausible as it may seem to many scientists, cannot be ruled out of science on that basis. Perhaps prayer can act at a distance on an unwitting recipient as gravity can; perhaps it cannot. True scientists will want to examine the evidence, form a provisional opinion, and remain open to new evidence.

Thus, the medical power of prayer presents no challenge to science. On the contrary, the array of double-blind studies, government research proposals, and foundation grants represent the workings of science. Theories are presented and tested. Some are falsified; some are tested further. The power of prayer may still be outside of mainstream medicine, but a scientific process is under way to determine whether it should remain there or move inside. As with all science in the real world, the process will often be slow, controversies will erupt, and politics and personalities will play a role. But gradually a consensus will be reached.

Thus, it is not science that is threatened by the current infatuation with the medical power of prayer—it is religion. And it is threatened not by the possibility that science will find that prayer is useless. It is threatened by the possibility that science will find that prayer works.

Grouping Prayer with Other Therapies

Consider what it would mean for science to say that prayer "works." It would mean that in controlled settings that can be replicated at will prayer has a measurable affect on a measurable symptom. Prayer can then be neatly domesticated and categorized. It will be like aspirin or acupuncture—indicated for arthritis, not indicated for pancreatic cancer.

This is the way prayer is currently presented in the bulk of the medical work that touts its effectiveness as medicine. At the Mind Body Study Group in the Duke University Medical Center, specialists, including radiologists and oncologists, combine traditional medical therapies with approaches like positive thinking, therapeutic touch, and, of course, prayer.[16] Dr. Larry Burk, the radiologist who heads the group, calls this approach "complementary medicine," because it combines traditional and nontraditional approaches.[17] At bottom, Burk says, we are studying "how emotions affect the immune system."[18]

Dr. Herbert Benson similarly presents prayer as one item on a medical menu. As head of Harvard University's Mind/Body Medical Institute, Benson has long stressed the therapeutic benefits of the relaxation response, a state of bodily calm, and remembered wellness, a technique through which a patient draws on his desire for health.[19] Benson has patients utilize prayer to achieve the relaxation response and to remember wellness, and he argues that, taken together with other self-help strategies such as nutrition, this approach can alleviate hypertension, insomnia, infertility, and other ailments.[20] But prayer is far from the only road to these results, in Benson's view. To elicit the relaxation response, Benson presents a table of possibilities: religious people can "choose a prayer" (the table suggests "Our Father who art in heaven" for Protestants or Catholics, "Sh'ma Yisroel" for Jews), whereas nonreligious people can choose a "secular focus" (the table suggests focus words like "ocean" and "calm").[21] In order to remember wellness, Benson offers a similar menu: "Remember the smell of incense at church, or the tranquillity you felt picking up stones from the beach on Cape Cod. . . . Remember the doctor who really cared about you or the chaplain who prayed with you in the hospital."[22] And although Benson believes that humans are "wired for faith," that faith can, in his view, be satisfied without a belief "in God per se"; indeed, the experience of God is the same "[w]hether God is conjured as an opiate for the masses, as Karl Marx suggested, or whether God created us to believe in an experience that is ever-soothing to us."[23]

Dr. Larry Dossey, who is cochair of the Panel on Mind/Body Interventions at the National Institutes of Health's Office of Alternative Medicine, also sees prayer as one type of medical intervention among others. He has argued explicitly that "the body does not distinguish between prayer and meditation,"[24] and he groups the controversial area of intercessory prayer with "shamanic healing, diag-

nosis at a distance, telesomatic events, and . . . noncontact therapeutic touch."[25]

A brief look at noncontact therapeutic touch will give you a sense
of the type of therapies linked by Dossey and others with prayer. In
therapeutic touch a trained practitioner moves her hands in a pat-
tern a few inches away from the patient's body in an effort to reduce
pain and promote healing. The technique, developed about twenty-
five years ago by Delores Krieger and Dora Kunz, is based on the
belief that every human body is surrounded by an energy field—a
belief that supporters relate to Chinese concepts of Qi, east Indian
concepts of prana, and Western ideas of quantum mechanics. The
practitioner manipulates the patient's energy field. Both the scientific basis and the efficacy of this therapy are quite controversial,[26]
but the basic belief of practitioners is that this is a scientifically ex-
plicable and measurable therapy.

The Office of Alternative Medicine in the National Institutes of
Health also groups prayer with a variety of nontraditional secular
approaches to medicine. One early group of research projects
funded by the office included using prayer to treat drug addiction,
yoga for alcoholism, and hypnosis to aid the mending of broken
bones.[27]

Perhaps the ultimate proof that prayer is coming to be seen as a
form of medicine is the growing interest in its negative effects. Medicine, after all, can be misused, and to some of its proponents prayer
is no different. Thus, Larry Dossey has warned about "toxic
prayer"—one person praying for harm to befall another—and has
suggested ways to strengthen the "psychospiritual immune system"
to alleviate the problem.[28]

From a scientific perspective it makes perfect sense to lump
prayer with other alternative therapies. If prayer is going to be
weighed and measured by scientific standards, it cannot be viewed
as special in any way. A controlled test for the efficacy of prayer will
look much like a similar test for the efficacy of meditation or therapeutic touching. Indeed, prayer will be compared with other therapies and combined with them as researchers deem appropriate. And
there is no reason, so long as the scientific approach is taken, for

prayer to be ruled out of bounds. In the end, of course, the evidence might or might not be forthcoming on the power of prayer, but there is no reason medical researchers should not consider the possibility, and there is no reason to withhold useful therapies from individuals who need them. If you need to lower your blood pressure, and prayer can do that for you, your doctor should tell you so, and you should be free to use that approach.

Of course, there could be various theological objections to the idea that prayer could work in the way that scientists might discover. Suppose prayer with a chaplain is shown to help 75 percent of patients who are recovering from heart surgery. We might ask why God would help 75 percent rather than 80 percent or 100 percent. And we might wonder why prayer works more often with people recovering from heart surgery than with people who have been shot through the heart. And some people of faith might wonder whether the success or failure of a double-blind study itself might reflect God's attitude toward the study. Scientists, who do not have to square their work with a theory of God's omnipotence, do not have to worry about these problems, but others might.

At the most general level, thoughtful theologians will be alert to the danger of accepting falsifiability as the measure for the efficacy of prayer. From a religious perspective, God need not confine his interventions in the world to those that are testable or replicable. Whether we use the term "miracle" or not, there may be events in the world that we simply will never understand at a human level.

Still, in the end, it is possible as a matter of Judeo-Christian theology that prayer could have effects that are limited and scientifically measurable, whatever other effects it may also have. Though it does not answer all of our questions, science does enable us to gain some understanding of the material world, and prayer may operate in part in that world. Thus, the argument of some religious leaders that we should not "test God" in the laboratory is unpersuasive because testing prayer is not the same as testing God.[29] Although neither God's existence nor his ultimate nature is scientifically testable, many aspects of the natural universe are. And human health is not completely outside of that realm. The vast majority of

Jews and Christians reject the central Christian Science teaching that "Mind is All and matter is naught"[30] and the corollary idea that traditional medicine, because it proceeds from the mistaken idea that matter is real, cannot provide real benefits.[31] To most of us, the physical world, including our bodies, exists and often follows discoverable patterns. So just as scientists cannot rule out the possibility that prayer has limited measurable effects, people of faith cannot rule out that possibility either.

The Distinctive Power of Prayer

So where is the risk, where is the harm, with the current infatuation with the medical power of prayer? The risk is that prayer will come to be seen as nothing but a form of medicine. In other words, just as we have seen in other contexts, the limited, measurable effects that science identifies with a phenomenon come to be seen as the whole story. If that happens with prayer, it will lose its distinctive contribution to our understanding of ourselves and our place in the cosmos.

It is a commentary on the times that we have to step back for a moment to recall what that distinctive contribution is. For too many people petitionary prayer, that is, prayer that asks God to grant our requests, has come to be nothing more than a kind of erratic vending machine, a means for trying to get a desired result. But petitionary prayer in the Judeo-Christian tradition means much more. It offers an opportunity to affirm our faith, to understand our limits, and to accept what life brings us whether or not it accords with our wishes.

These are traditional ideas, but they are ideas that are sometimes forgotten in our rush to see everything in a scientific and medical context. The heart of the Protestant perspective on prayer has been ably stated by the philosopher D. Z. Philllips.[32] He imagines religious parents with a dying child praying that the child may live. They understand that they cannot force God to act in a certain way. Indeed, they "recognize that things can go either way;

the child may live or it may die."[33] They recognize that some things are "beyond their control, and [they] seek something to sustain them which does not depend on the way things go, namely, the love of God."[34]

The Catholic theologian Karl Rahner has described petitionary prayer as a mingling of "the greatest boldness with the deepest humility," because it combines "a great measure of 'self-will' (for one presents to Him one's *own* desires) with a supreme degree of submissiveness (for one *prays* to Him whom one cannot compel, persuade or charm, but only beg)."[35] Such prayer, if done with "faith in the power of the Being to whom it is addressed and not merely in the power of prayer," can transform our lives: we become less egotistic and less resentful if we must join others in accepting bitter outcomes.[36]

Similar themes emerge from the Jewish perspective. Professor Jakob J. Petuchowski of Hebrew Union College stresses that petitionary prayer does not convey any information to God that he previously lacked. Rather, it helps us to recognize our dependence on God and to realize that we are not alone in the universe. It can even make us less egotistical when we pray as part of a larger community.[37] Rabbi Harold S. Kushner's popular writings stress a somewhat different perspective: petitionary prayer does not always work because some things are "too hard even for God." Still, petitionary prayer helps because we realize that since "God is on our side, we manage to go on."[38]

So petitionary prayer from a traditional religious perspective awakens us to our limits, to the existence of something greater than ourselves, and to the possibility that we can accept what happens even if things do not go our way. There is no logical reason that these valuable goals cannot exist alongside the possibility that petitionary prayer is good for our health. If I am facing heart surgery, and I offer prayers within a traditional religious framework for a successful outcome, there is no reason these prayers cannot raise the odds of that outcome while also reminding me of my place in a much larger universe.

The Threat to Prayer's Traditional Role

But there is a real danger that the scientific and the medical perspective will gradually crowd out the distinctive religious values of prayer. At a time when doctors are speaking out publicly about the medical benefits of prayer—indeed, at a time when those ideas show up regularly on the best-seller lists—religious leaders should speak out clearly and often about the other purposes of prayer. Some have done so,[39] but to date their influence has been limited. There is nothing wrong with doctors spreading the word about what they believe to be a valuable medical treatment, but that should not be the only voice in the public square. The religious values at stake here—humility, acceptance, understanding—are not trivial. But in our modern culture those values could easily be swamped by the latest scientific findings.

It is easy to see the risk. Consider the reported comments of the Reverend Robert Yim, a Catholic priest and chaplain at a hospital in Saint Louis: "Pastoral care is not just the hold-the-hands, comforting thing of just the spiritual, but we also ought to have measurable clinical outcomes for what we do."[40] But "comforting" does not capture all of what religion can do, and an emphasis on clinical goals does not capture all of what a priest can offer. In a society as saturated as ours is by science and by a desire for self-fulfillment, other messages can simply get dropped. Consider the practical advice the *Arizona Republic* has offered its readers: "If prayer has been missing from your life, consider revisiting it. There is medical evidence that prayer affects recovering patients. If it works for them, it may work for you."[41]

Recent years have seen a tremendous growth in the use of prayer circles and other forms of spiritual healing in mainline Protestant, Catholic, and Jewish groups.[42] In many churches, congregants pray weekly or daily for a long list of sick people. When President Clinton injured his knee, worshipers at the Foundry Memorial United Methodist Church in Washington, D.C., where Clinton had worshiped, prayed for his recovery.[43]

It is possible that the bulk of these prayers are offered in large part to gain the traditional humbling sense that petitionary prayer can bestow. But there are reasons for skepticism. As Dr. Dale Matthews, a leading proponent of prayer as medicine, says, trivializing religion is "a real danger when we attempt to embrace religion only for its health benefits."[44]

The particular danger here is that the interest in prayer is really being fueled not by any religious sentiments but by a broader embrace of unconventional therapies. It is the same phenomenon we saw with modern creationism: a distrust of "mainstream science," combined with a continued infatuation with the scientific method, leads not to an emphasis on spiritual values but to an emphasis on narrowly mechanistic explanations. The problem from the religious perspective is not that these explanations are controversial but that they point away from the distinctive contributions religion can make. The Reverend John Koenig, academic dean of the General Theological Seminary in New York, has linked the growth of spiritual healing in recent years in part to the growth of alternative medicine.[45] Rev. Koenig points out that this link is fueled by a suspicion of the medical establishment and a distrust of managed health care.[46]

So it is reasonable to suspect that for many Americans the increase in prayer for the sick has more to do with the increased interest in homeopathy and acupuncture than with any spiritual rebirth. On a variety of fronts, many Americans are trying and succeeding to get doctors to change their ways. Prayer is just one more example. Indeed, many Americans now link prayer directly with doctors: a recent poll showed that 64 percent of those surveyed believe doctors should pray with patients who request it.[47]

The halo effect of science in America today is so powerful that it is hard to imagine resisting it, even to the extent of retaining values alongside the values of science. We can imagine a test of this hypothesis. Suppose an impressive new study comes out linking prayer with a 75 percent greater likelihood of managing the pain associated with arthritis. The medical community would publicize this de-

velopment, as they should. In my view, it would be cause for celebration if mainstream religious groups balanced the scales a bit by
issuing statements noting the work of the doctors but stressing that
prayer also serves deeper goals of acceptance, understanding, and
community. From my perspective, it would be healthy if ministers,
priests, and rabbis preached sermons making the same point—
prayer is not primarily a new form of aspirin; it serves timeless goals
and teaches us about our limits. Perhaps all of this would help ordinary people of faith who read about the study to think of prayer
in its rich spiritual context.

At present, my hopes are not likely to be realized. Religious
groups and clergy would most likely join the medical profession in
touting the new arthritis study, perhaps briefly mentioning that
there are other reasons to pray as well. And ordinary people will
come to think of prayer even more as simply another potion rather
than in a broader context.

For millennia people have offered prayers in times of need. For
millennia to come people will do the same. I have no desire to rec-
ommend anything else. Prayer offers solace, release, a sense of our
limits, and, yes, it might offer medical benefits as well. But if modern trends continue, the medical view will dominate our thoughts at
the expense of everything else. If this seems unduly gloomy, consider
the following comparison.

Suppose a new controlled scientific study at a major university
demonstrates that playing jazz while corn is growing produces
larger ears of corn than playing no music at all. Let us imagine even
that playing jazz produces better corn than playing any other form
of music. Now the agricultural experts who conducted this study
would understandably be excited. They would not only announce
their results, but they would also continue their research in an effort
to find the best kind of jazz to play.

Their work would be widely praised, as it should be. Producing
a greater yield from any agricultural crop can reduce prices, thus
making food more available for all. But there is one effect we would
not expect. Jazz musicians would not alter the course of their cre-
ative work to become corn production specialists. Jazz critics would

not begin assessing new music in light of its corn-growing potential. Wynton Marsalis would not become a farmer.

The reason is that jazz has its own history, traditions, values, and goals. It does not want to be just a better fertilizer, or even primarily a better fertilizer. There would be nothing wrong with using jazz to grow better corn, but that would not become the work of jazz musicians.

Why can we not expect the same result when studies show that prayer reduces the pain associated with arthritis? I hope that it is not because we have forgotten that prayer has its own history, traditions, values, and goals. But it is reasonable to wonder.

5

How Free Speech and Due Process Protect Religion

If I mention to religious friends the preoccupation with science that I see when religious leaders discuss developments in genetics or medicine, I am often told that people of faith feel they have to hide that faith. They do not feel free, for example, to discuss publicly the notion that the soul might play a vital part in our lives. In particular, there is a powerful perception that the American legal system is hostile to religion—that the constitutionally mandated separation of church and state has pushed religion to the sidelines in public debate. Science, by contrast, is perceived to be both lawful and popular in America. Thus, I am told, it is hardly surprising that, consciously or not, religious leaders are pulled toward scientific arguments and explanations.

Depicting Religion as a Victim in the Courts

The public statements of some of America's religious leaders and their supporters certainly provide support for this view. Ralph Reed, executive director of the Christian Coalition, has written that "[t]he zealous disdain for religion in American jurisprudence amounts to intolerance. The full weight of American culture, law, and politics leans heavily against those who seek to bring their faith to bear in the larger society."[1] Michael Novak of the American Enterprise Institute has said, "If you just look at the way our courts deal with the word 'religion,' they almost always surround it with pejorative words, like 'divisive' and 'dangerous.' They treat it like a disease that has to be quarantined."[2]

When the U.S. Supreme Court in 1997 struck down the Religious Freedom Restoration Act, this refrain reached a crescendo that continues to this day. The executive director of the Baptist Joint Committee announced that "[t]he First Amendment has just been gutted by the Supreme Court."[3] A spokesman for the National Council of the Churches of Christ called the decision "a profound national wrong,"[4] and the general counsel for the United States Catholic Conference said that without the act religious organizations confront "chaos."[5]

And these were the mild reactions. The most common comparison offered in 1997 was to the Supreme Court's 1857 *Dred Scott* decision. Rabbi David Saperstein, director of the Religious Action Center of Reform Judaism, said that when the Court struck down the act it "abdicated its most solemn responsibility, the protection of our liberties," by rendering a decision that "will go down in history with Dred Scott."[6] A coalition of Protestant and Catholic leaders announced that "[o]ur present circumstance is shadowed by the memory of the infamous Dred Scott decision of 1857. Then, the Court, in a similar act of raw judicial power, excluded slaves of African descent from the community of those possessing rights that others are bound to respect."[7] The spokesman for the National Council of the Churches of Christ made the comparison explicit: "As the Dred Scott decision of a century ago was for African-Americans, so [the Court's decision] is for religious Americans today."[8]

Dred Scott v. Sandford, the most notorious Supreme Court decision in American history, found that neither black slaves nor their descendants could be considered citizens of the United States, that they were not protected by the Bill of Rights, and that Congress could not emancipate slaves because that would deprive slave holders of their "property."[9] The decision helped bring on the Civil War and was reversed by the three post–Civil War amendments to the Constitution.[10]

I know that in our contemporary culture it is fashionable to claim the status of victims. But comparing religious Americans today with slaves before the Civil War sets some kind of record. And rhetoric like this makes a difference. If people of faith mistakenly believe that they have no fair chance to participate in American debate and to shape American values, it is understandable that they will retreat. When new technologies emerge, scientific perspectives will seem to offer a safe and attractive avenue for discussion. But the loss of the distinctively religious point of view will harm everyone.

And the loss is needless. American legal doctrine does not oppress religion. It is essential that people of faith and their leaders have a clear sense of American constitutional law in this area. When they do, they will realize that although all of their hopes may not be realized, they are free to play a vital and distinctive role in political debate. Shedding the mantle of victimhood will be empowering.

To understand the constitutional status of American religion requires a broad perspective. This chapter gives an overview of the area and then focuses on the free speech and due process protections that shield religious speech and the right to use religious schools. The next chapter covers the free exercise of religion clause, showing how it protects faith and practice, and why the fate of the Religious Freedom Restoration Act will have very little practical effect on America's religious communities. Chapter 7 analyzes the nonestablishment requirement in the Constitution. Here religion is undeniably restricted in American life, but, as we shall see, some of those restrictions may work to the advantage of the religious perspective. Chapter 8 explains why it is perfectly lawful and legitimate for religious values to play a role in shaping legislation.

The Constitutional Framework for American Religion

The First Amendment to the U.S. Constitution provides that "Congress shall make no law respecting an establishment of religion, or prohibiting the free exercise thereof."[11] The first part is the establishment clause; the second is the free exercise clause. These clauses, like the rest of the Bill of Rights, were originally intended to limit only the federal government.[12] Indeed, the statement that Congress could not establish religion was designed in part to protect state establishments from federal interference.[13] After all, about half of the states had religious establishments when the United States was founded.[14] In Massachusetts, for example, tax dollars went toward the education and salary of Congregationalist ministers.[15] But the last of the state establishments was dissolved in 1833,[16] and the Fourteenth Amendment, adopted after the Civil War, altered the relationship of the federal and state governments.[17] In the 1940s the U.S. Supreme Court held that because of the Fourteenth Amendment the states were bound by both the free exercise and establishment clauses; thus, states today cannot have established churches.[18]

So everyone agrees today that the entire American government is bound by free exercise and nonestablishment principles. Unfortunately, that pretty much exhausts the area of agreement about the religion clauses. The religious leaders cited above are convinced that court decisions and government policies put their free exercise rights at risk. Opponents of organized religion are similarly convinced that every tax exempt church and public reference to God constitutes an illegal establishment of religion.

Both sides, of course, are guilty of exaggeration. But some of the controversy here is understandable given the tension between the two clauses. A broad reading of either one immediately seems to violate the other. Consider a young Catholic, drafted to serve his country, who finds himself stationed far from any church. Under the circumstances he might plausibly insist that his right to free exercise of religion is infringed unless the military provides a priest to celebrate Mass. From this soldier's point of view, the military chaplain program is not just a fine idea, it is a constitutional necessity. But a non-Catholic taxpayer may have a very different perspective when he sees his tax dollars going to support a priest. From this vantage point, the chaplain program is not just a bad idea, it is an unconstitutional establishment of religion.

To date the military chaplaincy programs have survived constitutional attack,[19] although it is worth noting that James Madison thought they were unconstitutional.[20] The broader point is that there can be serious difficulties when litigation arises under the religion clauses. In chapters 6 and 7 we will look at free exercise and establishment cases in order to understand how religion can intersect with public life in specific controversial areas. We will find that in many respects the rules are relatively clear and relatively favorable to religion.

But before doing that it is vital to understand what is at stake and what is not in litigation concerning the religion clauses. There is a real danger here of missing the forest for the trees. To a considerable extent litigation over the religion clauses does not implicate the most important freedoms for people of faith in America. In particular, the freedom of religious people, religious leaders, and religious groups to speak out in public debate is constitutionally protected by the free speech clause of the U.S. Constitution. And the vital freedom to send children to religious schools is constitutionally protected by the Constitution's due process clause.

These constitutional protections are not undercut in any way by the continuing debates over the scope of the free exercise and establishment clauses. Nor are these protections at risk as the membership and ideology of the Supreme Court changes over time. The cases we will be focusing on here are stable decisions that have stood the test of time. They provide the framework for understanding the controversies surrounding the religion clauses, and they provide the fundamental basis for a religious role in American public debate that focuses on humility, faith, and values.

Free Speech and Religion in the Public Square

Americans are justly proud that our First Amendment prevents the government from "abridging the freedom of speech, or of the press; or the right of the people peaceably to assemble, and to petition the Government for a redress of grievances."[21] The right of free speech covers all levels of government[22] and helps create a society in which wide open debate is the norm.[23]

But we often forget that the right of free speech includes religious speech. The Supreme Court made that point forcefully over a half-century ago and has never deviated from it.

On April 26, 1938, Newton Cantwell, a Jehovah's Witness, was preaching his faith on Cassius Street in New Haven, Connecticut.[24] Cantwell would typically knock on doors, ask permission to play a record on his portable phonograph, and then try to sell the book described on the record. He would also solicit contributions. One of Cantwell's records, "Enemies," attacked religious systems other than Cantwell's own as instruments of Satan and singled out the Roman Catholic Church for particularly harsh and offensive criticism.[25] About 90 percent of the residents of Cassius Street were Catholic, so Cantwell's message was not happily received. At one point he stopped two Catholic men on the street and, with their permission, played the record "Enemies." Both were furious and were tempted to hit Cantwell. Before any violence took place, he picked up his materials and left.[26]

Cantwell was tried and convicted on two counts: soliciting for religious or charitable contributions without obtaining a certificate required by state law and inciting a breach of the peace. The U.S. Supreme Court unanimously reversed both convictions in an opinion by Justice Roberts. On both counts its analysis combined a recognition of free exercise of religion values with traditional free speech doctrine.

As to the requirement of obtaining a certificate before soliciting, the Court felt this gave too much discretion to a state official to approve or disapprove religious speech in advance. Such a prior restraint, the Court held, was "obnoxious to the Constitution" under settled free speech law.[27] The Court's discussion of the breach of peace conviction began with the observation that "a State may not unduly suppress free communication of views, religious or other, under the guise of conserving desirable conditions."[28] Since there was no "clear and present danger to a substantial interest of the State,"[29] Cantwell's speech had to be protected, no matter how unpleasant or unpopular it might be:

In the realm of religious faith, and in that of political belief, sharp differences arise. In both fields the tenets of one man may seem the rankest error to his neighbor. To persuade others to his own point of view, the pleader, as we know, at times resorts to exaggeration, to vilification of men who have been, or are, prominent in church or state, and even to false statement. But the people of this nation have ordained in the light of history, that, in spite of the probability of excesses and abuses, these liberties are, in the long view, essential to enlightened opinion and right conduct on the part of the citizens of a democracy.[30]

This was the unanimous opinion of a remarkably diverse court—it was joined by conservatives like Justice McReynolds, centrists like Justice Stone, and liberals like Justice William O. Douglas. Commentators have emphasized that *Cantwell* remains to this day a "strong First Amendment case."[31]

And how could it be otherwise? The public utterances of religious laypeople, leaders, and organizations helped create the United States and have informed every major public debate since its creation, including slavery, prohibition, the civil rights movement, and the Vietnam War.[32] Protecting free speech without protecting religious speech is inconceivable in American history and law. As Justice Brennan wrote when the Supreme Court unanimously struck down a state law barring clergy from holding political office, we cannot "place religious discussion, association, or political participation in a status less preferred than rights of discussion, association, and political participation generally."[33] Or, as Justice Scalia more recently put it, "a free-speech clause without religion would be *Hamlet* without the prince."[34] The problem for American religion is not that it lacks the ability to speak out. The problem is its modern tendency, when the subject matter turns scientific, to lose its distinctive voice.

Now the right to free speech protects you from government censorship—it does not entitle you to taxpayer money to disseminate your views. If you believe American foreign policy is misguided, you have a right to speak out, but you have to do it on your own dollar. The same is true with religious speech. But traditional free speech doctrine does provide that if the government creates a public forum—a setting where people are free to express their views— then the government cannot discriminate against speakers based on the content of those views.[35] If, for example, a corner of a public park is set aside for speeches, the government cannot forbid speeches by Republicans or speeches that favor abolishing the income tax.

The application of this principle to religious speech has caused controversy, since religious speech on public property strikes some as an establishment of religion. But over the past quarter-century the Supreme Court has made clear that here—just as with Newton Cantwell's right to preach—traditional free speech protections include religion. If the government sets up a public forum, it cannot discriminate against religious speech.[36]

The pivotal modern case began at the University of Missouri at Kansas City (UMKC).[37] As a public institution, UMKC is subject to the limitations of the First Amendment.[38] In 1977 UMKC had a policy of encouraging the activities of student organizations; indeed, it provided facilities for the meetings of over one hundred student groups. It refused, however, to allow a religious group named Cornerstone to conduct its meetings in those facilities. Cornerstone was an organization composed of evangelical Christian students from many denominations. Its meetings, which were open to the public, typically involved prayers, hymns, Bible commentary, and religious discussions. UMKC took the position that it was allowed to prohibit the use of university buildings "for purposes of religious worship or religious teaching."[39]

The U.S. Supreme Court, by a vote of eight to one, told UMKC it was wrong. Justice Powell's opinion for the Court was a strong one. Of course public universities are free to make academic judgments concerning what may be taught, and the like. And of course public universities should not endorse particular religious teachings. But when the university creates an open forum for use by student groups, it is neither making academic judgments nor endorsing the views of any of those groups. UMKC hardly concedes that it is endorsing the views of the Young Socialist Alliance, a group eligible to use its facilities.[40] And Cornerstone should not be worse off than the Young Socialist Alliance. "Religious worship and discussion," the Court stressed, "are forms of speech and association protected by the First Amendment."[41]

An important application of the Cornerstone case came in 1993 when every member of the Supreme Court agreed that public schools could not bar a group from after-hours use of its facilities solely because the group had a religious viewpoint.[42] Under New York law, local school boards control the use of school property when school is not in session. One local board opened its schools for "social, civic and recreational" purposes but denied a church group the right to show a film series that promoted Christian family values.[43] Justice White's opinion for the Court found a clear violation of free speech principles: the First Amendment forbids the government from regulating speech so as to disfavor some viewpoints, and religious viewpoints are included in that protection. New York admitted that a nonreligious film about child rearing would be allowed under its rules, so it was not free to ban a religious perspective on that subject.[44]

These cases establish an important principle. Religious speech cannot be the subject of discrimination when the government chooses to create an open forum. Of course, difficult issues remain. In 1995 the Supreme Court considered whether the University of Virginia, which provides funds for student publications, could withhold such funds from religious groups.[45] The money in question came from student fees, and the direct payment of state money to a religious group could be seen as different from the neutral provision of an open forum. Nonetheless, the Court adhered to the thrust of its earlier decisions and held that because of free speech principles the university could not discriminate against religion— the money had to be made available for religious organizations just as it was made available for others. The Court did leave open the possibility that a student could be exempted from paying the mandatory fee if he felt it caused him to support speech with which he disagreed.[46]

But these complexities should not divert us from the main point. Free speech principles fully protect religious speech from government censorship and from exclusion from public forums. Moreover, another bedrock constitutional principle—the right to due process of law—also protects religious values without invocation of the religion clauses.

Due Process and the Right to Attend Religious Schools

The U.S. Constitution provides that neither the federal nor the state government may deprive any person "of life, liberty, or property, without due process of law."[47] Until the late nineteenth century the Supreme Court had interpreted this phrase as providing only procedural protections.[48] In other words, the government had to follow certain steps before taking away something of yours; but if those steps were followed, you had no further due process claim. The notion that you are entitled to this sort of procedural due process remains vital today.[49]

But beginning in the 1890s, the Supreme Court began to rule that the due process clause provides substantive protections as well.[50] On this view, you have certain fundamental rights that the government cannot take away, no matter how elaborate the procedures employed. This notion, called substantive due process, has led to some of the most controversial decisions in American history. And it is easy to see why—when the unelected Supreme Court says that an individual's "property" or "liberty" has been taken away by a legislative enactment, the will of a democratic majority, at least in the short run, is being thwarted. It is one thing for the Court to overrule a legislature when relatively explicit provisions of the Constitution are at stake. The Fifteenth Amendment, for example, provides that "the right of citizens of the United States to vote shall not be denied . . . by any State on account of race."[51] So if a given state legislature, reflecting the views of its constituents, disenfranchises an unpopular racial minority, the Court will quite properly void the statute. The Constitution, after all, is the supreme law of the land.[52]

But substantive due process cases tend to be a lot murkier, since "property" and "liberty" are relatively vague terms. In 1905, for example, the Supreme Court struck down a New York law that limited the number of hours a baker could work to sixty a week.[53] The Court found that the law interfered with the "liberty" of employers and employees to make a contract.[54] This decision ushered in an enormously controversial series of cases in which the Court invalidated a host of modern labor and economic regulations, often on substantive due process grounds.[55] After decades of protest, battles with President Franklin Delano Roosevelt, and the appointment of new justices, the Court largely abandoned substantive due process in the area of economic regulation.[56] Indeed, in the late 1930s the Court began overruling some of its earlier cases, thus allowing the government, for example, to enact maximum hour and minimum wage laws.[57]

Liberals hated the substantive due process cases that thwarted economic and social legislation in the New Deal. But it is conservatives who have been outraged by the more modern use of substantive due process, under which "liberty" has been seen as including a right of privacy, leading to cases in which the Court has sharply limited the ability of legislatures to restrict contraception and abortion.[58] The most famous of these cases, *Roe v. Wade*,[59] is every bit as controversial today as the anti–New Deal substantive due process cases were in the 1930s.

Yet, there is one substantive due process case that has been embraced by liberals and conservatives alike. The unanimous 1925 decision in *Pierce v. Society of Sisters*,[60] holding that the government cannot ban private schools, has been cited by the Supreme Court down to the present day, with no justice challenging its validity.[61] And although *Pierce* never mentions freedom of religion, it has become a vital force for the maintenance and transmission of religious values in American society.

The *Pierce* controversy had its roots in the nativist feelings that swept the United States during and after World War I. Anti-German sentiment and the Red Scare fueled state and federal efforts to coerce immigrants to embrace "Americanization" by abandoning their native languages and demonstrating loyalty to public institutions.[62]

In Oregon, public pressure focused on the Roman Catholic community. Troubled by the growth of Catholic private schools and by the increasingly visible presence of Catholics in public life, Scottish Rite Masons circulated a petition in 1922 calling for a statewide vote on an initiative requiring all children between the ages of eight and sixteen to attend public school.[63] The petition easily received enough signatures to place it on the November 1922 ballot.[64]

In the ensuing campaign, the initiative was supported by the Masons, the nativist Federation of Patriotic Societies, and the Ku Klux Klan.[65] They argued that children should not be divided into "antagonistic groups" that would separate the nation into "cliques, cults and factions."[66] Opponents of the initiative, which included not only Catholics, but many Protestant leaders as well, maintained that the proposal was motivated by bigotry.[67] On November 7, 1922, the initiative was approved by a vote of 115,506 to 103,685.[68]

Immediately after the election, Oregon's Roman Catholic leadership decided to test the constitutionality of the statute. The Society of the Sisters of the Holy Names of Jesus and Mary, which ran several parochial schools in the state, became a plaintiff. The society was joined by the Hill Military Academy, a nonsectarian private boys' school. Catholic leaders helped pay the Military Academy's legal expenses because, as one of them put it, it was necessary "to show that the fight was not an exclusively Catholic one."[69]

The legal arguments of the Society of Sisters relied heavily on a Supreme Court decision that came down just one month before their lawsuit was filed. Nativist sentiment in Nebraska had led to passage of a statute that banned the teaching in any school, public or private, of any subject in any language other than English.[70] The statute was aimed at the German-American community, where young people typically went to private schools where instruction was in English, but where the German language was taught to those who had not learned it at home.[71] In *Meyer v. Nebraska*[72] the Supreme Court found the statute unconstitutional. In his opinion for the Court, Justice McReynolds relied squarely on substantive due process. He found that the "liberty" protected by the due process clause included both the economic right of language teachers to practice their profession and "the power of parents to control the education of their own."[73] Though acknowledging that the state had substantial power to "improve the quality of its citizens," he concluded that the complete prohibition on foreign language instruction infringed on "fundamental rights which must be protected."[74] Justice Holmes, joined by Justice Sutherland, dissented. Holmes was a critic of substantive due process who believed that the doctrine gave the courts too much power at the expense of the democratically elected legislature.[75] For him it was enough that the Nebraska statute did not pass "the bounds of reason."[76]

Given this precedent, the challengers to the Oregon ban on private schools had good reason for optimism. When *Pierce v. Society of Sisters* reached the Supreme Court in 1925, the attorney for the society stressed the Court's holding in the *Meyer* case.[77] The strategy was successful. Justice McReynolds, this time writing for a unanimous Court, struck down the Oregon ban on private schools on substantive due process grounds, relying heavily on *Meyer*.[78] Once again the Court found that liberty had been infringed both in economic terms—the destruction of the schools was the destruction of business—and in terms of parental rights to direct the upbringing of their children.[79] The Court expressed the latter right in ringing language:

> The fundamental theory of liberty upon which all governments in this Union repose excludes any general power of the State to standardize its children by forcing them to accept instruction from public teachers only. The child is not the mere creature of the State; those who nurture him and direct his destiny have the right, coupled with the high duty, to recognize and prepare him for additional obligations.[80]

This time there was no dissent from Justice Holmes. Every member of the Court—a diverse group including conservatives like Willis

Van Devanter, centrists like Chief Justice Taft, and liberals like Louis Brandeis—joined the opinion. That unanimity foreshadowed *Pierce*'s future. Economic substantive due process has fallen into disfavor, and privacy as a form of substantive due process remains intensely controversial, but the notion that parental control over a child's education is contained within the "liberty" substantively protected by the Constitution is accepted by every member of the Supreme Court.[81] Indeed, *Pierce v. Society of Sisters* is venerated throughout our society by liberals,[82] libertarians,[83] and conservatives[84] alike.

The Ultimate Safety Valve: Religious Schools Today

Although *Pierce* did not mention religion, parochial schools, the primary parties at interest in that case, remain its chief beneficiaries. By creating an impregnable constitutional right to religious education, *Pierce* has become the ultimate safety valve for religious freedom in the United States. Neither Congress nor any state legislature can take away the right to send your child to parochial school. And many Americans have taken up that invitation.

Over 10 percent of America's school children go to private schools, and the majority of those are in religious schools.[85] This puts over three million young people in sectarian schooling,[86] and that is not the end of the story. Home schooling, which has grown dramatically in recent years, may now reach as many as one million children, and once more the majority are involved for religious reasons.[87]

The states have the authority to regulate nonpublic schooling in a reasonable manner to assure that basic skills are mastered, but state government cannot, through the guise of regulation, destroy the essential character of private schooling.[88] Though there have been battles over the precise scope of regulation in certain areas, particularly teacher certification, the trend in most states has been toward legislative acceptance of a good deal of autonomy for nonpublic schools.[89] In any event, the ability of those schools to teach religious and moral values in specific classes as well as throughout the curriculum is clear.[90]

Parents of private school children pay tuition as well as taxes that support the public schools. We will discuss in chapter 7 the legality and desirability of providing taxpayer support for religious schools. But even in the absence of that support, many parents are able and willing to make the sacrifice, in part because religious school costs are often fairly low and the benefits, including academic achievement as well as values education, are often quite high.[91]

Religious schooling is not available for everyone who would want it, but it is a widely used and growing feature of American society. The vitality of religious schools and their solid basis in the U.S. Constitution is a striking rebuke to those who say that religion is a victim of American law. Religious schools provide one basis for the development of a grounding in humility, faith, and values, and the free speech clause fully protects the expression of views that result from such a grounding.

6

How the Free Exercise of Religion Clause Works Today

The Constitution shields American religion from government interference not only with the free speech and due process clauses, but also with explicit protection for the free exercise of religion. Free exercise principles clearly stop the government from suppressing religious beliefs or practices because it disagrees with them or finds them offensive.

Much more difficult questions arise when neutral laws aimed at genuine social problems incidentally affect religious practice. It is this area that has led to much of the outcry over alleged government hostility to religion in recent years, an outcry fueled when the Supreme Court struck down the Religious Freedom Restoration Act. But this difficult topic constitutes only a small corner of American law relating to religion. In order to keep matters in perspective, let us begin with the less controversial area of freedom from direct suppression before turning to the problem of incidental impacts on religion.

Protecting Religious Belief and Practice from Political Attacks

When the U.S. Supreme Court began to give content to religious freedom in the 1940s it stressed the centrality of the "freedom to believe."[1] The Court's first occasion to expand on this idea came in the unlikely form of a criminal prosecution for mail fraud.

In 1934 Guy Ballard, founder of the "I Am" religious movement, set forth his teachings in the book *Unveiled Mysteries.*[2] Ballard described how a young man he met on Mount Shasta, California, turned out to be an "ascended master" from an earlier century. This master led Ballard on a trip back in time during which he learned the mysteries of reincarnation and other teachings of great help to mortals. Ballard stressed in *Unveiled Mysteries* that these experiences "were as real and true as any human experience on earth."[3] After Ballard's death, his wife, Edna, and his son Donald were convicted of fraud because they sold Ballard's book and otherwise promoted his teachings as the true route to physical and spiritual improvement.[4]

During the course of its 1944 consideration of the Ballards' appeal, the U.S. Supreme Court turned to the question of whether a jury should consider the truth of the statements in *Unveiled Mysteries.* For example, Guy Ballard claims in the book that he actually met a young man on Mount Shasta. Should the government be allowed to introduce evidence that Ballard never went to Mount Shasta? Justice Douglas's opinion for the Court squarely holds that the jury should not examine the truth or falsity of Ballard's beliefs. "Men may believe what they cannot prove," Douglas wrote, adding that heresy trials in any form are forbidden under our Constitution.[5] The framers of that document were centrally concerned with protecting our spiritual life:

> Religious experiences which are as real as life to some may be incomprehensible to others. Yet the fact that they may be beyond the ken of mortals does not mean that they can be made suspect before the law. . . . Man's relation to his God was made no concern of the state. He was granted the right to worship as he pleased and to answer to no man for the verity of his religious views.[6]

Finally, the Supreme Court stressed a point that is fundamental in a society as pluralistic as ours. The Ballards' beliefs may "seem incredible, if not preposterous, to most people,"[7] but if those doctrines can be examined by the government, then the same can be done with the religious beliefs of any group; indeed, a "jury in a hostile environment" might attack "the Divinity of Christ."[8] The truth of religious belief is simply off limits to the government.[9]

It follows from the principles of *Ballard* that the government cannot punish religious practices it disagrees with any more than it can punish religious beliefs. If the government bans a prayer or a ritual simply because it finds it mistaken or distasteful, it runs afoul of the free exercise clause. Because outward manifestations of religious belief are central to most faiths, protecting beliefs alone from government persecution would not be adequate.

Since the Supreme Court became active in the religious-freedom arena in the 1940s there have been few occasions to consider government persecution of specific rituals. The reason is simply that such persecution is relatively rare in modern American life. In 1993, however, the Court was called upon to stop the city of Hialeah, Florida, from forbidding certain practices of the Santeria religion that the city found offensive.

Santeria, "the way of the saints," developed in Cuba when the African religion of the Yoruba people who had been brought as slaves absorbed major elements of Roman Catholicism.[10] Santeria adherents use many Catholic symbols and sacraments, but they also perform animal sacrifice as a way of showing devotion to their *orishas,* or spirits. The animals sacrificed include chickens, goats, and turtles. In Cuba the Santeria religion was persecuted, leading many of its adherents to flee to South Florida.[11]

When members of the Santeria faith leased land in Hialeah, Florida, and announced plans to open a church, the city council met in emergency session. The tenor of the debate suggests the prevalent attitudes toward the religion. Councilman Mejides stated that he was "totally against the sacrificing of animals."[12] Councilman Cardoso said that Santeria believers "are in violation of everything this country stands for."[13] When Councilman Martinez, who supported restricting the Santeria church, said that in Cuba "people were put in jail for practicing this religion," the audience applauded.[14] The council then passed a series of ordinances essentially making it un-lawful to "sacrifice" any animal within the city limits of Hialeah.[15]

Every member of the U.S. Supreme Court agreed that Hialeah had violated the free exercise of religion clause. The city was unable to argue persuasively that it was concerned with animal rights or with public health issues, since it did not ban fishing or the exter-mination of mice within a home, nor did the city prohibit hunters from disposing of their kill inside or outside their home as they saw fit.[16] As the use of the word "sacrifice" suggests, Hialeah's laws "had as their object the suppression of religion."[17] Whatever the law in Cuba, that is not allowed under the U.S. Constitution.

Reconciling Free Exercise with Neutral Laws

The Santeria case was an easy one on its facts, but it does suggest the most difficult question in the free exercise area. Suppose the city of Hialeah, because of a genuine and consistent belief in animal rights, had prohibited all killing of animals within its city limits. That law would not be aimed at suppressing a particular religious practice, but it would have the same devastating affect on Santeria adherents. Could those adherents successfully challenge the law on free exercise grounds?

The general problem here is easy to state and hard to solve. Can neutral government laws be allowed to infringe on religious free-dom? Anyone who tells you he has an easy answer is kidding you. If you believe religion must always be free from government con-trol, then you have to allow religions to practice snake handling even if it endangers the public or human sacrifice if it is part of someone's faith. If you believe religion must always yield to the law, then you have to allow a dry county in the South to lock up Catholics for celebrating the Mass or Jews for drinking wine at the Passover Seder. And no matter what your position in this area of the law, you are going to have to worry about legislatures that pretend to be acting on neutral grounds when in fact they are targeting a religious practice and about religions that pretend to have a certain ritual so they can be excused from an unpopular law.

Courts and legislatures have struggled with this problem throughout American history. A brief summary of that struggle is necessary to understand the current state of the law in this area.

The nineteenth-century emergence of what came to be known as the Church of Jesus Christ of Latter-Day Saints gave rise to the first extended Supreme Court treatment of free exercise versus statutory law. The church, whose members are popularly known as Mormons, taught that men should, if possible, practice polygamy. Polygamy was contrary to the teaching of virtually all other Christians. Moreover, the practice of plural marriage carried with it notions of sexual license that linked it in the minds of some with slavery.[18] The Republican Platform of 1856 pronounced that it was "the imperative duty of Congress to prohibit in the Territories those twin relics of barbarianism, polygamy and slavery."[19] In 1862 Congress passed and President Abraham Lincoln signed the Morrill Act, which made polygamy a crime in the territories of the United States, including Utah.[20] In 1875 George Reynolds, secretary to Brigham Young, was convicted under the Morrill Act and sentenced to two years imprisonment because, while married to Mary Ann Tuddenham, he had also married Amelia Jane Schofield.[21]

The U.S. Supreme Court unanimously rejected Reynolds's claim that his conviction violated the free exercise of religion clause.[22] The Court recited the evils of polygamy that had motivated Congress in passing the Morrill Act, including the view that polygamy is an "odious" practice, condemned at common law, that leads to "despotism."[23] As to the free exercise clause, the Court found that it deprived Congress of all power "over mere opinion,"[24] but that Congress retained the ability to regulate actions that violated the law. Actions, as opposed to beliefs, simply could not be exempted from valid laws on religious grounds. To hold otherwise "would be to make the professed doctrines of religious belief superior to the law of the land, and in effect to permit every citizen to become a law unto himself. Government could exist only in name under such circumstances."[25] The Court supported its argument with the classic extreme examples:

> Suppose one believed that human sacrifices were a necessary part of religious worship, would it be seriously contended that the civil government under which he lived could not interfere to prevent a sacrifice? Or if a wife religiously believed it was her duty to burn herself upon the funeral pile of her dead husband, would it be beyond the power of the civil government to prevent her carrying her belief into practice?[26]

From the *Reynolds* decision in 1879 until 1963 the Supreme Court, in the few cases that raised the issue, essentially adhered to the view that general laws could restrict religious practices.[27] During this period, as we saw in chapter 5, the Court stressed that free speech principles fully applied to religious speech, and that doctrine has never changed. But when it came to practices, religion enjoyed no special status until the Supreme Court's 1963 decision in *Sherbert v. Verner*.[28]

Adell Sherbert, a member of the Seventh-day Adventist Church, was fired by her employer, a textile-mill operator in Spartansburg, South Carolina, because she would not work on Saturday, the Sabbath for Adventists.[29] When her Sabbath observance prevented her from finding any work in Spartansburg, she applied for unemployment compensation, but her claim was denied. Unemployment compensation is unavailable if you fail, "without good cause," to accept suitable work, and the government found that Ms. Sherbert had no "good cause" for turning down jobs that required her to work on Saturday.[30]

Ms. Sherbert challenged the denial of benefits on the ground that her free exercise of religion had been abridged, and she succeeded in the U.S. Supreme Court. Even more remarkable than her victory was the approach the Court used in reaching its conclusion. Justice Brennan's opinion for the Court began by asking whether the disallowance of unemployment benefits imposed a burden on Ms. Sherbert's free exercise of religion. He concluded that it did, since "it put pressure upon her" to forego her Sabbath observance.[31] Brennan then asked whether any "compelling state interest" justified South Carolina in burdening Sherbert's free exercise.[32] The state maintained that it was concerned about the possibility that individuals would pretend that religious beliefs made it impossible for them to take jobs, thus unjustly getting unemployment compensation and diminishing the funds available for worthy recipients. But no one contended that Ms. Sherbert was faking her beliefs and the state had presented no evidence of an inability to deal with this problem should it arise. Only if the state could show that denying benefits to Sabbath observers was the least restrictive means of achieving a compelling state interest could it abridge free exercise, and no such showing had been made in this case.[33]

In order to understand the uproar that arose decades later over the Religious Freedom Restoration Act, it is imperative to understand the contrast between the *Sherbert* decision and the earlier *Reynolds* decision concerning bigamy. Although *Sherbert* did not overrule *Reynolds,* it took a fundamentally different approach. Indeed, the two basic positions that currently dominate judicial, legislative, and public debate over free exercise were on the table after *Sherbert* was decided in 1963.

Under the *Reynolds* approach, if a neutral, valid law impinges on religious activities, free exercise challenges must fail. The courts will still protect religious beliefs and religious speech, but once beliefs and speech become action, that action can be regulated or prohibited by a neutral law. Under this approach the courts will step in if a legislature, under the guise of regulating for some public good, does not pass a neutral law but instead singles out a religious practice. Thus, the Hialeah ordinance that prohibited the sacrifice of animals must fall because it was aimed directly at Santeria adherents— it did not prevent others from killing animals for sport or profit.[34] But a genuinely neutral state law that forbade the killing of all animals within a city's limits because of sanitation concerns could not be successfully challenged by the Santeria church—their sacrifices would have to stop.

Under *Sherbert* all of the protections for religious beliefs and speech as well as the protection against laws aimed at religious practices are preserved. But *Sherbert* provides a key additional protection, because under *Sherbert* religious observances might be exempted from the operation of a valid, neutral law. The *Sherbert* test provides that a neutral law cannot infringe on free exercise unless the law serves a compelling state interest. Suppose a city has a law that prevents the killing of all animals within city limits, and suppose this law is not aimed at any religion—it was actually passed for sanitation reasons. Nonetheless, the Santeria sacrifices would have a chance of continuing in that city. Since the antikilling law infringes on free exercise, even though it does so innocently, the question becomes whether a compelling state interest justifies the law and whether banning all killings is the least restrictive means of serving that interest. The government would have to introduce evidence that animal slaughter in all forms poses a threat to the health of the public and that no other form of regulation—for example, a requirement that after Santeria observances all sacrificed animals must be disposed of quickly and cleanly—would serve their goals. The outcome of this case is unclear, because it would depend on the specific showings the government might make to justify this hypothetical ordinance. But the Santeria religion would have a chance of success. Under *Reynolds* it would have none.

And indeed, after *Sherbert* was decided, the Supreme Court upheld free exercise claims in several cases. Some of them involved the denial of unemployment benefits to those who could not take jobs because their religious beliefs prevented them from working in a munitions factory[35] or, as in *Sherbert,* on their Sabbath.[36] The most dramatic decision came in 1972 when the Court, in an opinion by Chief Justice Burger, ruled that Amish children could be exempted from Wisconsin's compulsory school attendance laws.[37] The close-knit Amish community sent their children to school until the eighth grade, but Wisconsin law required attendance until age sixteen. The Amish believed that high school taught worldly values that were inconsistent with their religious commitment to a simple, rural life separate from modern society.[38] The Supreme Court analyzed the problem under *Sherbert* and found that Wisconsin's attendance law, though not aimed at the Amish, infringed on their free exercise.

Moreover, Wisconsin had failed to demonstrate a compelling interest in keeping Amish children in school after eighth grade.[39] The Court also invoked its decision in *Pierce v. Society of Sisters*,[40] in which it had emphasized the rights of parents to control the education of their children.[41]

In the era when the Court invoked the *Sherbert* test, it did not always rule in favor of free exercise claims. At times the government was able to demonstrate a compelling state interest, such as the need to collect taxes, that overcame a burden on religious freedom.[42] And sometimes *Sherbert* was not even applied when religious freedom was at stake. In 1986, for example, the Court rejected the claim of an Orthodox Jew that he be allowed to wear his yarmulke, a small skullcap, while on duty in the Air Force.[43] Although the Air Force's requirement of standardized uniforms burdened the claimant's free exercise, the Court deferred to the special needs of the military without undertaking a *Sherbert*-type analysis of whether there was a compelling state interest.[44] Still, from its inception in 1963 until its sudden demise in 1990, the *Sherbert* approach dominated the free-exercise-of-religion field. Religious groups might win or lose under this approach, but everyone knew the rules. As one commentator put it, it was an era when "free exercise doctrine in the courts was stable, the noisy pressure groups from the ACLU to the religious right were in basic agreement, and most academic commentators were content to work out the implications of the doctrine rather than to challenge it at its roots."[45]

All of that changed with the Supreme Court's *Smith* decision in 1990.[46] *Smith* began with the use of drugs in religious rituals and ultimately led all the way back to the *Reynolds* approach to free exercise.

Peyote is a hallucinogenic drug that is used in the sacraments of the Native American Church. The decision in *Employment Division v. Smith* came after the Oregon courts had ruled that the use of peyote, even for religious purposes, violated the state's ban on controlled substances.[47] The Native Americans affected by this decision maintained that their use of the drug was protected by the free exercise clause.

In the course of rejecting this claim, the opinion for the Court, written by Justice Scalia, rejected the compelling state interest approach in the free exercise area. The Court did not explicitly overrule any precedent, but it interpreted the cases that had used the compelling interest language very narrowly. *Sherbert,* for example, was said to be explained by the need to respect religion when making individual decisions as to who should be exempt from unemployment compensation requirements.[48] The decision excusing Amish students from high school was explained as involving not just the free exercise of religion but the more general due process right, stemming from *Pierce v. Society of Sisters,* to control the education of one's children.[49]

Having cleared the field of troubling precedent, Scalia stated for the Court the general approach to be used in free exercise cases. And here the Court quoted directly from the *Reynolds* antipolygamy decision of 1879: "Laws are made for the government of actions, and while they cannot interfere with mere religious belief and opinions, they may with practices. . . . Can a man excuse his practices to the contrary because of his religious belief? To permit this would be to make the professed doctrines of religious belief superior to the law of the land, and in effect to permit every citizen to become a law unto himself."[50]

Scalia argued that judges were ill suited to decide when religious beliefs were sufficiently central to be entitled to exemptions from general laws.[51] Neutral laws of general applicability should always be immune from free exercise challenge in the courts. Requests for accommodations should be made to the legislature:

It is . . . not surprising that a number of States have made an exception to their drug laws for sacramental peyote use. . . . But to say that a nondiscriminatory religious-practice exemption is permitted, or even that it is desirable, is not to say that it is constitutionally required. . . . It may fairly be said that leaving accommodation to the political process will place at a relative disadvantage those religious practices that are not widely engaged in; but that unavoidable consequence of democratic government must be preferred to a system in which each conscience is a law unto itself or in which judges weigh the social importance of all laws against the centrality of all religious beliefs.[52]

Smith was a bitterly contested five-to-four decision. The four dissenting justices would have retained the compelling-state-interest test, although one of them, Justice O'Connor, would have found that Oregon had a compelling state interest in disallowing all peyote use since the war on drugs is so difficult and so important.[53]

So it turned out that *Sherbert* was not as strong as it seemed. *Reynolds* had never been overruled, merely sidestepped, and now the same fate befell *Sherbert*. Changes in membership of the Court and the continuing appeal of the *Reynolds* formulation caused the pendulum to swing back. The compelling-state-interest test was dead—neutral laws defeated free exercise claims once again.

Academic commentary on *Smith* was largely negative, with many noting that it was anomalous to leave the protection of minority religious practices to the popularly elected legislatures, when minority rights are generally believed to be more secure in the hands of life-tenured federal judges.[54] Several state courts continued to follow the *Sherbert* approach in interpreting their own state constitutions.[55] But the most remarkable reaction to *Smith* came from the public at large.

The Rise and Fall of the Religious Freedom Restoration Act

Shortly after *Smith* was decided, a massive coalition of civil-liberties and religious organization began a push to overrule it. The movement brought together such unlikely allies as the National Association of Evangelicals, the Mormon Church, and the American Civil Liberties Union.[56] The *Sherbert* approach of allowing free exercise to at times overcome general laws really had become accepted by a wide range of the American public. The group proposed that Congress enact a federal law stating that courts should use the *Sherbert* compelling-state-interest test in deciding free exercise cases.

From the very beginning this effort faced a major constitutional problem. Because the U.S. Constitution is supreme over ordinary federal laws and because the Supreme Court has the final say in interpreting the Constitution, an act of Congress cannot typically overcome a Supreme Court decision.[57] Only a constitutional amendment can do that. The supporters of the movement to overrule *Smith* hoped to avoid this problem by relying on a broad reading of section 5 of the Fourteenth Amendment, which empowers Congress "to enforce" the provisions of that amendment.[58] The theory was that the *Sherbert* test was needed to enforce the religious freedoms that the Fourteenth Amendment makes applicable to the states.[59]

In any event, the political momentum of the movement to overrule *Smith* became enormous. Testimony before Congress centered on situations in which neutral laws had begun to burden religious practice after the *Smith* decision came down. Examples included autopsies performed on Jewish and Hmong individuals in violation of their religious beliefs as well as zoning and historic-preservation rulings that prevented churches from expanding.[60] Ultimately, in 1993 the Religious Freedom Restoration Act passed both houses of Congress by the kind of massive margins generally reserved for declarations of war.[61] When President Clinton signed the law, he remarked that the unusual alliance brought together by the law could only be explained by "the Power of God."[62]

The Supreme Court was unmoved. In the first case before it involving the Religious Freedom Restoration Act, the Court struck the statute down as beyond Congress's power.[63] The issue before the Court was not the validity of *Smith*—indeed, Justice O'Connor, who continued to oppose *Smith,* agreed that Congress had gone too far with the act.[64] The point was the fundamental doctrine that an ordinary statute cannot change the meaning of the Constitution. The Court rejected the claim that Congress was simply trying to "enforce" the Constitution. The statute instead worked "a substantive change in constitutional protections,"[65] which Congress cannot do.

The reaction to this decision, as we noted in the beginning of chapter 5, was swift and negative. The supporters of the Religious Freedom Restoration Act were less concerned with the ultimate question of congressional power than with the immediate impact on religious practice. That is why a coalition of Christian leaders said that the Court's decision striking down the act "creates chaos that genuinely imperils religious liberties,"[66] the leader of a Jewish religious group joined others in comparing the Court's action to *Dred Scott*,[67] and a leading civil libertarian said "the decision throws us back into the dark ages of religious liberty."[68]

The Legislative Role in Protecting Free Exercise

Smith certainly does not reflect judicial sympathy toward religious liberty. It remains an intensely controversial decision, and it may not represent the last swing of the pendulum. Three justices of the Supreme Court have written opinions saying the Court should consider overruling it and going back to the compelling-state-interest test.[69]

But the practical effect of *Smith* is much less dramatic than the counsels of doom from religious leaders would suggest. And the primary reason stems from *Smith* itself. The Court emphasized in that opinion not that religious exemptions from general laws were improper, but that such exemptions should be based on legislative rather than judicial judgments.[70] The Court noted with favor that some legislatures had taken such steps.[71] This is no small matter, since it makes clear that the Supreme Court does not regard legislative exemptions for religion to be an unconstitutional establishment of religion. Instead they are regarded as a permissible accommodation between church and state.[72]

The immediate and understandable response from opponents of *Smith* is that when minority rights are at stake, we can hardly expect popularly elected legislators to be willing to go out on a limb. Minority religions and minority religious practices are likely to be quite unpopular with most voters. Surely life-tenured federal judges are more likely to have the courage to protect those who lack power at the polls.

That is certainly the theory that has sustained judicial review in many areas, and it is a theory that appears to have a basis in fact. Consider, for example, free speech, where the Supreme Court has protected flag burners, a group not likely to win many legislative battles.[73] But with free exercise law the reality may be different than the theory suggests. Legislators may in fact be more solicitous of religion than the Supreme Court.

We can begin with *Smith* itself. Recall that the issue there was the use of peyote, a hallucinogenic drug, in Native American rituals. The majority of the Court ruled that it would not create any free exercise exception to Oregon's general ban on peyote. Justice O'Connor in dissent vigorously opposed the abandonment of the compelling-state-interest test; indeed, she said the Court's decision was "incompatible with our Nation's fundamental commitment to individual religious liberty."[74] But then Justice O'Connor went on to apply the compelling state interest in the peyote case before her. And she found that the state of Oregon did indeed have such an interest:

> Because the health effects caused by the use of controlled substances exist regardless of the motivation of the user, the use of such substances, even for religious purposes, violates the very purpose of the laws that prohibit them. . . . Moreover, in view of the societal interest in preventing trafficking in controlled substances, uniform application of the criminal prohibition at issue is essential to the effectiveness of Oregon's stated interest in preventing any possession of peyote. . . . For these reasons, I believe that granting a selective exemption in this case would seriously impair Oregon's compelling interest in prohibiting possession of peyote by its citizens.[75]

So in the end, Justice O'Connor concurred in the result reached by the majority in *Smith*—Oregon could prevent Native Americans from using peyote for religious purposes.[76] Life tenure does not make one immune from seeing a compelling interest in the war on drugs. But the truly remarkable thing about *Smith* is that after it was decided, the democratically elected Oregon legislature showed more sympathy than the Court had to religious practice. Although Native Americans make up a small percentage of the voters in Oregon, the legislature created an exception from its ban on peyote use for use in religious rituals, thus joining many other states and the federal government, which had done exactly the same thing.[77]

And this example does not stand alone. Recall that during the period from 1963 to 1990, when the compelling-state-interest test held sway, not all free exercise claims succeeded. Justices were willing at times to find government interests that outweighed free exercise,[78] just as Justice O'Connor did in the peyote case. And recall that when a Jewish member of the Air Force sought to wear a yarmulke, the Court did not even engage in a compelling-state-interest test—it chose instead to defer virtually without question to the needs of the military.[79] Yet, here again, the legislature proved more solicitous of religion than the Court. In response to the yarmulke decision, Congress passed a statute permitting members of the armed forces to wear religious apparel while in uniform so long as the item does not "interfere with the performance of the member's military duties" and is "neat and conservative."[80] Under this approach yarmulkes and other qualifying religious items may now be worn.[81]

The truth is that commentators, whether they supported the *Smith* decision or not, agreed that in the years prior to *Smith* the Court often rejected free exercise claims.[82] As one observer put it, "[a]lthough before [*Smith*] the federal judiciary theoretically stood ready to require free exercise accommodation in some cases, in reality such accommodation almost always came not from the courts but rather from legislatures."[83]

Under the circumstances, the *Smith* decision hardly represents a disaster for American religion. *Smith* invites legislative accommodation of religious practice, and that type of accommodation, already important before *Smith*, is likely to continue.[84] Of course, free exercise was marginally better off before *Smith*, when a religious exemption from a general law might be obtained, at least in theory, from either the courts or the legislature. And under *Smith* it is certainly possible that an unpopular minority religious practice will be stamped out by a broad legislative enactment, requests for legislative exemption will fail, and the courts will be of no help. It is understandable that *Smith* remains controversial.

But it is not understandable that American religious leaders would regard *Smith* as evidence that American society is hostile to religion or religious perspectives. The passage of numerous legislative exemptions for religious practice to general laws—indeed, the overwhelming passage of the Religious Freedom Restoration Act itself—demonstrates that American religion is not a weak, marginalized force in this country. And it is essential to keep in mind that the entire *Smith* controversy only concerns one corner of the law relating to freedom of religion. As we saw in the last chapter and in this one, free speech, due process, and the ban on singling out religious beliefs or practices on ideological grounds all combine to assure a major role for religion in American public life. In this country religious leaders can speak out about their beliefs, can educate their children in their faith, and can practice their religion free of political persecution. These are not small matters.

7

Banning Established Religion in Public Schools and Public Places

The constitutional ban on established religion undeniably limits the ability of religious groups to promote their beliefs in American society. In particular, because religious teaching is not allowed in the public schools, an opportunity to present traditional perspectives on moral issues is lost. At the same time, science is most definitely taught in the public schools, raising the perception that religion is at a disadvantage in competing with science. These concerns have led to persistent calls for government support for religious schools to reduce the financial burden on those who want to provide a religious education for their children.

But this is an area where people of faith should be careful of what they wish for. Government support for religious schools would bring increased government supervision that would weaken the very characteristics that led people to those schools in the first place. As we shall see, when the government supports religious displays in public places, the result is a watered-down brand of religion, the kind of religion in which Good Friday becomes synonymous with the Easter Bunny. As we examine the status of government support for science, the restrictions on religion in the schools and in public places, and the proposals for public support of private schools, we will see that the ban on government support for religion can be good news for religion. The freedom to hold and present moral views without fear of government suppression and to educate children in religious schools without government control puts people of faith in a position to speak out boldly on matters of values and provide a counterweight to the materialistic perspective of modern science. Indeed, the contrast between science's entanglement with government and religion's freedom from that same entanglement points the way for the appropriate public role for religion.

Government Support for Science

The constitutional position of science in America is favorable.[1] To begin with, scientific speech is covered by the First Amendment's free speech clause.[2] Thus, anyone can write an article presenting a controversial scientific theory, and the government cannot suppress that article even if it believes the theory is wrong.[3] Of course, this freedom is not boundless. Despite the desires of some scientists, First Amendment protection does not extend to the performance of experiments. The government can restrict or even ban the actual conduct of scientific research if that research poses a danger to the public—no one has a right to play with plutonium in their backyard.[4]

Up to this point, science enjoys constitutional protection similar to that of religion. But science can be established in a way that religion cannot. The Constitution provides for the direct funding of scientific research, although it bans the direct funding of religious rituals.[5] Most dramatically, the government clearly cannot make the Baptist church the established religion by funding Baptist ministers' salaries while declining to fund the salaries of other clergy. But that is precisely what the government can do with science. It can fund research into the theory that Alzheimer's disease is caused by the genes, while declining to fund research by those who believe that the disease is caused by toxins in the environment. The latter group is free to speak out in support of their views and to seek private funding to test those views, but in the real world of science those can be empty freedoms.[6] Without government support basic research is often impossible, and without that support the freedom to speak is of limited value—your speech is drowned out by the well-funded supporters of the majority view, who can easily label you a crackpot. The majority has not always been right in the history of science, and government policymakers would be wise to keep that in mind; but the bottom line is that at any given moment some scientific approaches benefit immeasurably from government support, while others wither away from the lack of that support.[7]

And even those scientists who receive government money do not go unscathed by the government's power to establish science. Government support for science typically comes with strings attached telling you how to go about your work and how to report your results.[8]

Scientists have come to accept their dependence on the government, although those who lose in the battle to get grants often complain loudly.[9] But religion would be much more threatened by dependence on government, particularly if religion is going to provide a critical and distinctive voice on values in American debate. As we turn to how the ban on established religion limits the transmission of values in the public schools, we will see that government involvement with religion could lead down a dangerous road.

Prayer in the Schools

The two pivotal cases concerning religion in the public schools were decided in the space of one year in the early 1960s. The influence of those decisions banning prayer in the public schools is felt to this day. The cases establish that not only prayer, but religious teachings in general, are off limits in public education.

The first case, *Engel v. Vitale,* began when the New York Board of Regents, a state governmental agency, composed a prayer and recommended that it be used in public schools throughout the state.[10] The prayer was brief:

> Almighty God, we acknowledge our dependence upon Thee, and we beg Thy blessings upon us, our parents, our teachers and our Country.[11]

When the prayer was said aloud in class at the beginning of each school day in New Hyde Park, New York, the parents of ten pupils brought suit, contending that New York had made a law "respecting an establishment of religion" in violation of the Constitution.[12] With only one justice dissenting, the U.S. Supreme Court agreed. Justice Black's opinion for the Court noted that although pupils could remain silent or leave the room when the prayer was said, "[w]hen the power, prestige and financial support of government is placed behind a particular religious belief, the indirect coercive pressure upon religious minorities to conform to the prevailing officially approved religion is plain."[13] But Black's opinion did not turn solely on the presence of coercion. He argued that history showed that when the government supported religion, it not only led to protests from those of different faiths, but it also caused people to lose respect for the very religion "that had relied upon the support of government to spread its faith."[14] Citing Madison, Black maintained that the ban on establishment, which extends even to minor government endorsements of religion,[15] is based on the principle that "religion is too personal, too sacred, too holy, to permit its 'unhallowed perversion' by a civil magistrate."[16]

In a sense, *Engel* was an easy case. Even those who are sympathetic to religion in the public schools are troubled by having the government actually write a prayer. But the *Engel* case had broader implications, as the Court made clear just one year later when it decided *School District of Abington Township v. Schempp*.[17] This case concerned school districts where verses from the Bible were read at the beginning of class each day. Challenges were brought by parents who were members of the Unitarian faith and others who were avowed atheists.[18] Again over a lone dissent, the Court found an unconstitutional establishment of religion. Justice Clark's opinion for the Court found that these Bible readings were "religious exercises" required by the State and thus improper, regardless of the fact that students could be excused.[19] The Bible was not accepted by all religious people, let alone atheists, and the government could not play favorites in the area of religion.[20]

These decisions had a major impact. By eliminating even brief prayers from the public schools, they made clear that more extensive religious devotions or teachings were clearly off limits. And though the Court emphasized that the Bible and religion could be taught in secular subjects such as history,[21] it was evident that such teaching would have to be done very carefully to avoid claims of religious indoctrination.

The public reaction to *Engel* and *Schempp* was immediate and strong. Religious and political leaders expressed shock and outrage, congressional hearings were held, constitutional amendments were offered, and state officials called for defiance of the decisions.[22] Although Earl Warren had not written either opinion, he was the chief justice, and these decisions were viewed by many as unjustified activism by the Warren Court. "Impeach Earl Warren" billboards sprung up beside many highways.[23]

Today prayer in the schools remains a controversial issue, with many Americans wishing it were permissible.[24] The Supreme Court, however, has remained firm on the subject. It turns out that the ban on school prayer was not a product of the liberal Warren Court, destined to be overturned. In 1992 the Court considered whether a prayer could be offered by a rabbi at the graduation ceremony of a public middle school in Providence, Rhode Island.[25] In an opinion by Justice Anthony Kennedy, an appointee of Ronald Reagan, the Court found the prayer to be an unconstitutional establishment of religion.[26] Kennedy emphasized that school officials decided whether a prayer should be given, chose the religious participant who would give it, and provided guidelines for the substance of the prayer.[27] Moreover, students at the graduation would feel pressure to participate in the prayer ceremony by standing.[28]

Four justices dissented from Kennedy's opinion,[29] and litigation continues over whether graduation prayers are permissible if they are organized by student groups rather than school officials.[30] But it would be a mistake to think that prayer in the everyday classroom is going to be allowed by the Court. The four dissenting Justices in the graduation case carefully distinguished the Warren Court school prayer cases, noting, for example, that class attendance, unlike graduation, is compulsory.[31] Perhaps the best indication of the continuing vitality of *Engel* and *Schempp* is that when the graduation prayer case was argued, the solicitor general, representing the administration of President Bush and asking that the prayer be allowed, did not call for the overturning of those cases; he conceded that classroom prayer was unconstitutional.[32]

The reality is that public schools are not available for the transmission of religious values in our society. And it really could not be otherwise, given that public schools serve Americans from so many different religious traditions. This is not the consequence of some recently discovered craze for diversity in American education. In 1854 the Maine courts considered the case of fifteen-year-old Bridget Donahoe of Ellsworth, Maine, who had been expelled from public school for her refusal to read from the King James translation of the Bible.[33] As a Catholic, Donahoe believed the Douay version was more accurate. The courts ruled against her, her expulsion was upheld, and the Jesuit missionary who had supported her was tarred and feathered by the residents of Ellsworth.[34] In 1859 the Massachusetts courts considered the complaint of an eleven-year-old Catholic, Thomas Wall, who had been struck on the hands for thirty minutes with a rattan stick because he refused to recite from the King James Bible.[35] The courts ruled against the young boy.[36]

Religious Americans today do not want to go back to that era. But the fact is that there are real differences today among Judeo-Christian approaches to fundamental religious questions; and, of course, the differences widen enormously when the numerous other religious traditions represented in America are taken into account. Even the most basic Judeo-Christian texts are less uniform than many realize. When the Supreme Court held in 1980 that the Ten Commandments could not be posted in public school classrooms in Kentucky, the Court relied on the fact that some of the Commandments, such as not using the Lord's name in vain, concerned the religious duties of believers.[37] Thus, the Kentucky statute requiring that they be posted constituted an establishment of religion.[38] But if the statute had been upheld, the next dispute would have been over what version of the Ten Commandments to post. There are differences in some of the commandments as given in Exodus and Deuteronomy.[39] Moreover, most Protestants treat "no other gods" as the first commandment and "no images" as the second, whereas Catholics group the two together as the first commandment.[40] Catholics end up with ten because, unlike Protestants, they separate into two commandments the prohibitions on coveting a neighbor's wife and a neighbor's goods.[41] Jews use still another way to reach ten.[42] And differences about the Ten Commandments can have considerable significance. For example, the dispute over whether the commandment is "you shall not murder" or "you shall not kill" is relevant to the debate over capital punishment and other moral questions.[43]

The Lure of Watered-Down Religion

The understandable reaction to these and other disagreements among the faith traditions represented in America today is to seek common ground, to find a way to introduce religious values into public schools without offending anyone. This is an understandable instinct. No one believes the public schools are the appropriate forum for resolving theological disagreements. As the experience of Catholics in the nineteenth century demonstrates, minority religions will not fare well if we just let majority perspectives hold sway.

But the effort to find common ground is likely to lead in a dangerous direction as well. The watered-down version of religion that results is weak broth indeed.

Consider the middle school commencement prayer that the Supreme Court disallowed in 1992. Rabbi Gutterman's invocation read as follows:

> God of the Free, Hope of the Brave:
> For the legacy of America where diversity is celebrated and the rights of minorities are protected, we thank you. May these young men and women grow up to enrich it.
> For the liberty of America, we thank You. May these new graduates grow up to guard it. For the political process of America in

which all its citizens may participate, for its court system where all may seek justice we thank You. May those we honor this morning always turn to it in trust.

For the destiny of America we thank You. May the graduates of Nathan Bishop Middle School so live that they might help to share it.

May our Aspirations for our country and for these young people, who are our hope for the future, be richly fulfilled.

AMEN[44]

This is not the kind of prayer a rabbi offers in a synagogue. This is the kind of prayer you get when school officials provide clergy with guidelines recommending that prayers be composed with "inclusiveness and sensitivity."[45] This is, in short, an example of America's civil religion, the bland set of nonthreatening principles that affirm a generalized belief in a rather generalized God. As we noted above, Justice Kennedy's opinion for the Court found government support for even this sort of religion to be unconstitutional.[46] Ralph Reed, executive director of the Christian Coalition, criticized Kennedy's decision on the ground that the Court should have allowed "this innocuous prayer."[47]

But something is very wrong here. Innocuous prayer is a contradiction in terms. Or at least it should be. It is precisely when prayer gets watered down that it loses any distinctive meaning or function. When prayer takes place within a meaningful framework of faith it can carry powerful messages about humility, hope, and our relationship to God. When prayer is innocuous, it is no rival to the materialistic view of the world. The middle school invocation above does not offer any alternative to the secular mainstream. It lives in that mainstream. As we saw in chapter 4, innocuous prayer is easily swept up into the scientific worldview. It becomes at best a kind of aspirin or acupuncture, not a path toward faith and humility.

Real religion may be the real winner in the commencement prayer case. If the case had come out the other way, the public schools might have become the incubators of the sort of empty prayer that ill serves religion in the long run. It is far better for public school students to experience meaningful prayer and religion outside of school.

The Unhappy Fate of Christmas, Hanukkah, and Good Friday

The truth is that attempts to circumvent the ban on established religion are likely to harm religion as a distinctive moral voice in America. The fate of Christmas and Hanukkah in the public square, and the emerging threat to the meaning and observance of Good Friday, demonstrate the point. The story of these holidays should serve as a warning when we consider government involvement in religion.

The judiciary's unfortunate involvement in the meaning of Christmas became headline news in 1984 when the U.S. Supreme Court considered whether the annual Christmas display erected by the city of Pawtucket, Rhode Island, violated the establishment clause. Pawtucket won the case, but the victory was not good news for American religion, at least if religion is to be distinguished from shopping.

The Pawtucket litigation and the cases that followed engendered an enormous amount of discussion among lawyers because the cases revealed the Court's inability to settle on an approach to establishment clause jurisprudence.[48] From our perspective, the most important thing is not the legal categories the Court employed but rather the impact of the decisions on the nature of religion in the public square.

The challengers to Pawtucket's Christmas display focused on the inclusion in that display of a crèche, which depicted the Nativity scene with figures including the Infant Jesus, Mary, and Joseph.[49] The crèche is certainly a religious symbol. But Chief Justice Burger's opinion for the Court emphasized that the crèche had to be analyzed "in the context of the Christmas season."[50] Burger noted that the Nativity scene, "like a painting, is passive"; taken as a whole, "[t]he display engenders a friendly community spirit of goodwill in keeping with the season."[51] He listed the elements of the display that surrounded the crèche:

> [A] Santa Claus house, reindeer pulling Santa's sleigh, candy-striped poles, a Christmas tree, carolers, cut-out figures representing such characters as a clown, an elephant, and a teddy bear, hundreds of colored lights, a large banner that reads SEASONS GREETINGS.[52]

Burger noted as well that the entire display was put on by the city "in cooperation with the downtown retail merchants' association . . . in the heart of the shopping district."[53] Under the circumstances, the display was allowed.[54]

Reaction to the Pawtucket decision was swift. Lower courts considering the constitutionality of Christmas displays put up by various local governments had to decide whether the secular holiday trappings neutralized the Christian religious message. Some judges could not believe that they had been put in this position. One judge derided the "'St. Nicholas too' test—a city can get by with displaying a crèche if it throws in a sleigh full of toys and a Santa Claus, too."[55] Another said that the Supreme Court was "requiring scrutiny more commonly associated with interior decorators than with the judiciary."[56] And many noted that the Court's decision, wittingly or unwittingly, seemed to further the notion that Christmas was not a fundamentally religious holiday, but rather a secular holiday with a considerable emphasis on consumerism. As Professor Philip Kurland wrote, "[the Court's] treatment of the crèche symbol further detracts from the religious significance of the Christmas holiday, a holiday which every year, at least in this country, pays more homage to Mammon than to God. I would think that devout Christians might take umbrage."[57]

Then things got worse. In 1989 the Supreme Court considered the constitutionality of two holiday displays located on public property in downtown Pittsburgh. The first was a crèche placed on the courthouse steps, the second a Hanukkah menorah erected next to the city's Christmas tree.[58]

The Court was deeply divided, in terms both of reasoning and of results. Four justices would have allowed both displays;[59] three would have allowed neither.[60] The balance of power lay with Justices Blackmun and O'Connor, who voted to disallow the crèche but to allow the menorah–Christmas tree combination.[61] And the fears that judges and commentators had after the Pawtucket case were realized in the Pittsburgh decision. The crèche on the Pittsburgh courthouse steps was found to be unconstitutional precisely because it stood alone:

> Here, unlike in [Pawtucket], nothing in the context of the display detracts from the crèche's religious message. The [Pawtucket] display comprised a series of figures and objects, each group of which had its own focal point. Santa's house and his reindeer were objects of attention separate from the crèche, and had their specific visual story to tell. . . . Here, in contrast, the crèche stands alone: it is the single element of the display on the Grand Staircase.[62]

As to the Hanukkah menorah, Justice Blackmun noted that, like the crèche, it is a "religious symbol: it serves to commemorate the miracle of the oil as described in the Talmud."[63] And indeed, the menorah, a lamp with eight lights, is used in the celebration of Hanukkah, a Jewish holiday that marks the rededication of the Temple after its recapture from outside forces in 164 B.C. But in Pittsburgh, the city placed the menorah next to a Christmas tree and a sign saluting liberty. Taken as a whole, this display did not, in Blackmun's view, endorse the Christian and Jewish faiths, but "rather simply recognizes that both Christmas and Chanukah are part of the same winter-holiday season, which has attained a secular status in our society."[64]

Once again, the Court had bolstered those forces in our society that make it seem that only the secular world counts. Religion can hardly be a counterweight to materialism when it is presented as part of the shopping season. As Professor David Cobin pointed out in commenting on the Pittsburgh case, the Court had failed to recognize Roger Williams's seventeenth-century warning that the church is a garden in the wilderness that is threatened when government enters:

The effect of these decisions is to encourage local governments to denigrate religious symbols and empty them of their religious meaning. In Roger Williams' terms, the Supreme Court is encouraging local governments to plant the weeds of secularism in the garden of religion. . . . Governmental sponsorship and display of religious symbols uniquely accelerates societal abandonment of traditional religion.[65]

I must admit that when I discuss these concerns with friends, a common reaction is to treat Christmas and Hanukkah as lost causes. Even for many people of faith, these holidays are seen as primarily secular, seasonal shopping days. If that is true, I think it is quite a loss. But no one should assume that the losses will stop there. Lower court decisions reacting to various intersections of church and state have begun to treat Good Friday as a secular holiday as well.

When taxpayers brought suit challenging a Hawaii statute declaring Good Friday a state holiday, the government of Hawaii argued successfully that Good Friday was not chosen because of any religious significance.[66] The court was persuaded by evidence that "the Good Friday holiday has become a popular shopping day in Hawaii and businesses have benefitted from the three-day weekend created as a result of the holiday."[67] What is more, having Good Friday off means that "citizens are better able to enjoy the many recreational opportunities available in Hawaii."[68]

Of course, that is not the only meaning of Good Friday. In states with less favorable climates than Hawaii, the courts have told us that it is observed so that citizens can travel as they begin their spring vacation. In successfully supporting the closing of a county courthouse on Good Friday against an establishment clause challenge, officials from the Kentucky Transportation Cabinet testified that highway traffic on Good Friday was third in volume, behind only the Fourth of July and Thanksgiving traffic.[69] The court concluded that "[i]n many Northern Kentucky communities, [Good Friday] is the traditional start of spring vacation. This area is usually experiencing chilly weather in March and early April, and, as reflected by the Kentucky Transportation Cabinet Statistics, many Kentuckians spend Good Friday traveling to warmer areas."[70] A similar rationale allowed the courts to uphold the closing of public buildings on Good Friday in Michigan.[71] Under the circumstances, it is not surprising that a Maryland court, in the course of rejecting a challenge to the closing of schools on Good Friday, concluded that the entire Easter period has become "a highly secularized holiday."[72]

Under these decisions, the government can "observe" Good Friday. But I am not inclined to see these decisions as victories for religion. Indeed, I found it refreshing when a court held that government recognition of Good Friday in Illinois was unconstitutional, noting that "Christians believe that Jesus Christ was crucified on a Friday afternoon in the spring and that he rose from the dead the following Sunday."[73]

Of course, many factors are at work here. The commercialization of Christmas, Hanukkah, and Good Friday was not caused by judicial decisions rejecting establishment-clause challenges to public observances of those holidays. These decisions, however, do more than recognize that commercialization. They add to the problem by putting the imprimatur of the judiciary on the notion that holy days have become shopping days. And this is a very real risk of mixing government and religion in our pluralistic society. The inevitable result—since no single religious vision can be given full sway—is a watered-down civil religion that provides little counterweight to secularism.

The experience with government recognition of religious holidays demonstrates that watered-down religion in the public square is easily swallowed up in a materialistic society. Materialism in the sense of gift buying at all costs is not identical to materialism in the sense of a scientific image of who we are. But they are related. Both stress the material world of dollars, cents, and atoms and ignore the spiritual world of faith, humility, and values.

The spiritual world can best inform our lives if it is presented powerfully within a particular faith tradition. As the holiday cases demonstrate, that cannot happen in the public square if religion joins hands with government. It can happen when religious leaders stand on their own feet, practice their faith, and speak forcefully as they have every right to do under our Constitution.

Government and Religious Schools: The Danger of Vouchers

It is understandable that people of faith want not only the right to speak out, but also the right to raise their children within a particular tradition. This brings us to the issue of schooling, because there is no doubt that schooling plays a vital role, perhaps second only to the family, in shaping attitudes toward faith and values. As we have seen above, and as the holiday cases reinforce, meaningful religious teaching in the public schools is simply not going to happen in our pluralistic society. There are only two possibilities in the long run if religion is pursued in the public schools—suppression of whatever faith system is in the minority in a given school district or weakening religion to the point of irrelevance. Neither of these results is desirable. For those who use the public schools, the road to a meaningful moral upbringing can and should take place outside of those schools. As we will discuss in later chapters, the presence of science in the public schools and in our society generally should not block that road. Religious leaders can and should make clear that on matters of ultimate values, science does not provide the answers.

But for those who use private religious schools, there is an enticing possibility for strengthening the role of religion without offending minority religions or watering down the faith. Government support for religious schools would do the trick. As we noted in chapter 5, the constitutional right to send your children to religious school is the ultimate safety valve, but it can be expensive because parents pay tuition on top of the taxes needed to support the public schools. Many make the sacrifice. But perhaps more would do so if public aid could reduce the financial burden.

There have been many proposals over the years to channel public money to religious schools. An examination of the most far-reaching of those proposals—the voucher system—will reveal some of the opportunities and risks of government involvement with religion in this area.

Voucher plans are designed to help parents pay the cost of educating their children. The basic idea is that the state government would give parents a voucher worth a certain amount of money, which can be used to help pay the tuition for any school covered by the plan. The goal would be to help with tuition payments at private schools, including parochial schools.[74]

Voucher plans, which have been tried at times on a limited basis, are controversial for many reasons.[75] Some of the controversy concerns issues completely apart from religion. Proponents of vouchers want to give lower-income families the opportunity to utilize private schools, particularly when the public schools in a given community are ineffective. Vouchers could further that end and perhaps inspire the public schools to improve in order to attract students. Opponents of vouchers note the high cost in taxpayer dollars and point out that private schools could still decide who to admit and could still charge tuition higher than the voucher amount. Vouchers might thus help only the top tier of those with lower incomes, leaving public schools with reduced support in the community and an even more difficult educational task.[76]

But much of the debate over vouchers has concerned the relationship between church and state. As we have noted, most private schools in the United States are religious; thus, if they are eligible for the program, religious schools would be the biggest beneficiaries of vouchers. This prospect has caused an outpouring of debate over the constitutionality of voucher programs.[77]

The debate is a complex one because the U.S. Supreme Court has not directly confronted the issue, nor has it provided clear guidance. The Court's entire approach to the establishment clause has been marked by controversy, with different tests being propounded by different justices.[78] In some areas the Court's results have been consistent—prayer in the schools, for example, is not permitted. But in the area of government aid to religious schools, the results have been as confused as the doctrine. Over the years state governments have tried a variety of tax benefits, subsidies, and programs to provide goods and services in order to help out parochial schools. The Supreme Court has upheld some of these efforts but has struck down others, all the while trying to prevent direct government support for or entanglement with religion though allowing aid that manages in a neutral way to help parents provide a good education for their children.[79] No one believes that the government can directly pay the salary of clergy who teach courses in religion or, on the other hand, that the government is barred from building roads that might help someone get to a religious school. But once you start looking in between the extremes, the cases get difficult, and the Court has been deeply divided.

Because teaching in a religious school can involve the transmission of religious values in classes like history or civics, the Court has attempted to monitor how aid would play out in an endless variety of plans. Some indication of the problems the Court has faced is that in one case it allowed state aid for books and in another it barred state aid for maps.[80] Fortunately, the Court did not have to consider state aid for atlases.[81]

In recent years the Court, while remaining divided, has seemed to become more receptive to state aid to private schools, including church schools. In one case the Court, reversing earlier precedent, allowed New York to send public school teachers into parochial schools to provide secular remedial instruction to disadvantaged children.[82] Some observers believe this means the Court would uphold a voucher program covering all private schools, including religious schools; other analysts are not so sure.[83]

This is not the place to predict what the Court might do if a voucher program came before it. The more important question from our perspective is whether vouchers, if upheld, would be good news for American religion. It is vital to keep in mind that even if the Court finds voucher programs to be constitutional, that does not mean they have to be implemented. Should church leaders push for the passage of voucher programs?

There certainly are benefits to such programs. Properly run religious schools—and there are many—provide an enormous benefit to American society. By teaching and reinforcing religious values during the school day, they help build the kind of citizens who can enrich American life. Those who receive a solid education infused with a sense of faith and humility are fortunate indeed. From my point of view, the point is not that religious schools can teach creation science rather than evolution. Indeed, as I have argued above, creation science has it exactly backwards—it exalts the scientific method in a mistaken and misguided quest to strengthen religion. But religious schools can talk about and teach distinctive religious values in a way public schools cannot. A Catholic school, for example, can use its translation of the Bible, its approach to the Ten Commandments, and much more in reaching its goals. If vouchers make this experience available to a wider range of students, I believe that would be a benefit not only for those students and their families, but for the society as a whole.

But the danger is that vouchers will undermine the very experience they are trying to help. Current regulation of private schools is relatively minimal. But when government money comes, government control is often close behind. Voucher programs will initially be touted as simply providing money to parents and not compromising what is taught in private schools. But I am not optimistic that voucher programs will remain so benign.

Supporters of religious schools must realize that the voucher concept originally stemmed not from a concern with religion but from a desire, motivated by economic theory, to introduce competition into the educational system.[84] One of the earliest voucher proposals provided that schools affiliated with churches could qualify for a program restricted to secular private schools by dividing themselves up into a secular and a "religious part organized as an after school or Sunday activity."[85] But this, of course, would undermine the greatest strength of religious schools—the ability to bring values education into many traditional subjects.[86]

Even if vouchers are available for religious schools in their traditional undivided form, the problems will not go away. Taxpayers will want to be sure that public money is being spent in a way that the public desires, an approach that will prove dangerous for any school with a distinctive approach. The modern trend toward performance standards in education, whether they be local, state, or national, will put pressure on schools to alter their curricula. As one analyst of vouchers put it, "funding of religious institutions opens the door for . . . control of religious institutions."[87]

Experience in other countries demonstrates that this problem is a real one. In France, government support for Catholic schools is said to have ended many of the distinctive features of their curriculum, whereas a German study found that "[t]he choice of a publicly supported Catholic school . . . may not offer real pedagogical differences, given substantial government regulation and pressure for uniformity."[88] An umbrella study of government support for private schools in six nations concluded:

> For those who believe strongly in religious schooling and fear that government influence will come with public funding, reason exists for their concern. Catholic or Protestant schools in each of the nations studied have increasingly been assimilated to the assumptions and guiding values of public schooling. This process does not [even] seem to be the result of deliberate efforts . . . but rather of the difficulty, for a private school playing by public rules, to maintain its distance from the common assumptions and habits of the predominant system.[89]

Of course, a private religious school might retain the freedom to opt out of voucher programs. But that school would face an even more difficult financial crunch than it faces today—it would be competing not only with free public schools but with those private schools that accepted government vouchers and the attendant regulation and were thus able to offer, in effect, lower tuition.[90]

If vouchers come, they will pose a difficult dilemma. Compliance with government policies in areas ranging from education for the disabled to the appropriate coverage in a history course could come with the vouchers and could undermine a religious school's goals. My own sense is that the ultimate safety valve of private education will be best preserved if government involvement with private schools is minimized.

8

The Overlap between Religious Values and Law

The ban on government-established religion prevents the government from promoting the practice of any particular faith. But this ban does not mean that religious beliefs must be kept out of political debate. As we saw in chapter 5, the free speech clause in the Constitution fully protects the expression of religious views. It would be odd indeed if those views had to somehow be kept out of the political arena. Fortunately, that is not the law.

There is needless confusion on this point. Some Americans, including both supporters and opponents of traditional religion, seem to have the idea that if a clergyman or a devout citizen presents arguments based on religion in favor of a bill, passage of that bill would somehow constitute an "establishment of religion." That has never been the case. But this vague sense of unease about religious discourse contributes to a climate in which public discussions are robbed of a helpful perspective. In the next chapter I will discuss how the religious point of view can provide a healthy counterweight to the scientific perspective in a variety of areas, and I will note the prudential concerns that bear on deciding when presentation of an explicitly religious perspective is appropriate. In this chapter I want to clear the way by explaining the legal framework.

If any law inspired by religious beliefs was an invalid "establishment of religion," we would live in an odd society indeed. Theft would be lawful, not to mention murder. The biblical origin of many of our laws is clear.[1] As the legal scholar John Hart Ely has written, "[t]o taint as illegitimate bases of governmental choice all customs and commands which have roots in our nation's religious heritage would be to place in constitutional doubt large segments of our criminal and other law."[2] Supreme Court Justice Sandra Day O'Connor has been more blunt. Noting that many statutes blend secular and religious elements, she observes that "[c]haos would ensue if every such statute were invalid under the Establishment Clause."[3]

As we noted in the preceding chapter, the Supreme Court has struggled to develop a workable approach in the establishment of religion field. One consistent theme, however, has been that a statute with a valid secular purpose is not rendered unconstitutional because it was religiously inspired and continues to draw support from religious values.[4] It is when legislation serves solely religious aims that it becomes suspect, as it must in a society as diverse and free as ours.

Justifying Sunday Closing Laws

The judicial decisions upholding Sunday closing laws provide a good illustration of how this area of the law has developed. Once a central feature of American life, Sunday closing statutes gradually became unpopular and today have largely been repealed. But the decision to repeal or retain Sunday restrictions has been made by elected legislatures, not by courts. Despite the religious origins of these laws, they have not been found to constitute an establishment of religion.

Sunday closing laws have a venerable history, stretching back at least to Constantine's edict in 321 A.D.: "Let all judges and all city people and all tradesmen rest upon the *venerable day of the sun.*"[5] Like countless closing laws to follow, Constantine included an exception: "But let those dwelling in the country freely and with full liberty attend to the culture of their fields; since it frequently happens that no other day is so fit for the sowing of grain, or the planting of vines; hence, the favorable time should not be allowed to pass, lest the provisions of heaven be lost."[6]

Scholars debate whether Constantine's edict sprang from Christian motives.[7] But it is clear that the English laws that influenced the American colonists had a religious character. The first major English Sunday law, the statute of Henry VI in 1448, noted "the abominable injuries and offences done to Almighty God, and to his Saints, . . . because of fairs and markets upon their high and principal feasts," and therefore ordained that such fairs and markets should close on Sundays, Good Friday, and the major feast days.[8] The colonial Sunday statutes—and every colony had one—were also clearly designed to enforce the Fourth Commandment by limiting a variety of activities, including work and sport.[9] The Delaware statute, for example, recited that violation of the Lord's day acts "to the great Reproach of the Christian Religion," whereas Georgia legislation noted that "keeping holy the Lord's day is a principal part of the true service of God."[10]

When the Bill of Rights was added to the Constitution in 1791, state establishments of religion were not automatically abolished. The First Amendment's nonestablishment clause originally applied only to Congress, not to the states. As we saw in chapter 5, it was the post–Civil War Fourteenth Amendment that applied the nonestablishment clause to the states, a point the Supreme Court did not resolve until the 1940s.

Nonetheless, from the earliest days in this country there was often a recognition that state law should not mandate purely religious practices. And in the Sunday-closing-law context there was a recognition early on that a day of rest served secular as well as religious ends. Thus, a Massachusetts act of 1792 required observance of "the Lord's Day" not only for religious reasons but because that observance promoted "the welfare of a community, by affording necessary seasons for relaxation from labour and the cares of business" and because ceaseless labor caused "great damage [to] the community, by producing dissipation of manners and immoralities of life."[11]

Beginning in the nineteenth century numerous judicial opinions dealt with the legality of Sunday closing laws, or "blue laws," as they were often called.[12] Challenges were brought by those who observed a different Sabbath and those who simply wanted to work on Sunday. These challenges were almost uniformly unsuccessful. The courts typically found that an enforced weekly day of rest was good for workers and that since it was expedient to choose one day, there was no bar to choosing the day most people would prefer. A Pennsylvania Supreme Court decision from 1848 is typical:

> All agree that to the well-being of society, periods of rest are absolutely necessary. To be productive of the required advantage, these periods must recur at stated intervals, so that the mass of which the community is composed, may enjoy a respite from labour at the same time. They may be established by common consent, or, as is conceded, [by] the legislative power of the state. . . . When this happens, some one day must be selected, and it has been said the round of the week presents none which, being preferred, might not be regarded as favouring some one of the numerous religious sects into which mankind are divided. In a Christian community, where a very large majority of the people celebrate the first day of the week as their chosen period of rest from labour, it is not surprising that that day should have received the legislative sanction.[13]

With the exception of an 1858 California decision, every nineteenth-century state high court to consider the matter upheld Sunday closing laws, and the California court reversed itself in 1861.[14] Moreover, in three decisions between 1885 and 1900, the U.S. Supreme Court upheld Sunday closing laws.[15] The Court said in 1885:

> Laws setting aside Sunday as a day of rest are upheld, not from any right of the government to legislate for the promotion of religious observances, but from its right to protect all persons from the physical and moral debasement which comes from uninterrupted labor. Such laws have always been deemed beneficent and merciful laws, especially to the poor and dependent, to the laborers in our factories and workshops and in the heated rooms of our cities.[16]

But the acid test came in 1961 when the U.S. Supreme Court finally confronted Sunday closing laws with the clear understanding that states were forbidden just as strictly as Congress was from establishing religion. What is more, this was the Earl Warren Court, a body not afraid to assert a vigorous separation of church and state, as we saw in the school prayer context.

The 1961 case began when seven employees of a large discount store in Anne Arundel County, Maryland, were indicted for the Sunday sale of a three-ring loose-leaf binder, a can of floor wax, a stapler, and a toy submarine.[17] By the 1960s, Maryland's blue laws had become a patchwork affair, with the sale of some items allowed—such as milk, tobacco, and gasoline—and with different rules for different counties.[18] The appellants, however, had clearly sold forbidden items, and so they argued, among other things, that Maryland's Sunday closing laws constituted an establishment of religion.[19]

Chief Justice Earl Warren's opinion for the Court squarely rejected this claim. He noted the strongly religious origin of the Sunday closing laws, but he noted as well the secular purpose they served by providing a benefit to workers at the same time that they enhanced labor productivity.[20] Warren pointed out that a variety of modern labor statutes limited hours of employment and that both unions and trade associations supported modern Sunday closing laws.[21] Warren rejected the argument that Maryland was required to allow every worker to choose which day of the week he would like off:

> [T]he State's purpose is not merely to provide a one-day-in-seven work stoppage. In addition to this, the State seeks to set one day apart from all others as a day of rest, repose, recreation and tranquility—a day which all members of the family and community have the opportunity to spend and enjoy together, a day on which there exists relative quiet and disassociation from the everyday intensity of commercial activities, a day on which people may visit friends and relatives who are not available during working days.[22]

And Warren, of course, also made the point that laws cannot fall because secular reasons coincide with religious ones—this would forbid legislation against murder and theft because these crimes are "also proscribed in the Decalogue."[23]

Sunday closing laws are largely gone. Both secular and religious groups have abandoned them as the desire and need to conduct commerce every day of the week has outweighed the social and family values that Warren identified.[24]

But though the closing laws are gone, Warren's reasoning is not. Statutes will not be struck down because they further a religious perspective, so long as they serve secular goals as well.

Striking Down Solely Religious Statutes

Of course, there can be lively disputes over whether a particular statute really has a secular purpose, and reasonable people can differ on that question. But the Supreme Court has taken what one scholar has called a "generous" view of the definition of secular and thus has only rarely struck down legislation on the ground that it has a purely religious goal.[25]

The best way to get a sense of the Court's approach here is to look at the most controversial case where legislation was found wanting under the establishment clause because it had a solely religious purpose. In 1985 the Court struck down an Alabama statute that authorized a one-minute period of silence in all public schools "for meditation or voluntary prayer."[26] At first glance, this appears inconsistent with allowing Sunday closing laws. Surely there is a secular purpose in having students quiet down for a minute. But a closer look at the statute and its history makes the Court's decision more plausible. At a minimum, nothing the Court said undercuts the approach taken in the Sunday closing area.

The key to understanding the Court's decision is to realize how the Alabama statute the justices struck down changed earlier Alabama law. In 1978 Alabama enacted a statue that authorized a one-minute period of silence in all public schools "for meditation." The constitutionality of that statute was not before the Supreme Court, and as we shall see, the Court had good things to say about it. What was before the Court was a 1981 statute that changed the earlier statute to say "meditation or voluntary prayer."[27]

Justice Stevens's opinion for the Court began by noting that the 1978 statute had the effect of "protecting every student's right to engage in voluntary prayer during an appropriate moment of silence during the schoolday."[28] "Nothing," the Court emphasized, "prevented any student from engaging in voluntary prayer during a silent moment of meditation."[29] So what happened in 1981? What did the Alabama legislature do? The Court found that the only explanation offered in the state legislature for the addition of the needless words "or voluntary prayer" was the statement by Senator Donald Holmes that this change was an "effort to return voluntary prayer" to the public schools.[30] When Senator Holmes was asked in the later litigation over the 1981 law whether he had any purpose for the legislation other than returning voluntary prayer to the public schools, he said that he did not.[31]

So the Supreme Court was confronted with an odd case. The 1981 law had, the Court emphasized, "*no* secular purpose. . . . The State did not present evidence of *any* secular purpose."[32] In the view of the Court, students had every right to pray during the moment of silence before 1981. The 1981 enactment was an effort by the state to "characterize prayer as a favored practice."[33] Although the 1981 law could be seen as nothing more than symbolic, the Court felt that it had to be vigilant against any state action that either endorsed or disapproved of religion.[34] If Alabama could encourage private prayer, another state could discourage it. Neither is appropriate.

Perhaps Alabama's action in 1981 was sufficiently meaningless that the Court should have let it pass. My own view is that prayer is such a serious religious activity that neither the state of Alabama nor any other government entity should tell people whether or when they should be doing it. But for our present purposes, it is clear that this decision hardly calls into question the host of laws that serve both secular and religious ends. Justice O'Connor's concurring opinion stresses this point. O'Connor begins by emphasizing that "[n]othing in the U.S. Constitution as interpreted by this Court or in the laws of the State of Alabama prohibits public school students from voluntarily praying at any time before, during, or after the schoolday."[35] She notes that the moment of silence provided by the earlier legislation facilitated voluntary prayer.[36] She agrees with the Court that Alabama has improperly endorsed religious activity, and she emphasizes, in language we noted above, that "[c]haos would ensue" if the Court tried to strike down every statute where religious and secular interests intersect.[37]

Religious Involvement in the Abortion Debate

Thus, the establishment clause does not prohibit religious perspectives from being brought to bear on the vast majority of public policy issues. The abortion controversy is an example of an area of major importance in which the Court has recognized that religion cannot be kept out of the debate.

The Supreme Court's 1973 decision in *Roe v. Wade,* holding that a ban on abortion in the early stages of pregnancy violates a woman's constitutional right to privacy, ignited a national controversy.[38] Many opponents and supporters of *Roe* used religious arguments. This is hardly surprising, since the moral status of the fetus is a matter that has been addressed for centuries by numerous faith systems.[39]

The use of religion in this area quickly came to a head when Congress, beginning in 1976, prohibited the use of federal funds to reimburse the cost of abortions under the Medicaid program except under narrow circumstances.[40] This restriction—generally known as the Hyde Amendment because it was originally sponsored by Representative Henry J. Hyde—meant that some needy women would not be able to obtain abortions.

The Hyde Amendment was promptly challenged in court, and the litigation reached the Supreme Court in the 1980 case of *Harris v. McRae.*[41] Opponents of the Hyde Amendment argued that Congress had improperly burdened the constitutional right of poor women to get an abortion, a contention rejected by the Court over the dissent of four justices.[42] The opponents argued as well that the amendment constituted an unconstitutional establishment of religion because it was based on the Roman Catholic view that life begins at conception. In other words, because Catholic opposition to abortion fueled the restrictions contained in the Hyde Amendment, that amendment had to fall. A majority of the Court rejected this argument as well, and on this point the dissenting justices were silent.[43]

Justice Stewart's opinion for the Court in *Harris* on the establishment of religion issue is important because it is so routine. In other words, there is nothing about abortion that changes the analysis we have already seen. Stewart begins by citing *McGowan v. Maryland,* the Sunday-closing-law case, for the proposition that a statute does not violate the establishment clause because it "happens to coincide or harmonize with the tenets of some or all religions."[44] He then adds the inevitable observation that the opposition of major religions to stealing does not prohibit the state from criminalizing that behavior.[45] Stewart says that there are secular opponents of abortion who believe that the fetus should be protected from conception, and thus "the fact that the funding restrictions in the Hyde Amendment may coincide with the religious tenets of the Roman Catholic Church does not, without more, contravene the Establishment Clause."[46]

The view that religious beliefs can play a role in the public debate over abortion remains dominant among Supreme Court justices and legal scholars as well.[47] It could hardly be otherwise. Abortion involves fundamental moral judgments. Although secular philosophers certainly have something to say about those judgments, so do the great religious traditions so well represented in American society. People have participated from varying faith perspectives in every great social debate in American history, from slavery to the civil rights movement down to the present day. Abortion is no different. As it happens, on abortion our faith traditions have a variety of perspectives—the Roman Catholic opposition to abortion in virtually all circumstances is, for example, not shared by all Protestant and Jewish groups.[48] Indeed, some Jewish scholars believe that abortion is mandatory when the life of the mother is in danger.[49] No citizens should be left out of this debate because their positions stem from their most deeply held beliefs.

Here again, it is not the law that prevents the presentation of a distinctive religious perspective. Here—as with genetics, prayer, evolution, and other issues—there is the risk that religion will be seduced by science and that the abortion issue will be drained of its moral significance by an exaggerated reliance on technical findings.

Formulating a thoughtful position on abortion involves learning what one can of medical reality, including the nature of the fetus, its relation to the pregnant woman, the risks of various procedures, and the like. But although technical knowledge may be necessary for an ultimate position, it is not sufficient. As one scholar put it, "[w]hether a fetal organism at a given stage is a person with a right to life is *not* a scientific question, calling for the discovery of some deeply hidden though essentially biological fact. Facts . . . are highly relevant . . . but human personhood is not itself a state that can be observed under a microscope."[50]

This has not stopped people from trying to find a scientific answer to the abortion question. For some, opposition to abortion stems from a belief that from the moment of conception you are genetically a unique human being, indeed that a fertilized ovum contains "everything you are today. Nothing has been added . . . except nutrition."[51] Others maintain that since a fertilized egg has the potential to split into identical twins up to roughly the fourteenth day after conception, there is no "person" until that point.[52] Still others, also referring to identical-twin evidence, emphasize twins' different fingerprints at birth (even though they have the same genetic code) as proof that a fetus is not fixed at the moment of conception.[53] For others, the key moment is when brain wave activity occurs, or when life is possible outside the womb.[54]

None of these observations is going to dissolve the conflict over abortion. Maybe a little science fiction will help make this point. In Robert J. Sawyer's novel *The Terminal Experiment,* a scientist discovers that a small, weak electrical field departs the body at the moment of death. Although little is known about this field, it is quickly dubbed the soulwave. Before long an experiment on pregnant women finds that the soulwave arrives in the fetus between the ninth and the tenth week of pregnancy. I am sure you can guess what impact this has on the abortion debate—none at all:

> The front-page editorial in the November issue of *Our Bodies,* newsletter of the group Women in Control, headquartered in Manchester, England, denounces the discovery of so-called fetal soulwaves as "yet another attempt by men to impose control over women's bodies." . . . [I]n Toronto, Ontario . . . the organization Defenders of the Unborn [announced] "Abortion prior to the arrival of the soulwave is still a sin in the eyes of God. . . . For the first nine weeks of pregnancy, the fetus is a temple, being prepared for the arrival of the divine spark."[55]

No technical fact is going to work any magic solution here, particularly for those of us who believe, in the Judeo-Christian tradition, that humans are more than just genes. Technical data will have to be supplemented by insights drawn from religion, from philosophy, and from moral intuition. In American culture today, science acts like a giant magnet, but at times we have to resist it. To their credit, a large number of participants in the abortion debate understand this. They believe deeply that the fetus deserves moral respect as against the claims of the mother, or conversely that the mother's rights as a person should not give way to an entity that lacks personhood. And whether or not these views come from a traditional religious base, they have every right to be heard in public debate.

A Christian Nation?

The broad outline that emerges from our look at the legal status of religion would be agreed on by a wide range of judges and scholars. There will always be divisions over difficult cases, but certain basic principles are clear. Free speech allows Americans of all religious faiths to profess those faiths just as it allows Americans with no religious beliefs to present their point of view. Due process protects your right to send children to religious schools, and the free exercise of religion means that the state cannot single out an unpopular religious practice for condemnation. The ban on established religion prevents the government from supporting a religion or mandating its observance, but it does not prevent religious perspectives from playing a role in the debate leading up to the passage of statutes.

This is a legal regime that leaves a great deal of room for the flourishing of a variety of faiths, and, in fact, numerous religions thrive in America today. But, despite claims occasionally heard in political debate, this is not remotely a legal regime that creates a "Christian nation." It is far from clear that most American Christians would want such a nation—merging church and state can be bad for the church, and most Christians neither fear nor dislike a diverse society. Nonetheless, the idea that somehow our Constitution creates a "Christian nation" pops up frequently enough that it is worth tracing to its source.

To give the "Christian nation" idea its due, we should look at its most thorough and public airing. On April 23, 1988, an Arizona Republican Party activist wrote to Justice Sandra Day O'Connor asking for details on a Supreme Court decision saying this is a Christian nation.[56] On May 19, 1988, O'Connor replied, "You wrote me recently to inquire about any holdings of this Court to the effect that this is a Christian nation. There are statements to such effect in the following opinions."[57] O'Connor's letter then cited specific passages from three decisions.[58] In January of 1989 the Arizona Republican Party adopted a resolution proclaiming America to be a Christian nation.[59]

As we will see, the opinions O'Connor cited obviously do not establish that this is a Christian nation. But before looking at those opinions, it should be noted that O'Connor's letter was most likely drafted by an unthinking staff member and signed as part of an enormous pile of daily correspondence.[60] O'Connor later issued a statement of "regret" that her letter had been used in a "political debate,"[61] and her own judicial decisions reflect an appreciation for America's religious diversity. Indeed, she has ruled that displaying a nativity scene on the courthouse steps "has the unconstitutional effect of conveying a government endorsement of Christianity."[62]

Nonetheless, the "Christian nation" idea has taken on a life of its own, so we should look at the passages O'Connor cited. The first appears in an opinion for the Court by Justice William O. Douglas upholding a New York City program that permitted public school students to leave school under certain circumstances for religious instruction or devotional exercises.[63] In the cited passage, Douglas wrote, "We are a religious people whose institutions presuppose a Supreme Being. We guarantee the freedom to worship as one chooses. We make room for as wide a variety of beliefs and creeds as the spiritual needs of man deem necessary."[64]

Two points have to be made here. First of all, Douglas nowhere calls this a "Christian nation." He is, in fact, celebrating religious diversity. In the preceding paragraph of the very same opinion, he gives as examples of the uses of released time not only Catholics attending mass on a Holy Day of Obligation and Protestants attending a family baptismal ceremony, but also Jews being excused for Yom Kippur.[65] Second, Douglas later explained that his reference to Americans as "a religious people whose institutions presuppose a Supreme Being" was a recognition that "[t]he Puritan influence helped shape our constitutional law and our common law. . . . But those who fashioned the First Amendment decided that if and when God is to be served, His service will not be motivated by coercive measures of government."[66] In another reflection on his statement that we are "a religious people," he wrote, "The First Amendment leaves the government in a position not of hostility to religion but of neutrality. The philosophy is that the atheist or agnostic—the nonbeliever—is entitled to go his own way."[67]

The second passage cited by O'Connor provides even less support for the "Christian nation" idea. The reference is to an opinion by Justice Felix Frankfurter concurring in the Court's decision to uphold Sunday closing laws. Frankfurter wrote:

> Religious beliefs pervade, and religious institutions have traditionally regulated, virtually all human activity. It is a postulate of American life, reflected specifically in the First Amendment to the Constitution but not there alone, that those beliefs and institutions shall continue . . . free of the dictates and directions of the state. However, this free-

dom does not and cannot furnish the adherents of religious creeds entire insulation from every civic obligation.[68]

There is simply nothing here to suggest that Justice Frankfurter, a Jew, was describing America as a "Christian nation."

The final passage cited in Justice O'Connor's letter is the only one that actually uses the "Christian nation" language. The reference is to an 1892 decision of the Supreme Court in a case called *Church of the Holy Trinity v. United States.*[69]

In 1885 Congress passed a statute making it unlawful for any person or organization to "encourage the importation or migration of any alien" into the United States. A few years later the Church of the Holy Trinity in New York contracted with E. Walpole Warren of England to come to this country to be their pastor. When Warren did come here, the United States brought suit.

The U.S. Supreme Court held, in an opinion by Justice David Brewer, that, as a matter of statutory construction, the 1885 statute did not apply to the contract made by the church, and thus Warren was free to serve as pastor. Looking at the legislative history and the purpose of the act, the Court found that Congress intended only to stop the flow of "cheap unskilled labor" that was flooding the market, not to restrict the migration of "brain toilers," who were in short supply.[70] Justice Brewer went on to note that it was particularly clear that Congress did not mean to restrict the migration of clergy. We are, Brewer said, "a religious people. This is historically true."[71] He then cited the long history of Christian groups settling the early colonies and the continued influence of religion and Christianity on American society. He concluded:

> These, and many other matters which might be noticed, add a volume of unofficial declarations to the mass of organic utterances that this is a Christian nation. In the face of all these, shall it be believed that a Congress of the United States intended to make it a misdemeanor for a church of this country to contract for the services of a Christian minister residing in another nation?[72]

Justice Brewer, the son of Congregational missionary parents and himself a Sunday school teacher, clearly felt strongly about the importance of the Christian influence on American history, an influence that is undeniably great.[73] In 1905 Brewer even published a series of lectures under the title *The United States: A Christian Nation*.[74] But in that book Brewer argued that although America was a Christian nation, "the government as a legal organization is independent of all religions."[75] Even in the *Holy Trinity* opinion itself, Brewer did not suggest that Christianity enjoyed some favored status among American religions. In arguing that Congress could not have intended to exclude the immigration of clergy, he gives as an example the unlikelihood that Congress meant to void a contract made by a "Jewish synagogue with some eminent Rabbi."[76]

One could certainly debate precisely what Brewer meant by describing this country as a Christian nation and whether that description is apt. But in no sense did his comment in *Holy Trinity* create any kind of binding legal precedent concerning the meaning of the Constitution. The comment, written over a century ago, was not necessary to the resolution of the case, and it appeared in an opinion that concerned statutory construction rather than the meaning of the Constitution.

So in legal terms the United States is not a Christian nation. But it is a nation in which, as we have seen, free speech and the right to educate your children provide vital protections for people of faith, free exercise protects religion from discrimination, and the ban on established religion protects against the smothering embrace of government while allowing religious perspectives to shape public debate. Religious leaders can confront scientific perspectives in a meaningful way under our system. The issue is not the right to speak. The issue is the content of what is said.

9

Hearing Religion's Distinctive Voice

When word of a new scientific development reaches the public, it is understandable that people of faith and their leaders may want to speak out. Clearly, they have a right to do so. What matters is what they say.

On many issues, different faiths within the Judeo-Christian tradition will have different reactions. There is no reason to expect that Catholics and Baptists will always react in the same way to issues raised by genetic research, nor that either group will see things exactly as Jews do. There is no point in attempting to get around this reality. Observations that grow out of a deeply felt and deeply understood religious tradition are far more likely to be meaningful than watered-down platitudes designed to be inoffensive.

Despite this concern, I am comfortable noting, as I did in earlier chapters, that reactions based on a wholesale adoption of the materialistic worldview of science are not an appropriate or useful point of departure for any of the groups within the Judeo-Christian tradition. Beyond that it is difficult to talk about how religion ought to react to developments in modern science without violating my own premise that a vague American civil religion is no substitute for the real thing. Nonetheless, I believe it is incumbent on me to give some sense of the types of responses I believe we would hear if America's religious leaders could get over their infatuation with science whenever they read of a new discovery. I hope I can avoid the vacuous nature of many broad-based pronouncements without misrepresenting the substance of relevant portions of the

Jewish and Christian traditions. If nothing else, I may be able to point the way toward more specific statements that people could make when speaking from within their own faith traditions.

I am well aware that the relationship of religion and science, and thus the reaction of people of faith to scientific advances, has varied throughout history.[1] It could hardly be otherwise given the countless cultural, political, and legal environments in which religion and science have met. My concern is with the Judeo-Christian tradition within American society today. What can people of faith say now about the results of modern research?

Of course, on many occasions people of faith will simply want to applaud and study the latest findings from the world of science. Both Judaism and Christianity in our era are open to learning more about the natural world; in fact, they often actively support the scientific endeavor.[2] But scientific perspectives are not the only perspectives, and there are times when religious leaders and others will want to make that clear.

From my point of view, the central religious message that provides a distinctive counterweight to science revolves around ideas of humility, values, and faith. I will try to discuss these ideas and, in each case, offer an example of what religion might say in light of specific scientific developments.

The Central Message of Humility, Values, and Faith

Humility in the Judeo-Christian tradition flows from our status as people in the presence of God. For many of us, there is a profound message in Micah:

> And what does the Lord require of you
> But to do justly,
> To love mercy,
> And to walk humbly with your God?[3]

Nowhere is our humility more central than in our attempts to understand God. In the Bible he often appears as a cloud, escaping our full apprehension.[4] The book of Job teaches that we simply are not able to fully comprehend his ways or his purposes. When bad times befall Job, he and his friends agree that human understanding is limited, but it is only after God speaks to Job out of the whirlwind that they realize how absolute those limits are.[5]

Even these modest observations have implications for how we react to some of the rhetoric of modern science. Consider the world of modern physics. Dazzled by their own increasing comprehension of physical laws, and eager to build appreciation and support for their efforts, modern physicists have chosen some extraordinary language to describe their work. Those of us who draw from traditional religion a sense of deep humility are in a good position to offer a polite dissent when physicists begin to tell us about "the God Particle,"[6] or "the mind of God,"[7] or about "seeing the face of God."[8] The well-known optimism of scientists may serve them well as they try to understand more and more about nature.[9] And for some researchers an underlying faith that there is an order in the universe may be a necessary precondition to doing physics.[10] Einstein, for example, saw his own work as a "search for harmony" in nature.[11]

But the theologizing of many modern scientists appears to come not from a humble faith, but from scientific hubris.[12] The physicist Leon Lederman attempted to bolster the case for funding a high energy accelerator by writing a book, in a mock biblical style, that identified a subatomic particle, the Higgs Boson, as the God Particle.[13] The Higgs Boson, we are told, has this status because if we learn more about it we will be able to fill in missing pieces in the latest unified scientific theory:

> And how do we learn more about it? Since it is Her particle, we can wait, and if we lead an exemplary life, we'll find out when we ascend to Her kingdom. Or we can spend $8 billion and build us a Super Collider in Waxahachie, Texas, which has been designed to produce the Higgs particle.[14]

This turned out to be both bad politics—Congress declined to build the collider—and questionable theology, but this sort of terminology is increasingly common among scientists.[15] Though Lederman seems tongue in cheek, Stephen Hawking, in *A Brief History of Time,* seems very solemn when he tells us that his research into unifying theories in physics offers an understanding of the "mind of God."[16] And astronomer George Smoot, after discovering phenomena in background radiation that support the big bang theory of creation, announced that it was "like seeing the face of God."[17]

These are not isolated incidents. Modern physicists routinely refer to the unified theory they are now seeking as the Theory of Everything.[18] The physicist Steven Weinberg has written that "it is an irresistible metaphor to speak of the final laws of nature in terms of the mind of God."[19]

Physicists may want to try to resist this metaphor, or at least to modify it. A moderate amount of humility might introduce the notion that scientists two hundred years from now are unlikely to see present-day scientists as having understood everything. And the idea that physics has a special pipeline to an understanding of God reflects a remarkable degree of hubris. It may well be that we can learn, in our halting, imperfect way, something about God as we learn something about particles and cosmic radiation. But we can also learn something about God as we learn something about poetry, and about our fears, and about our children. Physics can be important and fascinating without being Everything.

One of the hardest things to learn is how we ought to live our lives. When we turn to the subject of values, it is particularly hard to proceed without going into the details of a particular religious tradition. But one observation that we can safely make about the Judeo-Christian approach is that values indeed exist, that is, there are human actions that deserve to be praised and those that deserve to be criticized. This central belief is not a scientific insight. Science by its nature is deterministic; it seeks mechanical explanations. Even though modern physics teaches that probabilities play an inevitable role in understanding the behavior of subatomic particles, it does not teach us whether free will or virtue is there.

Thus, if a purely scientific model is applied to human behavior, there is always the danger that values will drop out of the picture.

If we are nothing but molecules in motion, a virtuous act is no different from a reflex action.

There have been times in the history of science when the impulse to eliminate human autonomy and moral accountability from the picture has been strong. Darwinian evolution provided a particularly powerful temptation. The social Darwinism of Herbert Spencer, the eugenics movement, and many other chapters in modern history show the dangers of collapsing beliefs about the way things are into beliefs about the way things ought to be.[20] The naturalistic fallacy—that the factual *is* can be transformed into the normative *ought*—is not only bad logic; it is dangerous. The fact that slavery exists does not make slavery right.

Of course, in principle any complete mechanistic, deterministic system for explaining human behavior can try to reduce morality, as well as poetry and everything else, to the workings of molecules or genes or economic forces. But belief in such a theory could hardly be based on science. Such complete systems, by their nature, are utterly untestable. After all, it can always be said that the person doing the test as well the person evaluating the results is nothing but a product of the very forces under study. If a test purports to falsify Marxism, the true believer can always say that the test is nothing but the work of the ruling class.

Modern evolutionary biologists are generally more cautious in this respect than some of their predecessors. They typically argue that although our genes predispose us in certain directions, they do not provide the last word. Thus, E. O. Wilson, a founder of sociobiology, has written that "[w]hen any genetic bias is demonstrated, it cannot be used to justify a continuing practice in present and future societies. . . . Genetic biases can be trespassed, passions averted or redirected, and ethics altered."[21]

Nevertheless, the work of Wilson and others often seeks to show the limits of human capabilities, including moral capabilities, in light of our genetic heritage.[22] In the course of doing that it is easy to get carried away. Although in his book *Consilience* Wilson says that natural instincts can be "subdued," he at times appears to limit moral sentiments to nothing more than the product of genes and the environment, and he suggests that the ethical *ought* "is just short-hand for one kind of factual statement, a word that denotes what society first chose (or was coerced) to do, and then codified."[23] Under that view of morality, the most frightening societies in history can lay claim to doing what ought to be done. Meaningful moral discourse must go beyond that.

Or consider Steven Pinker's use of evolutionary biology to explain human behavior in his book *How the Mind Works*.[24] Pinker states quite clearly that morality cannot be reduced to genetics, indeed that science cannot answer the question "How did *ought* emerge from a universe of particles and planets, genes and bodies?"[25] But in his enthusiasm for the implications of research about the evolution of altruism, he tells us that "the moral emotions are designed by natural selection to further the long-term interests of individuals and ultimately their genes,"[26] and he gives us examples:

> *Liking* is the emotion that initiates and maintains an altruistic partnership. It is, roughly, a willingness to offer someone a favor, and is directed to those who appear willing to offer favors back. . . .
> *Sympathy,* the desire to help those in need, may be an emotion for earning gratitude. If people are most grateful when they most need the favor, a person in need is an opportunity to make an altruistic act go farthest.[27]

To at least one scientist reviewing this work, Pinker is here providing "fortune cookie mottoes," while vastly overstating what evolution can tell us about the human mind.[28] In any event, we all, scientists and nonscientists alike, have to be much more careful when we look at the biological aspects of human behavior. The vast majority of us do not believe that we can be reduced to our genes, and there is nothing in science that can compel that belief. Nothing requires us to see a person in need solely as an opportunity for the efficient dispensing of our goodwill.

Let us back up for a minute, and put the role of genetics and values in a more sensible context. First of all, as scientists would happily grant, genes alone, apart from the environmental context, determine nothing. You can breed roses for generations so that your seeds will produce only the bright red variety; but if you put those seeds in a vat of acid, you will not get bright red roses. It is only in certain environments that genetic characteristics can be expressed. And the interaction between the environment and genes remains enormously complex.

More importantly, as we have seen, if values have any meaning, they cannot be fully determined by a combination of genetic and environmental factors. In 1800 slavery may have existed in part for many reasons—social, political, economic—but the fact that it existed did not make it right. We have to keep reminding ourselves that what is does not imply what ought to be.[29]

Of course, empirical reality can constrain our moral choices. If I lack the real world ability to abolish all of the poverty on earth in the next five minutes, it is hard to argue that I am morally bound to do that. But that does not mean that I am free to ignore poverty altogether; I still have to decide what, if anything, I should do to improve the lot of others. As the philosopher Bernard Williams has written:

> The important point is that evolutionary biology is not at all directly concerned with the well-being of the individual, but with the fitness, which is the likelihood of that individual's leaving offspring. The most that sociobiology might do for ethics lies in a different direction, inasmuch as it might be able to suggest that certain institutions or patterns of behavior are not realistic options for human societies.[30]

Most religious leaders, like most scientists, are well aware that we must make difficult moral choices within the confines of our human capabilities. But there sometimes is a temptation to look to science, indeed to genetics, for a quick fix to a difficult moral dilemma. Consider the matter of the morality of homosexual conduct, an issue that requires everyone, including people of faith, to remember that *is* does not imply *ought*. Whenever a new study suggests some biological basis for homosexuality, both sides in the debate rush to use the data. For some church leaders, a genetic basis means that homosexuality is inborn and thus cannot be considered wrong, and therefore practicing homosexuals should be welcomed into the church.[31] To other religious leaders, the same scientific evidence indicates that homosexuality is a disease that should be cured, just as we seek cures for other genetic ailments, such as cystic fibrosis.[32] On this view, homosexuality is a problem that should be done away with.

But of course, scientific evidence alone cannot answer the ultimate moral issue. Suppose there is a strong genetic predisposition to homosexual behavior. We still have to decide whether to structure the environment to encourage or discourage homosexual behavior or whether to be indifferent to it. If there is a strong genetic predisposition to alcoholism, we have to make that choice: we can subsidize liquor sales, forbid them, tax them, or leave them to the market. We have to make the same decisions when we learn that genes dispose one to running fast or jumping high. Genes do not come with labels saying "disease" or "virtue" or "matter of indifference." Certain traits, such as physical aggression, can be rewarded in some settings, such as football, and condemned in others, such as street crime. We simply have to make the difficult moral choices. Each religious tradition will have to search its own soul about homosexuality; science will not provide the ultimate answers.

And science will be even less valuable when we seek ultimate answers on final questions of faith. As to the necessity of faith, there is a consensus that extends beyond those with traditional religious beliefs. Many scientists, for example, regardless of their formal religious affiliations, have testified that a faith in the order of the universe has shaped their work. Perhaps the best known example is the testimony of Albert Einstein:

> Quantum mechanics is very impressive. But an inner voice tells me that it is not yet the real thing. The theory produces a good deal but hardly brings us closer to the secret of the Old One. I am at all events convinced that *He* does not play dice.[33]

Many scientists who disagree with Einstein about quantum theory nonetheless recognize that there are limits on what human reason can tell us about the physical world around us.[34] Of course, there are dissenters to any view. Richard Dawkins, the popular exponent of evolutionary biology, has written that there is no room for faith in his world—"[F]aith," he says, "seems to me to qualify as a kind of mental illness."[35] Dawkins will have to do battle with a legion of philosophers of science, who know that scientists, like the rest of us, must make some important assumptions if they are to rely on the evidence of their senses, on generalizing from what they see, and on the notion that the way things worked yesterday requires that they work that way today.[36] Most of are aware that faith in our senses and in the stability of phenomena is needed to function in the world. And I suspect that even Dawkins has some articles of faith. They just grow out of a different tradition. He has written, after all, that "DNA sequences are the gospel documents of all life, and we have learned to decipher them."[37]

But although science, like every other human endeavor, rests on certain assumptions, traditional religion embodies additional articles of faith that go beyond the concerns of science. In some settings, that traditional faith can provide a counterweight when public discussion becomes too focused on narrow material concerns. The debate over physician assisted suicide provides an important example.

As modern technology has extended our ability to keep people alive even when many brain functions have stopped, the question of when medical treatment should cease has become extremely controversial. The debate has been driven by technological developments beginning with the artificial respirators of the 1950s and continuing with the more advanced life-support devices available today.[38] Much of the recent controversy has focused on the legal question of whether a patient who wishes to end his life but is unable to do so himself should be allowed to call on a physician for help. The U.S. Supreme Court has held that states may bar physician assisted suicide,[39] but the Court has left open the possibility that dying patients may have a right to obtain pain relief, even when that medicine "would hasten their deaths."[40]

The question of pain relief is a vital one, but it is not the only one. For many Christians, the question of life's end inevitably raises a central article of faith—death as a gateway to eternal life. Christian leaders who share this faith can play an invaluable role in counseling those faced with a terminal illness.

One would expect that when terminal illness looms, medicine, science, and law would at least share the stage with traditional religion. Regrettably, that is not always the case. In many instances, church leaders have not publicly discussed the spiritual decisions involved with the end of life.[41] According to David H. Smith, director of the Poynter Center for the Study of Ethics and American Institutions, many mainline religious leaders have abdicated their public responsibility, leaving discussions dominated by secular supporters of "death with dignity."[42] In some cases, churches have not even reached their own members with instruction and counseling. Joanne Lynn, director of the Center to Improve Care of the Dying at George Washington University, has lived with this:

> How often I hear: "My father went to church his whole life. He was a leader in the church and very much a member. But he got old and sick, and when he most needed someone to visit, to give Communion, we had to beg the church to show up."[43]

Fortunately, we have an excellent example of the important contribution traditional Christian perspectives can make in what has become in our society too much a purely legal and medical matter. The Episcopal Diocese of Washington, D.C., has produced a report on assisted suicide and euthanasia that presents a thoughtful discussion of the many ways that Christian perspectives can inform this debate. At the risk of emphasizing one part of the discussion over the others, let me present a passage that combines the traditional opposition to suicide with a Christian understanding of the limits of medicine:

> There are values that are weightier than that of life. We are called to risk—not take—our lives at times for the sake of God and others. Christ implicitly indicated this when he observed that the good shepherd lays down his life for the sheep (John 10:10). . . . Nothing in the central Christian tradition requires us to extend our lives for as long as possible, even though they are valuable . . . Christians, while called by God to life, have reason not to fear death. We see death as that oc-

casion when the love and power of God in Christ will break forth in its fullness. The meaning that Christians find in death is not the nothingness of final extinction, but the complete revelation of the being and love of God.[44]

This is the kind of report that can make a difference. The varying perspectives of those in the Jewish and Christian traditions can add immeasurably to the lives of their own members and of the society at large.

And on a broader scale, the focus on humility, values, and faith that traditional religion supplies can wisely temper our reaction to the advances of modern science. We can respect modern physics, biology, and medicine without believing that they present the final account of everything, the end of values, and the alleviation of pain as the solution to all of our problems.

The Places Where Religion Should Be Heard

If religion is to make a useful contribution to our society, it must be heard in a variety of settings. Yet enormous controversy swirls around the appropriate place where religious sentiments might be aired in American public debate. Although the legal right of people of faith to speak out is unassailable, difficult prudential questions arise when religious people try to find their voice in our diverse society. If we begin our analysis of this issue by looking first at the more intimate settings for religious speech, we can clarify the choices that remain in the broader marketplace of ideas.

Individuals ought to clarify their own stance in relation to modern science before worrying about how to address others. From national spokesmen for religious coalitions to prominent clergy to parishioners, the starting point is often reading in the newspaper about the latest developments in astronomy or genetics or medicine. The starting assumption should never be "this changes everything." It probably does not. A clear understanding of the science involved will typically reveal matters of great interest and the possibility of reshaping some of what we know about the natural world and our options in dealing with it, but it will rarely be anything that bears directly on ultimate value choices.

In educating our children, a similar dynamic is at work. Traditional secular science education is nothing to be feared. The more one learns about the substance of science and the scientific method, the more one learns about what science can and cannot do. Science does not tell people how to live their lives, and good science teachers do not spend class time on that subject. If you meet a bright young person with an utterly secular, materialistic view of the world, do not blame his science classes. The problem in the moral education of children is not too much science, it is too little education in philosophy, ethics, and the doctrines of their faith. The last of these must be taught at home and within the church. You cannot entrust the teaching of the real substance of actual religious faith to the public schools. It violates our laws, it flies in the face of our religious diversity, and it is certain to lead to very bad teaching.

It is vital that values education take place at home and in the religious community. That is the best insurance against young people adopting the view that nothing matters in the world but science.

The threat posed by science in the absence of values education is real. It is too easy to laugh it off by pointing out that so many young people do poorly on their science tests. It is true that too many students not only receive no real religious education outside of school, but they also learn little or nothing about the scientific theories they purport to study in school. But that is not good news for religion. Although these students may misunderstand modern genetics, they learn the bigger and more dangerous message that there is nothing in the world except science. Science, after all, is taught in school and discussed in the media and apparently taken very seriously in our society. These students become easy prey for the kind of pop science or pseudoscience that uses the language of the real thing to build credibility without actually bothering with careful testing, replication of results, and the like. Bad science gives us the worst of both worlds—no real grip on the natural world and no place for spiritual values.

So religion's distinctive voice—its timeless message of humility, values, and faith—must be taught to the young. Only then can it serve as a counterweight to the materialistic perspective of science.

When individuals armed with a particular religious perspective seek to participate in national political debate, the issues become more complicated. For many of the matters I am concerned with, the national debate is not central. I think it would be a major step if individuals, understanding the limits of science, took responsibility within their own faith traditions for the moral choices they made, rejecting the view that they could pawn those choices off on the latest developments in genetics or physics. But there are times when a religious perspective on science does become relevant in broader debate. Consider, for example, the matter of assisted suicide. In light of the Supreme Court decision mentioned above, state legislatures have leeway in deciding whether to permit or ban physician assisted suicide. For though the Court held that individual rights could not overcome a state law forbidding the practice, it implied that the legislature of a state could, with appropriate safeguards, allow it. The essence of the Court's decision was that this matter should not be resolved in litigation but rather through the democratic process. Thus, Chief Justice Rehnquist's opinion for the Court concluded:

> Throughout the Nation, Americans are engaged in an earnest and profound debate about the morality, legality, and practicality of physician-assisted suicide. Our holding permits this debate to continue, as it should in a democratic society.[45]

Certainly there are explicitly religious perspectives that may be relevant to this debate. A proposed statute that would allow assisted suicide in a very wide range of cases might be questioned on the basis of traditional religious doctrines opposing suicide. On the other hand, a statute that prevented a physician from turning off elaborate life-support equipment might raise problems for those whose traditional faith emphasizes personal autonomy and the centrality of the spirit over physical existence in some settings.[46]

As we emphasized in chapters 5 and 8, the expression of religious perspectives in public debate is completely protected by the free speech clause and does not constitute an establishment of religion. How could it be otherwise? As Chief Justice Rehnquist said, assisted suicide raises moral issues. We are not limited to secular philosophers in discussing such issues. If an editorial writer is free to cite Mill or Kant, he is equally free to cite Jesus or Rabbi Akiba.

But the fact that an approach is legal does not mean that it is wise. A host of political theorists have raised questions about whether, in a diverse society such as ours, it is appropriate or prudent to introduce explicitly religious arguments into public debate. I respect these concerns, but I believe that in the vast majority of cases of the type we are concerned with here, there is no real problem with presenting religious views in the public square; in fact, important values are served when those views are aired.

The writings of scholars such as Kent Greenawalt, John Rawls, and Michael Perry are representative of the important work going on in this field. Greenawalt is identified with the view that legislators should not rely on religious arguments when they publicly discuss political issues.[47] Rawls maintains that religious justifications should not be advanced when society is addressing a fundamental question such as who can vote or hold property.[48] Perry takes a view that is more "congenial to the airing of religious arguments" than either Greenawalt's or Rawls's.[49] He would allow legislators and other citizens to rely on religious arguments, although when the subject is human well-being, they should not do so unless they can advance a secular argument that would lead to the same conclusion.[50]

These authors and others raise important concerns, such as the possibility that when a government official talks solely in religious terms, people of other faiths will feel excluded, or the possibility that unless a secular consensus can be reached on the fundamental structure of government, democracy in a diverse society will not be possible. And there is, of course, the practical concern that people of a particular religious faith will have difficulty winning allies if they cannot cast their arguments in broad terms. Finally, there is the reality that if a political majority of one faith enacted a law that was based solely on the tenets of that faith and served no other purpose—such as a law that everyone in a particular town must wear a cross—the nonestablishment ban in our Constitution would be violated.

These are very real concerns, although I would note, as others have, that we must also be cautious that we do not create a political culture in which a relentlessly secular perspective marginalizes people of faith.[51] Moreover, in many instances when religious perspectives are relevant, shutting them out weakens our political culture. As Michael J. Sandel has argued,

> At least where grave moral questions are at stake, it is not possible to detach politics and law from substantive moral judgment. But even in cases where it is possible to conduct political debate without reference to our moral and religious convictions, it may not always be desirable. The effort to banish moral and religious argument from the public realm for the sake of political agreement may end by impoverishing political discourse and eroding the moral and civic resources necessary to self-government.[52]

In any event, a full analysis of the arguments from political theory is beyond our scope. We are concerned here with more narrow questions. When a new development in genetics raises questions about human behavior, people of faith might speak about the matter with their families, religious leaders might issue public statements, and a legislator who happens to be religious might make a speech. In all of these situations, the speaker might make explicitly religious points. For example, some people of faith would assert that part of our God-given nature is free will and that our knowledge of genetics does not change that. In this setting no legal scholar or judge would question the right to religious speech. That right is at the absolute heart of our history and our freedoms. I believe as well that few, if any, political theorists would believe that it was somehow wrong in our pluralist society to speak publicly in this setting about religion. No one is being excluded from the political process, and no one is being alienated from the public debate, unless alienation results whenever you hear an argument you disagree with.[53] Even when legislation is under consideration, such as with the assisted suicide controversy, it does not threaten our political culture if among the arguments heard are those based on traditional religious views concerning suicide or the centrality of the spirit as opposed to the body. We would cut ourselves off from a large body of wisdom and from the felt beliefs of millions of fellow citizens if we lacked the strength to include these considerations along with the avalanche of arguments we will hear about the costs of medical care, the maximization of individual happiness, and the legal difficulties of determining intent when someone is disabled. In the real world of American culture today, the problem is not that when scientific issues arise we think too much about values.

A Personal Observation

An argument of the type I am making inevitably involves a personal element. I think my views on the appropriate balance between religion and science are reasonably grounded in the readings I have done and in rational analysis, but I freely concede that they are grounded in personal experience as well. In fairness, I believe I should write a bit about the two main influences on my thinking in this area. Samuel Scolnic, the rabbi at the synagogue I attended as a young man, and Benjamin Goldberg, my late father, might not agree with everything I have said here, but they certainly shaped my thinking.

Samuel Scolnic is a tall Texan who came to Congregation Beth El in Bethesda, Maryland, in 1956. My family belonged to Beth El, and I studied Judaism and Hebrew and went to services there for many years, while I was attending public schools. I celebrated my Bar Mitzvah and confirmation at Beth El, and my wife, Miriam, and I were married there by Rabbi Scolnic in 1969.

Rabbi Scolnic is a man of considerable learning and dignity, and his views on Judaism and public policy would merit careful study. I want to restrict myself now, however, to the impressions I gained as a youngster from him about religion and science. It always seemed to me that in Scolnic's sermons and classes, modern rationalism, including science, was accorded respect, but it did not dictate the agenda. Faith and tradition had their own strength. Scolnic was never trendy. He would sometimes talk about the matters of the day, but they never seemed like the only things that mattered.

Scolnic retired as rabbi at Beth El in 1988, although he continues to teach there. At the time of his retirement, the congregation published a collection of his sermons.[54] In one of them, he discusses the biblical passage in which Lot's wife, disobeying an order, looks back at the destruction of Sodom and is turned into a pillar of salt. The rabbi mentions that Israeli guides today point out salt formations near Sodom, but he says that whether those very formations date to biblical times "is quite unimportant."[55] What is important is the message. Scolnic points out that Lot's wife had lived in Sodom and that she might have looked back "out of nostalgia, out of wistfulness, out of sadness [or] out of concern and fear."[56] All are good reasons, but the message may be that, as difficult as it is in times of loss, sometimes you have to look forward:

> [T]he commandment to Lot and his family may have been intended for us as much as it was for the people to whom it was directed. By turning their eyes backward, they surely could not have affected the destruction of Sodom and Amorah, but they could affect their own future and their own destiny. With courage, with hope, with faith, they could leave the rubble of the past and move on to a more constructive future.[57]

These are not startling insights, but they are powerful ones. I am grateful that Rabbi Scolnic did not muddy the message by discussing, as some modern creation scientists do, the chemical process by which Lot's wife could become a pillar of salt.[58]

In his sermon on the dream in which Jacob sees a ladder stretching from earth to heaven with angels going up and down, Scolnic builds on a famous Chasidic interpretation.[59] The ladder should be understood as a human being, with feet on the earth but a head that could touch the heavens. The angels represent our thoughts, some noble, some evil. "Man," Scolnic emphasized, "is not a speck of matter, a bit of protoplasm that appears on earth for a second or two; his life is neither meaningless nor devoid of purpose."[60] And that purpose is not a small one:

> Wherever a person stands, whatever he may be doing, he has the capability of joining earth to heaven. He is the conduit, the medium between these two spheres. He is capable of turning wherever he stands into a holy place.[61]

Again, these are not novel sentiments. But again I am grateful, this time to have avoided the New Age insight that angels are essentially a marketing opportunity.

My father was tall, but he was definitely not a Texan. Before I was born, he moved from New York City to the Washington, D.C., area to work for the federal government as a physicist. He rose to head a major government laboratory that did research on night vision.

My father was a terrific guy, but for now I am just going to look at his views on science and religion. Like many scientists, my father tended to value his chosen field over other secular pursuits. He respected the work of novelists, economists, even lawyers, but he saved his highest admiration for great scientists. In our household, as in others, the word Einstein was essentially synonymous with genius.

But my father did not grant science unlimited jurisdiction. In particular, in the area of religion he was quite sure that no one knew all the answers. On those occasions when we listened to Rabbi Scolnic's sermons together, his reaction was typically "maybe."

Religious faith was in a separate sphere from his work at the laboratory. As a working physicist, he associated science with detailed observations, quantitative measurements, and elaborate, often unsuccessful, tests. When the weather was really cold and the sky was really dark, cutting edge night vision technologies did not always work the way they had in the lab. Science to him was not about metaphysics or even paradigms. It did not provide answers, or even very good metaphors, outside of its own realm. He and my mother taught values to their children through traditional rules and by the lives they led, not by equations.

At first glance, it might seem hard to provide a more straightforward, even obvious, set of ideas than those I first gleaned from my rabbi and my father. As I studied areas like the philosophy of science and constitutional law, I learned that the intersection between values and empiricism can be a complex and difficult field. But I also learned that allowing one to swallow the other serves the interests of neither.

10

Alternative Perspectives on Religion and Science

I believe that within America's legal culture today, religion can play a more vital role if it strips itself of unneeded scientific trappings. But I do not believe that the current confusion about the proper role of religion and science arises inevitably from something about the immutable nature of religion or science. Throughout Western history, the relationship of the Judeo-Christian tradition to science has fluctuated. Indeed, I could hardly call for limits on religion's overly attentive concern with the latest scientific findings if I did not believe these matters were open to reevaluation.

A brief exposure to the varying relationship between religion and science in Western and other traditions will help us gain some perspective on what I take to be the current imbalance in that relationship. I think it also will be useful to look at some sophisticated current attempts to use science to buttress religion to see what they imply about the role of religion in public debate. The spate of books with titles like *The Science of God* and *God: The Evidence* suggests that my concerns about the seductive nature of science may have some broader implications.

Other Places, Other Times

We are inclined today to think of modern science as beginning in Europe in the seventeenth century, with a particular emphasis on the appearance of Galileo's *Dialogue on the Two Chief World Sys-*

tems in 1632 and Newton's *Principia* in 1687.[1] But prior to that time, numerous efforts had been made to systematically understand the natural world, and Christianity had at times provided encouragement to those efforts. In the centuries before Galileo it was often difficult to separate religion and science.[2] For many the biblical concept of Creation served as a catalyst for understanding nature since that concept "implied a dependable order behind the flux of nature."[3]

When we turn to the modern scientific movement that Galileo began, we see Christianity both in conflict with religion and in support of it. Galileo, of course, was condemned by church officials and subjected to house arrest.[4] But it is equally true that in seventeenth-century England religion played a positive role in the development of modern science. Devout Puritans were disproportionally represented among early scientists, and Puritan schools placed science courses in their curricula.[5] Many scholars, following Robert Merton, believe that Calvinist theology, which emphasized this-worldly enterprise and understanding God through understanding nature, played a vital role in the creation of modern science.[6] At the time of the American Revolution, the dissenting theologians who helped found this country often supported science—in fact, the theologians and the scientists were often the same people.[7]

In the centuries that have followed, these patterns have been played out countless times and in countless ways. Religious leaders and individual people of faith have both supported and opposed science in a variety of settings, and Catholics, Protestants, and Jews have been represented on all sides of these controversies. Many notable theories have drawn science and religion together. In the seventeenth century, for example, the Jewish philosopher Baruch Spinoza closely identified God with the universe itself.[8] Contemporary notions of process theology, favored by some scientists, find God manifest in all of the relationships we see developing around us.[9]

Outside of the Judeo-Christian tradition there have been similar variations in the relationship between science and religion. Until roughly 1200 A.D., the Islamic faith supported considerable scientific achievement, particularly in astronomy; in later eras this tradition was often absent.[10] Today there are leaders in Islamic society who would reject those elements of science seen as "Western," whereas others believe Islam can be reconciled with all forms of science.[11] Buddhist teachings tend to accept science as part of a unified understanding of the world, although there can be tensions when science calls attention to itself and seeks to stand apart from "the organic wholeness of existence."[12]

I am not seeking in this book to make a sweeping philosophical or theological argument about the intrinsic nature of science and religion. I am well aware that for many people of faith there is no conflict between the two. I simply believe that today, in America, when policy matters are under consideration, the scientific worldview is not adequately balanced by some of the great teachings from the Judeo-Christian faith traditions.

Secular Limits on Science

I do not believe that it is only religion that can provide a counterweight to science. I recognize that there are many secular arguments about the limits of science, in fact, about limits on the human endeavor in general. Whether or not a given thinker is ultimately moved by spiritual concerns, it certainly is possible to frame such arguments without reference to any particular faith tradition.

In this century, Wittgenstein's dictum—"whereof one cannot speak, thereof one must be silent"—has resonated with many scholars.[13] And Camus certainly spoke to the limits of our understanding with his image of the absurd contradiction between the human desire for clarity and the irrational character of the world.[14] Contemporary philosophers have hardly assumed that science can answer all of our questions. The analytical philosophy of Bernard Williams, for example, distinguishes sharply between the realm of science and the realm of ethics.[15]

In the academic world the claims of science have also been under attack for many years from scholars who can be loosely categorized as postmodern or deconstructionist.[16] Following the work of people like Paul Feyerabend, these writers have maintained that the rational, neutral stance of science is a veneer that can be stripped away, revealing a series of contestable political assumptions.[17]

The merits and demerits of these secular arguments about the limits of science deserve the attention they have been given in academic life. But that should not obscure our view. Science is a big target in academe precisely because it wields such influence in our society. The point is not that outstanding, peer-reviewed science dominates our popular culture. Much of the science that seduces people of faith is shakier than that, and some of it ranges from bad science to a parody of science. But that is just my point. The scientific, materialistic worldview is so pervasive in our culture that people feel the need for a "scientific" argument even if none is available and even if none would be relevant. Feyerabend himself has noted that "fly-by-night mystics, prophets of a New Age, and relativists of all sorts" are happy to "view quantum mechanics as a turning-point in thought" without really dealing with the actual science involved.[18] Wendy Kaminer's critique of the self-help movement captures the way that science swallows up the modern world of personal fulfillment:

> New Age appropriates science, or tries to, in an effort to bolster its credibility and expand its market. New Age embraces pop neuroscience— . . . the science of brain wave machines that offer push-button Nirvana. Having trouble meditating . . . ? At an altered-mind-states gym in Cambridge or L.A. you can hook yourself up to an Inner Quest 111 or an MC^2Dreamachine. . . . [I]f the appropriation of science by self-styled spiritual leaders reflects some underlying ideological confusion, it does make sense commercially; that is, it makes money.[19]

Even the quixotic search for hidden messages in sacred texts—an activity as old as the texts themselves—today takes on a scientific aura. Modern students of the so-called Bible Code claim to have found in the Bible ancient predictions of events ranging from the assassination of Robert Kennedy to the details of the Gulf War.[20] But these predictions do not come from ordinary numerology or sudden revelation. They are made with computers, and they utilize "mathematics, computer science, and statistics."[21] "Nothing," we are assured, "is taken on faith."[22] Heaven forbid that faith should play a role in understanding the Bible.

It is precisely because science has seduced so many in our society, that it has reached so far beyond what even many scientists believe is its proper sphere, that the need for a reassertion of traditional religious values is so great.

Using Science to Find God

One traditional type of relationship between science and religion is driven by a search for harmony. Throughout the centuries, many people of faith, rather than challenging the results of science, have used those results to bolster their faith. Thus, Charles Kingsley, the Anglican clergyman and Darwin contemporary, was delighted with the theory of evolution, finding quite congenial the image of a God who had created a world that continually remade itself.[23]

In a series of books beginning about twenty years ago, John Polkinghorne has painstakingly examined the intersection of modern science and religion. Polkinghorne is a theoretical physicist and Anglican priest who serves as president of Queen's College, Cambridge.[24] I find his efforts impressive, in part because of the care he takes in defining his inquiry. Polkinghorne recognizes the great influence of science in Western culture, but he writes "not to submit to slavery to the spirit of the age," but rather to find "consonance" between what he experiences as a scientist and as a Christian.[25] Polkinghorne rejects the "prosy literalism" that would "turn the images of religion, whose function is to evoke eternity, into mundane descriptions of improbable facts," but he also rejects "a toned-down theology of a Cosmic Mind," adhering instead to traditional Christian beliefs.[26]

The balance Polkinghorne achieves between religious and scientific considerations is noteworthy. In reading some recent works by other authors who argue for the harmony between science and religion, I have sometimes had the sense that the scientific perspective is overwhelming everything else. Using modern science to prove the existence of God can be a dangerous enterprise. My own concern in this book is that religious people not let the latest scientific discoveries eclipse traditional teachings about faith and values. But a related concern is presented by recent works that use science to bolster religion. I certainly do not claim to be able to evaluate the strengths and weaknesses of these arguments on their own terms. But I do want to point out what I take to be some dangers in these efforts, because I believe the seductive pull of modern science is extraordinarily widespread in our culture.

Consider the sophisticated writings of Gerald Schroeder, a physicist who taught at the Massachusetts Institute of Technology before moving to the Weizmann Institute in Israel. In books such as *Genesis and the Big Bang* and *The Science of God,* Schroeder has combined a careful study of the first five books of the Bible in Hebrew with a detailed recounting of modern scientific discoveries. He finds that biblical and scientific descriptions of topics like the creation of the universe and the start of life on Earth present "identical realities but viewed from vastly different perspectives. Once these perspectives are identified, they coexist comfortably."[27]

The coexistence that Schroeder has in mind takes place at an extraordinary level of detail. For example, using relativistic conceptions of time based on Einstein's work, Schroeder maintains that the six days of creation can be understood to have lasted fifteen and three-fourths billion years, a "surprisingly good" match with modern cosmological theories.[28] The biblical basis for this notion of time stems from passages in Genesis that speak of the "generations of the heavens and the earth when they were created in the day that the Eternal God made earth and heavens."[29] And the fit is remarkably precise: Schroeder argues, for example, that day three in Genesis started 3.75 billion years ago and ended 1.75 billion years ago. Day three is when water first appears on Earth, and modern science tells us that water appeared about 3.8 billion years ago. Day three in Genesis also reports the emergence of plant life, including grass, whereas modern science puts that development much later than

Schroeder's chronology would suggest. Schroeder deals with this difficulty by arguing that the usual reading of the biblical text is a "misunderstanding"—better biblical interpretations have long suggested that grass may have appeared much later than day three.[30]

Without evaluating the merits of these arguments, I have two main cautions about the approach. First, basing a philosophy on the details of the latest scientific findings can mean basing it on shifting sands. Scientific estimates of the age of the earth and when it cooled and so on have changed quite a bit and may continue to change.

Recent developments offer an example. Like many observers, Schroeder is taken with the fact that certain of the constants that scientists find in the universe, such as those relating to the energy of the big bang, result in the development of life on earth, whereas slightly different constants would have made life impossible.[31] Since, under this argument, the exact measure of these constants becomes an important basis for religious belief, it is quite important to get the data right and not to include constants that lack a scientific basis. Schroeder himself discusses the most famous example of an utterly mistaken constant. Einstein's general theory of relativity seemed to demand that the universe either expand or contract over time. Einstein believed, however, that the universe was static. So Einstein introduced into his theory a cosmological constant, a repulsive energy force that would counteract gravity and enable the universe to stand still. A few years later, when Edwin P. Hubble discovered the expanding universe, Einstein renounced the cosmological constant, calling it the biggest "blunder" of his career.[32]

Schroeder, like other scientists, is unsparing in his description of Einstein's mistake. Einstein "rationalized away" conflicting data and published results "mutilated" by the cosmological constant.[33] Indeed, according to Schroeder, this constant "was no more than what a college freshman would call a 'fudge factor,' a totally subjective modification of the objective solution he was seeking."[34] Schroeder says the whole episode was one reason Einstein overlooked a description of the universe that would have been more in keeping with the biblical tradition.[35]

But science does not stand still. In 1998 the cosmological constant made a front-page comeback. Scientists had long believed that gravity should slow the expansion of the cosmos over time. Confronted with new data showing that cosmic expansion is in fact speeding up, an international team of scientists reluctantly concluded that Einstein's cosmological constant may in fact exist— space itself may be permeated by a repulsive force.[36]

I do not want to overstate this point. Nothing in these recent discoveries undercuts Schroeder's basic biblical analysis. And there is no guarantee that the cosmological constant will survive the next round of scientific data to come in. But that is precisely the problem. It is one thing to seek harmony between the perspectives of science and religion. It is another enterprise altogether to believe that the findings of science down to the decimal point in any given year must match up with religious teachings and texts. Achieving that end does not seem particularly worthwhile to me, and given how science changes, I am not sure it is readily achievable.

This brings us to my second concern with Schroeder's enterprise. Responding to scientific findings sometimes seems to put religion in a subservient position. Unless one is very careful, it can seem as though science is setting the agenda for religion. Consider Schroeder's discussion of dinosaurs. He tells us that he is often asked why the Bible does not mention dinosaurs, since science has demonstrated that they once existed. Schroeder responds that "[f]ortunately the bible does mention dinosaurs, though not by that name."[37] He then offers a lengthy analysis of the meaning of the Hebrew phrase *taninim gedolim,* which refers to one of the creatures God created on the fifth day. *Gedolim* means big, and although *taninim* is usually translated as something like *whale* or *alligator,* Schroeder concludes that it means reptile and that "big reptiles" means dinosaurs.[38]

My main concern here is Schroeder's use of the word "fortunately." It seems as though the Bible is being judged by whether it meets the arbitrary test of currently fashionable scientific concerns. After all, as Schroeder himself notes, the Bible does not appear to mention bananas or oranges.[39] Yet Schroeder does not feel the need to engage in a lengthy search for words that might be translated as *banana* or *orange*. At times it seems that science is running the show, and that can be troubling.

I have similar concerns about some of what appears in Patrick Glynn's book, *God: The Evidence*. Let me say again that I am not attempting an analysis of the substance of Glynn's argument. And I know that Glynn has a strong sense of limits. He clearly states, "I am not claiming that anyone today can reason his or her way to faith in God. This was not even true in my case."[40] Moreover, he recognizes that science alone cannot resolve issues of right and wrong.[41] But at times, like Schroeder, he seems to rest his analysis on the shifting sands of current science and to let science set his agenda.

Glynn, like Schroeder, is attracted to the idea that the fundamental constants in the universe all seem "fine-tuned" to assure the emergence of human life on earth.[42] As we have seen, this approach requires continued attention to the ever-changing world of science. More fundamentally, this approach has a circular quality that, at least for me, removes much of its appeal.

For Glynn, as for others, the basic argument for God that emerges from the nature of the physical constants we find in the universe is captured in the phrase "the anthropic principle":

> [T]he anthropic principle says that all the seemingly arbitrary and unrelated constants in physics have one strange thing in common— these are precisely the values you need if you want to have a universe capable of producing life. In essence, the anthropic principle [comes] down to the observation that all the myriad laws of physics were fine-tuned from the very beginning of the universe for the creation of man—that the universe we inhabit appeared to be expressly designed for the emergence of human beings.[43]

Among the laws Glynn cites are the relation of gravity to electromagnetism, the difference in mass between a proton and a neutron, and so on.[44] Basically, the notion is that it is extraordinarily unlikely—one chance in countless billions—that the world we are in could have happened by chance. God must have designed it.

I cannot speak for others, but my own faith is not enhanced by these observations. If I reach into a bowl containing a hundred trillion lottery tickets and I pull out the one belonging to Mary Smith, I do not doubt that she will feel lucky, perhaps even blessed. But from my point of view, I had to pull out someone's name—there was no grand design. Any name I picked would seem like a miraculous long shot. Moreover, the anthropic principle rests on the belief that ours is the only universe. Some scientists believe otherwise, which is why Glynn has to spend a fair amount of time arguing against those scientists who believe we are not able to observe all of the universes that exist.[45] I can honestly say that whether or not those scientific theories gain support from astronomical discoveries in the years ahead will have little impact on my spiritual life.

But for Glynn the most recent scientific discoveries take on remarkable importance. In fact, he says it is only in the last two or three decades that science has provided the crucial evidence in support of the anthropic principle because before that science depicted a random universe.[46] When it comes to belief in God, according to Glynn, "[r]eason no longer stands in the way, as it once clearly did."[47] Frankly, I believe that a large number of reasonable people believed in God in the millennia that preceded the 1960s. They were not disheartened by the state of science in their era, either because they could reconcile it with their view of God or because they believed it was not relevant to that view. They may also have recognized that the scientific explanations change over time.

For me the discussions about the anthropic principle recall the historic "argument from design." In 1802 William Paley, in his book *Natural Theology,* made the famous argument that the wonders of nature proved the existence of God. When you find a watch, you assume there must be a watchmaker; when you look at the intricacies of flowers and animals, you assume there must be a Designer.[48] This argument was not original with Paley, and it had been strongly criticized by David Hume, who noted the anthropomorphic nature of the discussion as well as the existence of imperfections in nature.[49] Moreover, Darwin's work undercut Paley for many since Darwin showed how natural selection could lead to intricate living mechanisms without any Grand Designer.[50] Nevertheless, the argument did not end there. For some, natural selection itself came to be seen as evidence of God's plan.[51]

This somewhat circular process may come to characterize the anthropic principle. Some new discovery in physics might well "explain" what previously appeared to be an unlikely coincidence and thus seem to undercut the anthropic principle. Yet that new discovery itself may suggest to some people that God is at work in a different way. There is nothing wrong with this process, but I am not one of those who finds it particularly compelling.

There is a very real danger that some devotees of the anthropic principle will lose sight of the nonscientific point. I am confident that Glynn and Schroeder would not fall in this category. But for others who are less careful, the focus on accounting in detail for the latest developments in the most esoteric and controversial areas of science can pull one away from the spiritual values that can inform everyday life. Mainstream followers of the Judeo-Christian tradition do not want to go as far as Spinoza did in identifying God with the impersonal cosmic order.[52] But a narrow adherent to the anthropic principle can sound like Spinoza on steroids.

Glynn's book ranges beyond astronomy and physics to evidence from psychology, medicine, and other fields that suggest to him that God exists. At times he argues strongly that the theory of evolution cannot convincingly account for the human belief in God and the consequences of that belief.[53] There certainly is a lively debate in this field. Even the sociobiologist E. O. Wilson, who believes that religion "can all eventually be explained as brain circuitry and deep, genetic history," has to concede that the issue is "far from resolved."[54] Even if you believe, as I do, that matters of ultimate faith cannot be determined by the scientific method, it is fascinating to read rival speculations on complex human behavior. Both Wilson and Glynn are arguing over the notion that the human body and mind are "wired for God."[55] Wilson believes the wiring stems from blind natural selection. Glynn believes it was put there by the Creator. My concern is that if we focus too much on whether we are wired for faith, we will become more concerned with the wiring than the faith.

11

Conclusion

Within a span of two months at the end of 1997, three of the most dissimilar magazines in the country had cover stories on the American people's quest for a stronger sense of spirituality. *Christianity Today,* which describes itself as a magazine of evangelical conviction, titled its story *Missing God at Church?*[1] The author described evangelical Christians who are unhappy with sermons that stress "immediate and timely application" of the Bible.[2] The churches, he maintained, "engineer 'worship experiences,' and yet heartfelt needs still go wanting."[3] What is really needed is "a service that is centered on God."[4]

Mother Jones is a magazine dedicated to investigative reporting that tells the reader on its masthead that it is named after an "orator, union organizer, and hellraiser." When its cover announced *Believe It or Not: Spirituality Is the New Religion,* one columnist was moved to say that it was "strange and marvelous stuff" to hear this "from a liberal muckraker."[5] The editor's essay at the beginning of the issue announced, "Marx did not recognize that our desire to connect with a transcendent power runs even deeper than our drive for economic satisfaction."[6] The essay criticized activists "righteously wedded to atheist or agnostic positions, as if the impulse to do good is best if it emanates from reason alone," argued that "all systems of belief or disbelief, including science, have suprarational foundations," and concluded that some of the most important principles in the universe "lie fundamentally beyond our comprehension."[7]

The *New York Times Magazine* titled its special issue *God Decentralized.* The introductory essay set out the theme:

The proportion of Americans who say they believe in God, who pray regularly and who attend religious services is just about the same as it was 50 years ago. There has, however, been a striking change in the nature of faith and worship. The religious institutions that used to deliver orthodox practice to the unquestioning masses are under challenge—not just by smaller institutions but by individuals who want to reshape religion for themselves. . . . The result is a time of spiritual ferment.[8]

These diverse voices reflect a broader reality in American life. A hunger for spiritual enrichment is widespread. It is felt by members of conservative churches and by secular activists. Obviously, the causes of this hunger are as numerous as its manifestations. I certainly do not believe that I have identified or could identify everything that is contributing to this sense that the spiritual side of life does not have enough sway. But I am convinced that one of the major problems here is the dominating presence of the scientific worldview in every corner of our lives. We look to scientific terminology whether the underlying research is good, bad, or indifferent and whether it is relevant or not. The costs are considerable. In particular, when science swallows up the religious perspective, an awful lot is lost.

Consider a news story that broke at precisely the time these magazines hit the newsstands. The story reported that researchers at the University of California at San Diego read a series of test words to patients suffering from an unusual form of epilepsy. This group was chosen because people with this type of epilepsy often report mystical experiences. When the electrical conductivity of the patients' skin was measured and compared with control groups, it was found that the patients tended to have unusually strong reactions to religious terms such as the word "God."[9] The scientists, believing that part of the brain's temporal lobe might be involved in this reaction, dubbed that brain part "the God module."[10]

The scientists can perhaps be forgiven for choosing a rather grandiose term for a rather limited finding. But of course the media immediately began talking about whether "the human brain might be hard-wired to hear the voice of heaven," despite the fact that a researcher pronouncing the word "God" might not be precisely the same thing. Most troubling from my point of view, however, were the comments of a Catholic priest on *NBC Nightly News:* "Here is a dimension of us searching for God. Call that a lobe or an antenna or a spiritual awakening. Call it what you like, but there's more to life than meets the eyes."[11] Of course, having heard from a priest, the newscasters interviewed a spokesman for Atheists United: "If there's a God module in the brains of people, there's also anti-God modules which result in people being atheists and agnostics."[12]

I do not find this to be a particularly fruitful interchange. If you take a materialistic point of view—if you equate a lobe with a spiritual awakening—you are not going to add much to the discussion of a scientific development.

On the final day of basic training at Fort Jackson, South Carolina, our drill sergeant, Hardin Dennis, let down his guard and chatted pleasantly with those of us who had just finished our eight weeks. One of my fellow trainees, emboldened by the casual atmosphere, proposed a wager. "Sergeant," he said, "I'll bet you I can do fifty pushups with my left hand." Sergeant Dennis smiled and replied, "I learned a long time ago never to bet on another man's trick."

Sergeant Dennis knew better than to let someone else set the agenda. Religious leaders, and the rest of us who sometimes seek a spiritual perspective, would be wise to keep that in mind. I would propose some simple steps that we might consider using when we hear of a new scientific development that is said to bear on moral issues and we are wondering how to react.

First, take a deep breath. An instant response, whether to the media or to a family member, is not necessary. In fact, sometimes an instant response is worse than none at all. It is easy to get caught up in the latest fads.

Second, consider whether this scientific development changes everything. It probably does not. It probably seeks to fill in some information about the natural world, while the basic balance between that world and the spiritual remains intact.

Finally, consider the possibility of pointing out those things that are not changed by the new development. There will be no shortage of people pointing out the new possibilities raised by advances in science. It may be useful to remember that fundamental value choices remain before us and perhaps even to note that a sense of humility remains appropriate. In sum, a timely response is not as important as a timeless one.

I am a strong supporter of science. As the son of a physicist, I suppose it is not surprising that the relationship of science to society has always fascinated me. I have written and lectured for years in defense of funding basic research even when the payoff in useful technology is distant and uncertain.[13] But my love for science does not mean that I think science is all there is. In fact, I believe that when science invades every corner of our lives, it is bad for both science and religion. If we ever end up asking scientists what our values are, we are going to end up unhappy with the answers and unhappy with the scientists.

We are more than the sum of our genes, our religious texts are more than science books, our prayers are more than medicine. We have the legal right to speak out about our faith, to educate our children in that faith, and to have our faith inform our moral and policy choices. The question is not whether we are free to make spiritual values temper material progress. The question is whether we will choose to do so.

Notes

NOTES TO CHAPTER 1

1. I have analyzed the role of science in American society in relation to our legal system in STEVEN GOLDBERG, CULTURE CLASH: LAW AND SCIENCE IN AMERICA (1994).

2. Sean O'Connor, *The Supreme Court's Philosophy of Science: Will the Real Karl Popper Please Stand Up?*, 35 JURIMETRICS J. 263, 276 (1995). Of course, Popper's work has hardly escaped criticism from other philosophers. Id. at 275–276.

3. KARL POPPER, REALISM AND THE AIM OF SCIENCE 175–176 (1992) (emphasis in the original).

4. JAMES TURNER, WITHOUT GOD, WITHOUT CREED: THE ORIGINS OF UNBELIEF IN AMERICA 262–267 (1985).

5. Id. at 267.

NOTES TO CHAPTER 2

1. Edmund L. Andrews, *Religious Leaders Prepare to Fight Patents on Genes,* N.Y. TIMES, May 13, 1995, at A1. An earlier version of this chapter appeared in Steven Goldberg, *Gene Patents and the Death of Dualism,* 5 S. CAL. INTERDISC. L. J. 25 (1996).

2. RICHARD JOHN NEUHAUS, THE NAKED PUBLIC SQUARE: RELIGION AND DEMOCRACY IN AMERICA (1984); STEPHEN L. CARTER, THE CULTURE OF DISBELIEF: HOW AMERICAN LAW AND POLITICS TRIVIALIZE RELIGIOUS DEVOTION (1993).

3. STEPHEN L. CARTER, THE CULTURE OF DISBELIEF: HOW AMERICAN LAW AND POLITICS TRIVIALIZE RELIGIOUS DEVOTION 51–52 (1993).

4. Peter L. Berger, *Religion in a Revolutionary Society,* in IRVING

KRISTOL (ed.), AMERICA'S CONTINUING REVOLUTION: AN ACT
OF CONSERVATION 143 (1975). It is unclear whether Eisenhower actu-
ally made this statement. See Richard John Neuhaus, *Who Needs God*,
NAT'L REV., Nov. 10, 1989, at 52.

5. STEPHEN L. CARTER, THE CULTURE OF DISBELIEF: HOW
AMERICAN LAW AND POLITICS TRIVIALIZE RELIGIOUS DEVO-
TION 23 (1993).

6. Id. at 48; see also RICHARD JOHN NEUHAUS, THE NAKED
PUBLIC SQUARE: RELIGION AND DEMOCRACY IN AMERICA 5–6,
156 (1984).

7. RICHARD JOHN NEUHAUS, THE NAKED PUBLIC SQUARE:
RELIGION AND DEMOCRACY IN AMERICA 19 (1984).

8. STEPHEN L. CARTER, THE CULTURE OF DISBELIEF: HOW
AMERICAN LAW AND POLITICS TRIVIALIZE RELIGIOUS DEVO-
TION 8, 51, 230 (1993).

9. Gustav Niebuhr, *Clinton Talks about Religion as His Anchor*, N.Y.
TIMES, Oct. 4, 1994, at A1.

10. Edmund L. Andrews, *Religious Leaders Prepare to Fight Patents on
Genes*, N.Y. TIMES, May 13, 1995, at A1.

11. Louis Freedberg, *80 Church Groups Ask for Ban on Gene Patents*,
SAN FRANCISCO CHRONICLE, May 19, 1995, at A1.

12. See, e.g., Tim Radforce, *Newsbites*, THE GUARDIAN [London],
May 25, 1995, at 1.

13. Stephen Green, *Case for Halt to Patenting Human Genes Spelled
Out*, SAN DIEGO UNION-TRIBUNE, May 19, 1995, at A16.

14. Reginald Rhein, *Gene Patent Crusade Moving from Church to
Court*, BIOTECHNOLOGY NEWSWATCH, June 5, 1995, at 1.

15. See the discussion under *Patenting Life: The Legal Background*,
infra.

16. See, e.g., PETER SINGER, ANIMAL LIBERATION 188, 192 (2d
ed. 1990) (Jewish and Christian traditions distinguish sharply between the
moral status of humans and other animals).

17. See the discussion under *Patenting Life: The Legal Background*,
infra.

18. "Congress shall have Power . . . to promote the Progress of Science
and Useful Arts, by securing for limited Times to Authors and Inventors the
exclusive Right to their respective Writings and Discoveries;" U.S. CON-
STITUTION, art. 1, sec. 8, cl. 8. This clause confers both the patent and

the copyright powers. See ROBERT PATRICK MERGES, PATENT LAW AND POLICY: CASES AND MATERIALS 36 (1992).

19. ROBERT PATRICK MERGES, PATENT LAW AND POLICY: CASES AND MATERIALS 36 (1992).

20. Kewanee Oil Co. v. Bicron Corp., 416 U.S. 470, 478 (1974).

21. Id. at 480–481.

22. Id. at 476.

23. See, e.g., Tilghman v. Proctor, 102 U.S. 707, 728 (1880) ("A machine is a thing. A process is an act, or a mode of acting. The one is visible to the eye,—an object of perpetual observation. The other is a conception of the mind, seen only by its effects when being executed or performed.")

24. ROBERT PATRICK MERGES, PATENT LAW AND POLICY: CASES AND MATERIALS 35 (1992).

25. Kewanee Oil Co. v. Bicron Corp., 416 U.S. 470, 475–476 (1974).

26. Robert Patrick Merges, *Intellectual Property in Higher Life Forms: The Patent System and Controversial Technologies,* 47 MD. L. REV. 1051, 1068 (1988).

27. See the Plant Patent Act of 1930, 35 U.S.C. §161; the Plant Variety Protection Act of 1970, 7 U.S.C. §2402.

28. Diamond v. Chakrabarty, 447 U.S. 303 (1980).

29. Id. at 305.

30. Id. at 307.

31. Id. at 309.

32. Id. at 314–318.

33. Ned Hettinger, *Patenting Life: Biotechnology, Intellectual Property, and Environmental Ethics,* 22 B.C. ENVTL. AFF. L. REV. 267, 270 (1995).

34. Id. at 270–271.

35. Rebecca Dresser, *Ethical and Legal Issues in Patenting New Animal Life,* 28 JURIMETRICS J. 399 (1988).

36. Reid G. Adler, *Biotechnology as an Intellectual Property,* 224 SCIENCE 357, 361 (1984).

37. A host of ethical and policy issues were canvassed in Rebecca Dresser, *Ethical and Legal Issues in Patenting New Animal Life,* 28 JURIMETRICS J. 399 (1988); Robert Patrick Merges, *Intellectual Property in Higher Life Forms: The Patent System and Controversial Technologies,* 47 MD. L. REV. 1051 (1988); and in Mark W. Lauroesch, *Note: Genetic Engineering: Innovation and Risk Minimization,* 57 GEO. WASH. L. REV. 100 (1988).

38. *The Genome Project: The Ethical Issues of Gene Patenting, Hearing before the Subcommittee on Patents, Copyrights, and Trademarks of the Committee on the Judiciary,* U.S. Senate, 102d Cong., 2d sess., Sept. 22, 1992, 8 (statement of Senator Hatfield).

39. Id. at 3 (statement of Senator Hatch).

40. Id. at 3–4. See also Rick Weiss, *What Is Patently Offensive? Policy on "Immoral" Inventions Troubles Legal, Medical Professionals,* WASHINGTON POST, May 11, 1998, at A21.

41. Daniel L. McKay, *Comment: Patent Law and Human Genome Research at the Crossroads: The Need for Congressional Action,* 10 COMPUTER & HIGH TECH. L. J. 465, 482 (1994).

42. Id. at 486.

43. Rebecca S. Eisenberg, *Patenting The Human Genome,* 39 EMORY L. J. 721 (1990).

44. Id. at 723–724.

45. Funk Bros. Seed Co. v. Kalo Inoculant Co., 333 U.S. 127, 130 (1948).

46. Diamond v. Chakrabarty, 447 U.S. 303, 309–310 (1980).

47. Rebecca S. Eisenberg, *Genes, Patents, and Product Development,* 257 SCIENCE 903, 904 (1992).

48. Parke-Davis & Co. v. H. K. Mullford & Co., 189 F. 95 103 (S.D.N.Y. 1911), aff'd, 196 F. 496 (2d Cir. 1912).

49. Rebecca S. Eisenberg, *Genes, Patents, and Product Development,* 257 SCIENCE 903, 904 (1992); ROBERT PATRICK MERGES, PATENT LAW AND POLICY: CASES AND MATERIALS 125 (1992).

50. Ned Hettinger, *Patenting Life: Biotechnology, Intellectual Property, and Environmental Ethics,* 22 B.C. ENVTL. AFF. L. REV. 267, 271, n. 24 (1995).

51. Rebecca S. Eisenberg, *Patenting the Human Genome,* 39 EMORY L. J. 721, 722 (1990).

52. Kevin Kelly, *The Elimination of Process: Will the Biotechnology Patent Protection Act Revive Process Patents?* 24 J. MARSHALL L. REV. 263 (1990); Jeremy Cubert, *U.S. Patent Policy and Biotechnology: Growing Pains on the Cutting Edge,* 77 J. PAT. & TRADEMARK OFF. SOC'Y 151 (1995).

53. See, e.g., Daniel L. McKay, *Comment: Patent Law and Human Genome Research at the Crossroads: The Need for Congressional Action,* 10 COMPUTER & HIGH TECH. L. J. 465, 488–494 (1994); Rebecca S.

Eisenberg, *Patenting the Human Genome,* 39 EMORY L. J. 721, 736–744 (1990).

54. See Ned Hettinger, *Patenting Life: Biotechnology, Intellectual Property, and Environmental Ethics,* 22 B.C. ENVTL. AFF. L. REV. 267, 291–295 (1995).

55. See Daniel L. McKay, *Comment: Patent Law and Human Genome Research at the Crossroads: The Need for Congressional Action,* 10 COMPUTER & HIGH TECH. L. J. 465, 495 (1994).

56. Louis Freedberg, *80 Church Groups Ask for Ban on Gene Patents,* SAN FRANCISCO CHRONICLE, May 19, 1995, at A1.

57. See, e.g., Susan Katz Miller, *Activists Join Forces against Animal Patents,* 137 NEW SCIENTIST 8 (1993).

58. Carl T. Hall, *Theologians Split over Gene Rights,* SAN FRANCISCO CHRONICLE, May 20, 1995, at B3.

59. Stephen Green, *Case for Halt to Patenting Human Genes Spelled Out,* SAN DIEGO UNION-TRIBUNE, May 19, 1995, at A16.

60. United Methodist Church Genetic Science Task Force, *Draft Report to Annual and Central Conferences,* 4 CHRISTIAN SOCIAL ACTION 17 (Jan. 1991).

61. *New Developments in Genetic Science,* THE BOOK OF RESOLUTIONS OF THE UNITED METHODIST CHURCH 325, 326, 338 (1992). The Book of Resolutions includes all resolutions, such as *New Developments in Genetic Science,* that have been approved by the General Conference of the United Methodist Church. Id. at 5. Only the General Conference speaks for the United Methodist Church in its entirety. Id.

62. See Reginald Rhein, *Gene Patent Crusade Moving from Church to Court,* BIOTECHNOLOGY NEWSWATCH, June 5, 1995, at 1.

It is of course impossible to know how many of the signers of the Joint Appeal subscribed to the Methodist perspective. The appeal itself was brief and subject to many interpretations. But the Methodist report, a lengthy document developed after numerous hearings and meetings, provides by far the most extensive religious justification for the opposition to the patenting of human genes. Some of the briefer statements issued by other religious leaders at the time of the Joint Appeal are described in Stephen Green, *Case for Halt to Patenting Human Genes Spelled Out,* SAN DIEGO UNION-TRIBUNE, May 19, 1995, at A16, and later in this chapter. For a summary and analysis of various earlier pronouncements of religious groups on biotechnology, see Thomas C. Wiegele, *Organized Religion and Biotechnology: Social Responsibility and the Role of Government,* in DAVID J. WEBBER (ed.), BIOTECHNOLOGY: ASSESSING SOCIAL IMPACTS AND POLICY IMPLICATIONS 17 (1990).

63. THE BOOK OF RESOLUTIONS OF THE UNITED METHODIST CHURCH 332–334 (1992).

64. Id. at 333.

65. Id. at 332. An introductory section of the report, "Our Theological Grounding," emphasizes that human beings are created "in the image of God," and have "inherent worth and dignity . . . irrespective of genetic qualities, personal attributes or achievements." Id. at 326–328. But as we shall see, when the discussion turns to gene patenting, these traditional ideas take on a remarkably materialistic flavor.

66. Id. at 332.

67. Id.

68. Id. at 331.

69. Id.

70. Id. at 330.

71. Id. at 329.

72. Dennis S. Karjala, *A Legal Research Agenda for the Human Genome Initiative,* 32 JURIMETRICS J. 121, 147 (1992). See also Rochelle Cooper Dreyfuss & Dorothy Nelkin, *The Jurisprudence of Genetics,* 45 VAND. L. REV. 313, 348 (1992) ("[G]enetic assumptions must be examined skeptically before they are allowed to alter concepts such as personhood, normalcy, responsibility, and culpability.").

73. STEVEN GOLDBERG, CULTURE CLASH: LAW AND SCIENCE IN AMERICA 130 (1994).

74. BRUCE MAZLISH, THE FOURTH DISCONTINUITY: THE CO-EVOLUTION OF HUMANS AND MACHINES 22–24 (1993).

75. J. Robert Nelson, *What Is Life?* 4 CHRISTIAN SOCIAL ACTION 4, 6 (Jan. 1991).

76. See chapter 1.

77. Id.

78. STEVEN GOLDBERG, CULTURE CLASH: LAW AND SCIENCE IN AMERICA 130 (1994).

79. See, e.g., John Horgan, *Can Science Explain Consciousness,* SCIENTIFIC AMERICAN, July 1994, at 88. A recent effort in the field is DAVID J. CHALMERS, THE CONSCIOUS MIND: IN SEARCH OF A FUNDAMENTAL THEORY (1996); for a critical review and a survey of

the area, see John R. Searle, *Consciousness and the Philosophers,* N.Y. REV. BOOKS, Mar. 6, 1997, at 43.

80. Steven Goldberg, *The Changing Face of Death: Computers, Consciousness, and Nancy Cruzan,* 43 STAN. L. REV. 659, 673–680 (1991).

81. Id. at 677–680.

82. Id.

83. Oliver Sacks, *Neurology and the Soul,* N.Y. REV. BOOKS, Nov. 22, 1990, at 44, 45.

84. Id. at 45.

85. Id.

86. Stephen L. Thaler, *Death of a Gedanken Creature,* 13 JOURNAL OF NEAR-DEATH STUDIES 149 (1995). See also Philip Yam, *As They Lay Dying,* SCIENTIFIC AMERICAN, May 1995, at 24.

87. THOMAS NAGEL, THE VIEW FROM NOWHERE 9 (1986).

88. John Horgan, *Can Science Explain Consciousness,* SCIENTIFIC AMERICAN, July 1994, at 90, 94. The term "mysterians" comes from the 1960s rock group, Question Mark and the Mysterians. Id. at 90. Fans of the era will recall their biggest hit, "96 Tears."

89. Id. at 90.

90. Id. at 94.

91. COLIN MCGINN, THE PROBLEM OF CONSCIOUSNESS: ESSAYS TOWARDS A RESOLUTION 6 (1991) (emphasis in the original).

92. For a thoughtful discussion of other religious reactions to genetics research, see Ronald Cole-Turner, *Religion and Gene Patenting,* 270 SCIENCE 52 (1995).

93. Mark J. Hanson, *Religious Voices in Biotechnology: The Case of Gene Patenting,* HASTINGS CENTER REPORT (special supplement), Nov.–Dec. 1997, at 13.

94. Stephen Green, *Case for Halt to Patenting Human Genes Spelled Out,* SAN DIEGO UNION-TRIBUNE, May 19, 1995, at A16.

95. Statement of Dr. Richard Land, National Press Club, Washington, D.C., May 18, 1995, at 1. Dr. Land did sensibly note that humans "are more than the sum of their DNA," id., but it is precisely that recognition that is undercut by granting such importance to ownership of DNA sequences.

96. See, e.g., John R. Searle, *Consciousness and the Philosophers,* N.Y. REV. BOOKS, Mar. 6, 1997, at 43 ("I suppose most people in our civilization accept some form of dualism. . . . But that is emphatically not the current view among [scientific and philosophical elites].")

97. See, e.g., Wray Herbert, Jeffery L. Sheler, & Traci Watson, *The World after Cloning*, U.S. NEWS & WORLD REPORT, Mar. 10, 1997, at 59.

98. Id.

99. Gina Kolata, *With Cloning of a Sheep, the Ethical Ground Shifts*, N.Y. TIMES, Feb. 24, 1997, at A1.

100. Id.

101. This was the 1997 recommendation of the National Bioethics Advisory Commission, a recommendation endorsed by President Clinton. Jodi Enda, *Clinton: No Cloning of Humans, but Experiments on Cells Are OK*, DES MOINES REGISTER, June 10, 1997, at 3.

102. See, e.g., Leon R. Kass, *The Wisdom of Repugnance*, THE NEW REPUBLIC, June 2, 1997, at 17.

103. The Catholic Church, for example, opposes cloning because it violates "the dignity both of human procreation and of the conjugal union." Wray Herbert, Jeffery L. Sheler, & Traci Watson, *The World after Cloning*, U.S. NEWS & WORLD REPORT, Mar. 10, 1997, at 59.

104. Even from a strictly physical perspective, a cloned human will not be as close to his donor as identical twins are to each other. The cloned human, for example, would carry a small fraction of DNA from the woman who provided the egg. And the old, adult cells that were used to create the clone might have undergone random mutations since the donor was an infant. Steve Kloehn & Paul Salopek, *A Matter of Identity: Most Maintain Clone Would Be Its Own Person*, DALLAS MORNING NEWS, Mar. 9, 1997, at 1. For a discussion of cloning and individuality, see John A. Robertson, *Liberty, Identity, and Human Cloning*, 76 TEXAS L. REV. 1371, 1411–1415 (1998).

105. Id. The National Bioethics Advisory Commission said that the religious leaders who testified before it rejected "genetic determinism." NATIONAL BIOETHICS ADVISORY COMMISSION, CLONING HUMAN BEINGS 50 (1997).

106. Carol McGraw & Susan Kelleher, *Can Cloning Also Give Life to a Soul? Religious Leaders and Scientists Wrestle with the Moral Issues Raised by the Technology*, ORANGE COUNTY REGISTER, Feb. 25, 1997, at A1.

107. Leslie Scanlon, *Cloning Technology Spawns Moral Dilemma, Words of Caution*, LOUISVILLE COURIER-JOURNAL, Apr. 7, 1997, at A1.

108. NATIONAL BIOETHICS ADVISORY COMMISSION, CLON-ING HUMAN BEINGS 50, 59 (1997).

109. Steve Kloehn & Paul Salopek, *Humanity Still at Heart, Soul of Cloning Issue: Scientists and Theologians Agree We Are Our Own Persons,* CHICAGO TRIBUNE, Mar. 2, 1997, at C1.

110. STEPHEN L. CARTER, THE CULTURE OF DISBELIEF: HOW AMERICAN LAW AND POLITICS TRIVIALIZE RELIGIOUS DEVO-TION 9 (1993).

NOTES TO CHAPTER 3

1. CHRISTOPHER P. TOUMEY, GOD'S OWN SCIENTISTS: CRE-ATIONISTS IN A SECULAR WORLD 259 (1994).

2. RAYMOND A. EVE & FRANCIS B. HARROLD, THE CRE-ATIONIST MOVEMENT IN MODERN AMERICA 15 (1991).

3. DOUGLAS J. FUTUYMA, SCIENCE ON TRIAL: THE CASE FOR EVOLUTION 69 (1995).

4. Id. at 69–70.

5. DOROTHY NELKIN, THE CREATION CONTROVERSY: SCI-ENCE OR SCRIPTURE IN THE SCHOOLS 26–27 (1982).

6. Id. at 26.

7. JON H. ROBERTS, DARWINISM AND THE DIVINE IN AMER-ICA: PROTESTANT INTELLECTUALS AND ORGANIC EVOLUTION, 1859–1900 17 (1988)

8. RONALD L. NUMBERS, THE CREATIONISTS: THE EVOLU-TION OF SCIENTIFIC CREATIONISM 141 (1992). See also DOROTHY NELKIN, THE CREATION CONTROVERSY: SCIENCE OR SCRIP-TURE IN THE SCHOOLS 28 (1982).

9. RONALD L. NUMBERS, THE CREATIONISTS: THE EVOLU-TION OF SCIENTIFIC CREATIONISM 141 (1992).

10. Id. at 14.

11. Id. at 16.

12. Id.

13. Id. at 17.

14. JON H. ROBERTS, DARWINISM AND THE DIVINE IN AMER-ICA: PROTESTANT INTELLECTUALS AND ORGANIC EVOLUTION, 1859–1900 96 (1988).

15. RONALD L. NUMBERS (ed.), 1 CREATIONISM IN TWENTI-

ETH-CENTURY AMERICA: A TEN VOLUME ANTHOLOGY OF DOCUMENTS, 1903–1961 xi (1995) (citing Alexander Patterson).

16. RAYMOND A. EVE & FRANCIS B. HARROLD, THE CREATIONIST MOVEMENT IN MODERN AMERICA 19 (1991).

17. RONALD L. NUMBERS (ed.), 1 CREATIONISM IN TWENTIETH-CENTURY AMERICA: A TEN VOLUME ANTHOLOGY OF DOCUMENTS, 1903–1961 xi (citing Alexander Patterson).

18. RAYMOND A. EVE & FRANCIS B. HARROLD, THE CREATIONIST MOVEMENT IN MODERN AMERICA 20 (1991); RONALD L. NUMBERS, THE CREATIONISTS: THE EVOLUTION OF SCIENTIFIC CREATIONISM 38–39 (1992).

19. CHRISTOPHER P. TOUMEY, GOD'S OWN SCIENTISTS: CREATIONISTS IN A SECULAR WORLD 31 (1994).

20. Id.

21. JON H. ROBERTS, DARWINISM AND THE DIVINE IN AMERICA: PROTESTANT INTELLECTUALS AND ORGANIC EVOLUTION, 1859–1900 24 (1988).

22. Id. at 24 (quoting Moses Stuart; emphasis in original).

23. Id. at 233–234; see also RAYMOND A. EVE & FRANCIS B. HARROLD, THE CREATIONIST MOVEMENT IN MODERN AMERICA 20 (1991).

24. RAYMOND A. EVE & FRANCIS B. HARROLD, THE CREATIONIST MOVEMENT IN MODERN AMERICA 20 (1991).

25. JON H. ROBERTS, DARWINISM AND THE DIVINE IN AMERICA: PROTESTANT INTELLECTUALS AND ORGANIC EVOLUTION, 1859–1900 237 (1988).

26. RAYMOND A. EVE & FRANCIS B. HARROLD, THE CREATIONIST MOVEMENT IN MODERN AMERICA 3–4, 20 (1991).

27. RONALD L. NUMBERS, THE CREATIONISTS: THE EVOLUTION OF SCIENTIFIC CREATIONISM 4 (1992).

28. For an excellent historical treatment, see EDWARD J. LARSON, TRIAL AND ERROR: THE AMERICAN CONTROVERSY OVER CREATION AND EVOLUTION (1989).

29. DOROTHY NELKIN, THE CREATION CONTROVERSY: SCIENCE OR SCRIPTURE IN THE SCHOOLS 30–33 (1982).

30. In particular, it weakened antievolutionism in the North. EDWARD J. LARSON, SUMMER OF THE GODS: THE SCOPES TRIAL AND AMERICA'S CONTINUING DEBATE OVER SCIENCE AND RELIGION 222 (1997). See also EDWARD J. LARSON, TRIAL AND ERROR:

THE AMERICAN CONTROVERSY OVER CREATION AND EVOLUTION 58–72 (1989).

31. Some of this image stems from the play and movie *Inherit the Wind,* which was never intended to be a balanced account of the Scopes trial and which, in fact, unfairly portrays Bryan as a mindless reactionary. EDWARD J. LARSON, SUMMER OF THE GODS: THE SCOPES TRIAL AND AMERICA'S CONTINUING DEBATE OVER SCIENCE AND RELIGION 239–246 (1997).

32. RONALD L. NUMBERS, 1 CREATIONISM IN TWENTIETH-CENTURY AMERICA: A TEN-VOLUME ANTHOLOGY OF DOCUMENTS, 1903–1961 vii (1995).

33. DOROTHY NELKIN, THE CREATION CONTROVERSY: SCIENCE OR SCRIPTURE IN THE SCHOOLS 30–33 (1982).

34. Id.

35. RONALD L. NUMBERS, THE CREATIONISTS: THE EVOLUTION OF SCIENTIFIC CREATIONISM 42–43 (1992).

36. CHRISTOPHER P. TOUMEY, GOD'S OWN SCIENTISTS: CREATIONISTS IN A SECULAR WORLD 49 (1994).

37. Id.

38. RONALD L. NUMBERS, THE CREATIONISTS: THE EVOLUTION OF SCIENTIFIC CREATIONISM 44 (1992).

39. Id. at 41–44. For a detailed account of Bryan's attitudes toward science, see JAMES GILBERT, REDEEMING CULTURE: AMERICAN RELIGION IN AN AGE OF SCIENCE 23–35 (1997). Gilbert notes Bryan's doubts about biblical literalism as well as Bryan's philosophical, as opposed to scientific, problems with evolution. Id. at 33, 35.

40. CHRISTOPHER P. TOUMEY, GOD'S OWN SCIENTISTS: CREATIONISTS IN A SECULAR WORLD 22 (1994).

41. RONALD L. NUMBERS, THE CREATIONISTS: THE EVOLUTION OF SCIENTIFIC CREATIONISM 204, 335–339 (1992).

42. CHRISTOPHER P. TOUMEY, GOD'S OWN SCIENTISTS: CREATIONISTS IN A SECULAR WORLD 31–32 (1994).

43. RONALD L. NUMBERS, THE CREATIONISTS: THE EVOLUTION OF SCIENTIFIC CREATIONISM 319 (1992).

44. Id. at 336.

45. See, e.g., PHILLIP E. JOHNSON, DARWIN ON TRIAL 4, 14, 113 (1991); see also PHILLIP E. JOHNSON, REASON IN THE BALANCE: THE CASE AGAINST NATURALISM IN SCIENCE, LAW, & EDUCATION (1995).

46. EDWARD J. LARSON, SUMMER OF THE GODS: THE SCOPES TRIAL AND AMERICA'S CONTINUING DEBATE OVER SCIENCE AND RELIGION 237 (1997).

47. CHRISTOPHER P. TOUMEY, GOD'S OWN SCIENTISTS: CREATIONISTS IN A SECULAR WORLD 32–34 (1994).

48. Id. The leading proponent of flood geology before Morris and Whitcomb was George McCready Price, who initially presented the idea in 1923. Id. at 33.

49. In the passages that follow, I will be relying on the 1961 edition. The book has been through numerous printings, and some revisions have been made. See, e.g., RONALD L. NUMBERS, THE CREATIONISTS: THE EVOLUTION OF SCIENTIFIC CREATIONISM 203, 209 (1992)

50. JOHN C. WHITCOMB, JR., & HENRY M. MORRIS, THE GENESIS FLOOD: THE BIBLICAL RECORD AND ITS SCIENTIFIC IMPLICATIONS xx–xxi (1961).

51. Id.

52. Id. at xix.

53. Id. at 55.

54. Id. at 63.

55. Id.

56. Id. at 55–62.

57. Id. at 344.

58. Id. at 80–86. For the use of an evolutionist's work, see p. 82, n. 4.

59. Id. at 253.

60. Id. at 353.

61. Id. at 328.

62. Id. at 10, n. 2.

63. DOROTHY NELKIN, THE CREATION CONTROVERSY: SCIENCE OR SCRIPTURE IN THE SCHOOLS 75 (1982).

64. Id. at 78–84.

65. See NATIONAL ACADEMY OF SCIENCES, SCIENCE AND CREATIONISM (1984).

66. DOROTHY NELKIN, THE CREATION CONTROVERSY: SCIENCE OR SCRIPTURE IN THE SCHOOLS 76 (1982).

67. DOUGLAS J. FUTUYMA, SCIENCE ON TRIAL: THE CASE FOR EVOLUTION 21 (1995).

68. PHILIP KITCHER, ABUSING SCIENCE: THE CASE AGAINST CREATIONISM 5 (1982).

69. DOUGLAS J. FUTUYMA, SCIENCE ON TRIAL: THE CASE FOR EVOLUTION 5 (1995).

70. See generally EDWARD J. LARSON, TRIAL AND ERROR: THE AMERICAN CONTROVERSY OVER CREATION AND EVOLUTION (1989).

71. Id. at 92.

72. 393 U.S. 97 (1968).

73. Id.

74. STEVEN GOLDBERG, CULTURE CLASH: LAW AND SCIENCE IN AMERICA 75 (1994).

75. EDWARD J. LARSON, TRIAL AND ERROR: THE AMERICAN CONTROVERSY OVER CREATION AND EVOLUTION 125–188 (1989).

76. Id. at 147. Larson is describing the defeats prior to 1978; in the text I describe the subsequent setbacks for creationism.

77. McLean v. Arkansas Board of Education, 529 F. Supp. 1255, 1267, 1269 (E.D. Ark. 1982).

78. Id.

79. Edwards v. Aguillard, 482 U.S. 578 (1987).

80. Id. at 593. Fundamentalist parents have also been unsuccessful in having their children excused from public school classes on free exercise of religion grounds when evolution and other secular subjects are taught. See Mozert v. Hawkins County Board of Education, 827 F. 2d 1058 (6th Cir. 1987), cert. denied, 484 U.S. 1066 (1988).

81. A 1991 Gallup Poll found that 47 percent of respondents supported the creation of man within the past ten thousand years, 40 percent said God has guided evolution, including the development of humans, over millions of years, and 9 percent said man evolved without God. Jim Dawson, *Evolution Fight Has New Form, but Emotions Have Endured,* MINNEAPOLIS STAR TRIBUNE, June 22, 1992, at A1. Similar earlier results are summarized in EDWARD J. LARSON, TRIAL AND ERROR: THE AMERICAN CONTROVERSY OVER CREATION AND EVOLUTION 157–158 (1989).

82. EDWARD J. LARSON, TRIAL AND ERROR: THE AMERICAN CONTROVERSY OVER CREATION AND EVOLUTION 92 (1989).

83. JOHN C. WHITCOMB, JR., & HENRY M. MORRIS, THE GENESIS FLOOD: THE BIBLICAL RECORD AND ITS SCIENTIFIC IMPLICATIONS xxi (1961).

84. Id. See also McLean v. Arkansas Board of Education, 529 F. Supp 1255, 1268 (E.D. Ark. 1982).

85. RAYMOND A. EVE & FRANCIS B. HARROLD, THE CREATIONIST MOVEMENT IN MODERN AMERICA 179 (1991).

86. McLean v. Arkansas Board of Education, 529 F. Supp. 1255, 1269 (E.D. Ark. 1982).

87. JOHN C. WHITCOMB, JR., & HENRY M. MORRIS, THE GENESIS FLOOD: THE BIBLICAL RECORD AND ITS SCIENTIFIC IMPLICATIONS 10 (1961).

88. CHRISTOPHER P. TOUMEY, GOD'S OWN SCIENTISTS: CREATIONISTS IN A SECULAR WORLD 259 (1994).

89. RAYMOND A. EVE & FRANCIS B. HARROLD, THE CREATIONIST MOVEMENT IN MODERN AMERICA 86 (1991).

90. Id. at 89–90.

91. STEPHEN L. CARTER, THE CULTURE OF DISBELIEF: HOW AMERICAN LAW AND POLITICS TRIVIALIZE RELIGIOUS DEVOTION 161 (1993).

92. RONALD L. NUMBERS, THE CREATIONISTS: THE EVOLUTION OF SCIENTIFIC CREATIONISM 339 (1992).

93. DOROTHY NELKIN, THE CREATION CONTROVERSY: SCIENCE OR SCRIPTURE IN THE SCHOOLS 195 (1982).

94. CHRISTOPHER P. TOUMEY, GOD'S OWN SCIENTISTS: CREATIONISTS IN A SECULAR WORLD 50 (1994).

95. EDWARD J. LARSON, TRIAL AND ERROR: THE AMERICAN CONTROVERSY OVER CREATION AND EVOLUTION 127 (1989).

96. CHRISTOPHER P. TOUMEY, GOD'S OWN SCIENTISTS: CREATIONISTS IN A SECULAR WORLD 259 (1994).

97. Id. at 34.

98. PERCIVAL DAVIS & DEAN H. KENYON, OF PANDAS AND PEOPLE: THE CENTRAL QUESTION OF BIOLOGICAL ORIGINS (2d ed. 1993).

99. Jay D. Wexler, *Of Pandas, People, and the First Amendment: The Constitutionality of Teaching Intelligent Design in the Public Schools,* 49 STAN. L. REV. 439, 452 (1997).

100. Erik Larson, *Darwinian Struggle: Instead of Evolution, a Textbook Proposes "Intelligent Design,"* WALL ST. JOURNAL, Nov. 14, 1994, at A1.

101. The text itself cites language from the Supreme Court's 1987 creationism decision. PERCIVAL DAVIS & DEAN H. KENYON, OF PAN-

DAS AND PEOPLE: THE CENTRAL QUESTION OF BIOLOGICAL ORIGINS 161 (2d ed. 1993). See also Jay D. Wexler, *Of Pandas, People, and the First Amendment: The Constitutionality of Teaching Intelligent Design in the Public Schools,* 49 STAN. L. REV. 439, 452–454 (1997).

102. Intelligent design theory dates back at least to the eighteenth-century theologian William Paley. Jay D. Wexler, *Of Pandas, People, and the First Amendment: The Constitutionality of Teaching Intelligent Design in the Public Schools,* 49 STAN L. REV. 439, 442 (1997).

103. Erik Larson, *Darwinian Struggle: Instead of Evolution, a Textbook Proposes "Intelligent Design,"* WALL ST. JOURNAL, Nov. 14, 1994, at A1.

104. THOMAS S. KUHN, THE STRUCTURE OF SCIENTIFIC REVOLUTIONS 172 (1962).

105. RAYMOND A. EVE & FRANCIS B. HARROLD, THE CREATIONIST MOVEMENT IN MODERN AMERICA 50 (1991). For an Orthodox Jewish perspective, see ARYEH CARMELL & CYRIL DOMB (eds.), CHALLENGE: TORAH VIEWS ON SCIENCE AND ITS PROBLEMS 254–258 (1988).

106. The Catholic position was reaffirmed by Pope John Paul II in 1996. See Randy Frame, *Pope Says Evolution "More Than a Hypothesis,"* CHRISTIANITY TODAY, Dec. 9, 1996, at 72.

107. RAYMOND A. EVE & FRANCIS B. HARROLD, THE CREATIONIST MOVEMENT IN MODERN AMERICA 45 (1991). For a more general discussion of the compatibility of science and religion, see George P. Smith II, *Pathways to Immortality in the New Millennium: Human Responsibility, Theological Direction, or Legal Mandate,* 15 ST. LOUIS U. PUB. L. REV. 447, 450 (1996).

108. Paul L. Holmer, *Evolution and Being Faithful,* 84 CHRISTIAN CENTURY 1491, 1494 (1967).

109. Stephen Jay Gould, *Impeaching a Self-Appointed Judge,* SCIENTIFIC AMERICAN, July 1992, at 119.

NOTES TO CHAPTER 4

1. Monica Fountain, *Care for Body and Soul: Chaplains Play Larger Role in Patients' Well-Being,* CHICAGO TRIBUNE, Nov. 27, 1994, at 1; Gary Thomas, *Doctors Who Pray: How the Medical Community Is Discovering the Power of Prayer,* CHRISTIANITY TODAY, Jan. 6, 1997.

2. Lee Bowman, *Does Prayer Aid Healing? Researchers Are Consider-*

ing Scientific Study of Whether and How Spirituality in Patients Affects Their Chances of Recovery and Long Life, PITTSBURGH POST-GAZETTE, July 29, 1996, at A6; Claudia Wallis, Faith and Healing: Can Prayer, Faith, and Spirituality Really Improve Your Physical Health? A Growing and Surprising Body of Scientific Evidence Says They Can, TIME, June 24, 1996, at 58; HAROLD G. KOENIG, IS RELIGION GOOD FOR YOUR HEALTH? 101–112 (1997).

3. Claudia Wallis, Faith and Healing: Can Prayer, Faith, and Spirituality Really Improve Your Physical Health? A Growing and Surprising Body of Scientific Evidence Says They Can, TIME, June 24, 1996, at 58.

4. LARRY DOSSEY, HEALING WORDS: THE POWER OF PRAYER AND THE PRACTICE OF MEDICINE 179–181 (1993); Gary Thomas, Doctors Who Pray: How the Medical Community Is Discovering the Power of Prayer, CHRISTIANITY TODAY, Jan. 6, 1997.

5. Kim Herald, Prayer as Good Medicine: Although Skeptics Abound, Some Doctors and Researchers Say Spirituality Is Good for Your Health, ORLANDO SENTINEL, Aug. 14, 1996, at E1.

6. Gary Thomas, Doctors Who Pray: How the Medical Community Is Discovering the Power of Prayer, CHRISTIANITY TODAY, Jan. 6, 1997.

7. LARRY DOSSEY, HEALING WORDS: THE POWER OF PRAYER AND THE PRACTICE OF MEDICINE (1993); HERBERT BENSON, TIMELESS HEALING: THE POWER AND BIOLOGY OF BELIEF (1996). Both Dossey and Benson have written other books in this area as well.

8. Kenneth L. Woodward, Is God Listening? NEWSWEEK, Mar. 31, 1997, at 57, 62.

9. Rick Weiss, New Lines of Research: Scientists Take a Look at Unorthodox Healing Arts, WASHINGTON POST, Nov. 9, 1993, at D7.

10. Michelle Bearden, Prescription for Prayer: Doctors Examine the Role of Faith in Healing, TAMPA TRIBUNE, May 19, 1996, at 1.

11. See, e.g., Irwin Tessman & Jack Tessman, Mind and Body, 276 SCIENCE 369 (1997) (review of BENSON, TIMELESS HEALING). The National Research Council has produced a largely critical survey of a variety of mind-body studies. See DANIEL DRUCKMAN & ROBERT A. BJORK (eds.), IN THE MIND'S EYE: ENHANCING HUMAN PERFORMANCE (1991). This study contains an interesting discussion of how the placebo effect itself may have a biochemical basis. Id. at 138.

12. A University of New Mexico study of alcoholics found the group

that was prayed for did not fare better than the non–prayed for group. Bill Broadway, *Researchers Explore Healing's Spiritual Side: Study Challenges Common Ideas on the Power of Prayer,* WASHINGTON POST, Apr. 27, 1996, at B7.

13. LARRY DOSSEY, HEALING WORDS: THE POWER OF PRAYER AND THE PRACTICE OF MEDICINE 181–186 (1993).

14. WILLIAM JAMES, THE VARIETIES OF RELIGIOUS EXPERIENCE 415 (1990).

15. Irwin Tessman and Jack Tessman, *Mind and Body,* 276 SCIENCE 369–370 (1997) (review of BENSON, TIMELESS HEALING).

16. Bill Hendrick, *Duke University Researchers Say Studies Confirm the Effectiveness of Unorthodox Treatments Such as Prayer and Therapeutic Touch,* ATLANTA JOURNAL AND CONSTITUTION, Nov. 18, 1995, at C1.

17. Id.

18. Id.

19. HERBERT BENSON, TIMELESS HEALING: THE POWER AND BIOLOGY OF BELIEF 15–22 (1996). Remembered wellness, in Benson's view, is essentially the placebo effect. Id. at 20.

20. Id. at 146–147.

21. Id. at 134–135.

22. Id. at 303–304.

23. Id. at 300, 305.

24. LARRY DOSSEY, PRAYER IS GOOD MEDICINE: HOW TO REAP THE HEALING BENEFITS OF PRAYER 91–92 (1996).

25. LARRY DOSSEY, HEALING WORDS: THE POWER OF PRAYER AND THE PRACTICE OF MEDICINE 41 (1993).

26. See, e.g., Mary Elizabeth Cronin, *Healing Hands—Therapeutic Touch Helps Reduce Pain and Anxiety and Speeds Healing,* SEATTLE TIMES, Jan. 1, 1997, at D1; Faye Flam, *Therapeutic Touch Pinches Mainstream Doctors: They, Physicists Claim It's Fake,* TIMES-PICAYUNE, Jan. 26, 1997, at A3.

27. Rick Weiss, *New Lines of Research: Scientists Take a Look at Unorthodox Healing Arts,* WASHINGTON POST, Nov. 9, 1993, at D7.

28. Larry Dossey & Caren Goldman, *Toxic Prayer,* NEW AGE JOURNAL, Dec. 1997, at 74, 79. See also LARRY DOSSEY, BE CAREFUL WHAT YOU PRAY FOR—YOU JUST MIGHT GET IT (1997).

29. LARRY DOSSEY, PRAYER IS GOOD MEDICINE: HOW TO REAP THE HEALING BENEFITS OF PRAYER 63 (1996).

30. MARY BAKER EDDY, SCIENCE AND HEALTH WITH KEY TO THE SCRIPTURES 109 (authorized ed., 1934 printing).

31. Id. at 107–164.

32. D. Z. PHILLIPS, THE CONCEPT OF PRAYER (1965). Major influences on Phillips include Kierkegaard and Wittgenstein. Id. at vii.

33. Id. at 120.

34. Id.

35. KARL RAHNER, THEOLOGICAL INVESTIGATIONS: VOLUME III, THE THEOLOGY OF THE SPIRITUAL LIFE 210 (1967; translated by Karl-H. and Boniface Kruger).

36. Id. at 211–213.

37. JAKOB J. PETUCHOWSKI, UNDERSTANDING JEWISH PRAYER 37–38 (1972). See also KAUFMANN KOHLER, JEWISH THEOLOGY SYSTEMATICALLY AND HISTORICALLY CONSIDERED 274–275 (1968).

38. HAROLD S. KUSHNER, WHEN BAD THINGS HAPPEN TO GOOD PEOPLE 129 (1983).

39. For a variety of views from a fundamentalist Protestant perspective, see WAYNE A. GRUDEN (ed.), ARE MIRACULOUS GIFTS FOR TODAY? (1996).

40. Lee Bowman, *Does Prayer Aid Healing? Researchers Are Considering Scientific Study of Whether and How Spirituality in Patients Affects Their Chances of Recovery and Long Life*, PITTSBURGH POST-GAZETTE, July 29, 1996, at A6.

41. PHOENIX ARIZONA REPUBLIC, Jan. 25, 1997, at D8 (the paper attributed these sentiments to Mike Vandermark's book WALL STREET & WILDFLOWERS.)

42. Diane Winston, *Hands-On Healing: Mainline Protestants Are Discovering Powerful New Spiritual Tool*, DALLAS MORNING NEWS, Mar. 1, 1997, at G1; Kenneth L. Woodward, *Is God Listening?* NEWSWEEK, Mar. 31, 1997, at 58.

43. Kenneth L. Woodward, *Is God Listening?* NEWSWEEK, Mar. 31, 1997, at 58.

44. DALE A. MATTHEWS, THE FAITH FACTOR: PROOF OF THE HEALING POWER OF PRAYER 282 (1998).

45. Diane Winston, *Hands-On Healing: Mainline Protestants Are Discovering Powerful New Spiritual Tool*, DALLAS MORNING NEWS, Mar. 1, 1997, at G1.

46. Id.

47. Ginger Thompson, *Prescription for Prayer,* BALTIMORE SUN, Feb. 13, 1997, at A1.

NOTES TO CHAPTER 5

1. RALPH REED, AFTER THE REVOLUTION: HOW THE CHRISTIAN COALITION IS IMPACTING AMERICA 49 (1994).
2. Michael Novak, *Think Tank: Is America Becoming Anti-Religious?* Television Broadcast, May 20, 1994.
3. John Dart & Lee Romney, *High Court's Ruling May Give Proposed Amendment a Boost,* L.A. TIMES, June 28, 1997, at B4.
4. Linda Greenhouse, *Laws Are Urged to Protect Religion,* N.Y. TIMES, July 15, 1997, at A15.
5. Prepared Testimony of Mark E. Chopko before the House Judiciary Committee, Federal News Service, July 14, 1997.
6. *Religious Action Center Calls Supreme Court Ruling a Blow to Religious Liberty,* U.S. NEWSWIRE, June 25, 1997, at 1 (statement of Rabbi David Saperstein, director of the Religious Action Center of Reform Judaism).
7. Ecumenical Leaders' Statement, *Charles Colson, Richard Neuhaus and a Diverse Coalition Calling for Christians to Vigorously Respond to Supreme Court Rulings on Religion,* July 2, 1997, at 3. See Larry Witham, *Coalition of Clerics Hits Court Rulings,* WASHINGTON TIMES, July 2, 1997 at A4.
8. Prepared Testimony of Rev. Oliver Thomas, special counsel, National Council of the Churches of Christ, before the House Judiciary Committee, Federal News Service, July 14, 1997.
9. Dred Scott v. Sandford, 60 U.S. (19 How.) 393 (1857).
10. EARL WARREN, A REPUBLIC IF YOU CAN KEEP IT 46 (1972).
11. U.S. CONSTITUTION, amend. 1.
12. Barron v. Baltimore, 32 U.S. (7 Pet.) 243 (1833).
13. *Rethinking the Incorporation of the Establishment Clause: A Federalist View,* note, 105 HARV. L. REV. 1700, 1703 (1992).
14. Id. at 1706, n. 42. The establishments were typically accompanied by some protection of free exercise. See STEPHEN M. FELDMAN, PLEASE DON'T WISH ME A MERRY CHRISTMAS: A CRITICAL HISTORY OF THE SEPARATION OF CHURCH AND STATE 150 (1997).
15. JOHN T. NOONAN, JR., THE BELIEVER AND THE POWERS THAT ARE: CASES, HISTORY, AND OTHER DATA BEARING ON

THE RELATION OF RELIGION AND GOVERNMENT 114, 116–117 (1987).

16. See School District of Abington Township v. Schempp, 374 U.S. 203, 255, n. 20 (Brennan, J., concurring).

17. Id. at 255, et seq.

18. Cantwell v. Connecticut, 310 U.S. 296 (1940) (free exercise); Everson v. Board of Education, 330 U.S. 1 (1947) (establishment). The application of the establishment clause to the states has been the cause of continuing criticism in academic literature. See, e.g., Akhil R. Amar, *The Bill of Rights as a Constitution*, 100 YALE L. J. 1131, 1157–1158 (1991).

19. Katcoff v. Marsh, 755 F. 2d 223 (2d Cir. 1985).

20. See Lee v. Weisman, 505 U.S. 577, 624–625 (1992) (Souter, J., concurring).

21. U.S. CONSTITUTION, amend. 1.

22. As originally drafted, the First Amendment only restricted the federal government; but, as with the religion clauses, the Supreme Court has held that the Fourteenth Amendment makes free speech protections applicable against the states. Gitlow v. New York, 268 U.S. 652 (1925).

23. See, e.g., New York Times Co. v. Sullivan, 376 U.S. 254 (1964).

24. State v. Cantwell, 8 A. 2d 533, 535 (Conn. 1939). Cantwell was accompanied by his sons, but their conviction for breach of the peace was reversed before the case reached the U.S. Supreme Court. Id.

25. Cantwell v. Connecticut, 310 U.S. 296, 309 (1940).

26. Id. at 309.

27. Id. at 306, n. 7 (citing Near v. Minnesota, 283 U.S. 697 [1931]).

28. Id. at 308.

29. Id. at 311.

30. Id. at 310.

31. WILLIAM W. VAN ALSTYNE, FIRST AMENDMENT: CASES AND MATERIALS 754, n. 19 (2d ed. 1995).

32. James E. Wood, Jr., *Introduction: Religion and Public Policy,* in JAMES E. WOOD, JR., & DEREK DAVIS (eds.), THE ROLE OF RELIGION IN THE MAKING OF PUBLIC POLICY 1–10 (1991).

33. McDaniel v. Paty, 435 U.S. 618, 640 (1978) (Brennan, J., concurring in the judgment).

34. Capitol Square Review and Advisory Board v. Pinette, 115 S. Ct. 2440, 2446 (1995).

35. See, e.g., Healy v. James, 408 U.S. 169 (1972).

36. For a survey of developments in this area, see Michael Stokes Paulsen, *A Funny Thing Happened on the Way to the Limited Public Forum: Unconstitutional Conditions on "Equal Access" for Religious Speakers and Groups,* 29 U.C. DAVIS L. REV. 653 (1996).

37. Widmar v. Vincent, 454 U.S. 263 (1981).

38. See, e.g., Healy v. James, 408 U.S. 169 (1972).

39. Widmar v. Vincent, 454 U.S. 263, 265 (1981).

40. Id. at 274.

41. Id. at 269. Justice White, in his dissent, did not maintain that letting Cornerstone use school facilities constituted an establishment of religion; he simply maintained that the university should be free to decide whether or not to allow religious uses of its facilities. *Id.* at 282.

42. Lamb's Chapel v. Center Moriches Union Free School District, 113 S. Ct. 2141 (1993).

43. Id. at 2144.

44. Id. at 2147.

45. Rosenberger v. Rector, 115 S. Ct. 2510 (1995).

46. The Court's decision was five to four, and one member of the majority—Justice O'Connor—held open this possibility. Id. at 2527 (O'Connor, J., concurring).

47. U.S. CONSTITUTION, amend. 5 (federal government); U.S. CONSTITUTION, amend. 14 (state government).

48. See, e.g., The Slaughter-House Cases, 83 U.S. (16 Wall.) 36, 80–81 (1872).

49. See, e.g., Zinermon v. Burch, 494 U.S. 113 (1990).

50. See, e.g., Allgeyer v. Louisiana, 165 U.S. 578 (1897).

51. U.S. CONSTITUTION, amend. 15.

52. U.S. CONSTITUTION, art. 6.

53. Lochner v. New York, 198 U.S. 45 (1905).

54. Id.

55. LOUIS FISHER & NEAL DEVINS, POLITICAL DYNAMICS OF CONSTITUTIONAL LAW 199 (1992).

56. Id.

57. See, e.g., West Coast Hotel Co. v. Parrish, 300 U.S. 379 (1937).

58. LOUIS FISHER & NEAL DEVINS, POLITICAL DYNAMICS OF CONSTITUTIONAL LAW 199–200 (1992).

59. Roe v. Wade, 410 U.S. 113 (1973).

60. Pierce v. Society of Sisters, 268 U.S. 510 (1925).

61. See, e.g., Washington v. Glucksberg,117 S. Ct. 2258, 2267 (1997).

62. Mark L. Adams, *Fear of Foreigners: Nativism and Workplace Language Restrictions,* 74 OR. L. REV. 849, 858, 861 (1995).

63. WILLIAM G. ROSS, FORGING NEW FREEDOMS: NATIVISM, EDUCATION, AND THE CONSTITUTION, 1917–1927 148–153 (1994). The initiative exempted some children, including those who were disabled or who lived a long distance from public schools. Id. at 151.

64. Id. at 150.

65. Id. at 151.

66. Id. at 152.

67. Id. at 158.

68. Id.

69. Id. at 161.

70. See, e.g., Bill Ong Hing, *Beyond the Rhetoric of Assimilation and Cultural Pluralism: Addressing the Tension of Separatism and Conflict in an Immigration-Driven Multiracial Society,* 81 CALIF. L. REV. 863, 917 (1993).

71. WILLIAM G. ROSS, FORGING NEW FREEDOMS: NATIVISM, EDUCATION, AND THE CONSTITUTION, 1917–1927 2 (1994).

72. 262 U.S. 390 (1923).

73. Id. at 401.

74. Id.

75. See, e.g., Lochner v. New York, 198 U.S. 45, 74 (1905) (Holmes, J., dissenting.)

76. Bartels v. State of Iowa, 262 U.S. 404, 412 (1923) (Holmes, J., dissenting). *Bartels* was a companion case to *Meyer v. Nebraska*—the Holmes dissent applied to both. See Meyer v. Nebraska, 262 U.S. 390, 403 (1923).

77. Pierce v. Society of Sisters, 268 U.S. 510, 516 (1925) (argument of William D. Guthrie).

78. Id. at 534.

79. Id. at 534–535.

80. Id. at 535.

81. See, e.g., Justice Brennan's unchallenged assertion concerning the *Meyer* line of cases: "I think I am safe in saying that no one doubts the wisdom or validity of those decisions." Michael H. v. Gerald D., 491 U.S. 110, 142 (1989) (Brennan, J., dissenting). Stephen Carter has said that *Pierce* is "almost certainly" the Supreme Court opinion "most supportive of the survival of religious communities." STEPHEN L. CARTER, THE DISSENT

OF THE GOVERNED: A MEDITATION ON LAW, RELIGION, AND LOYALTY 35 (1998).

82. Barbara Bennett Woodhouse, *"Who Owns the Child?"*: *Meyer and Pierce and the Child as Property,* 33 WM. & MARY L. REV. 995, 996 (1992). Woodhouse herself is a rare critic of these decisions. Id.

83. Id.

84. David M. Smolin, *Essay: The Jurisprudence of Privacy in a Splintered Supreme Court,* 75 MARQ. L. REV. 975, 1063 (1992).

85. William Sander & Anthony C. Krautmann, *Catholic Schools, Dropout Rates, and Educational Attainment,* 33 ECON. INQ. 217 (1995).

86. Total private school enrollment in 1997 was about 6 million. Peter W. Cookson, *New Kid on the Block? A Close Look at America's Private Schools,* 15 BROOKINGS REVIEW 22 (1997).

87. Jack MacMullan, *The Constitutionality of State Home Schooling Statutes,* 39 VILL. L. REV. 1309, 1311 (1994); Jack MacMullan, *Increase in Home Schooling Opens Market for Materials,* TULSA WORLD, Aug. 30, 1996, at D3.

88. See generally E. Vance Randall, *Private Schools and State Regulation,* 24 URBAN LAWYER 341 (1992); Ira C. Lupu, *Home Education, Religious Liberty, and the Separation of Powers,* 67 B.U. L. REV. 971 (1987).

89. See Neal Devins, *Fundamentalist Christian Educators v. State: An Inevitable Compromise,* 60 GEO. WASH. L. REV. 818 (1992).

90. The religious atmosphere in some private schools has played a role in cases striking down aid to those schools, a topic we will turn to in chapter 7, but the Court has never suggested that apart from public aid there is any legal infirmity in a school having such an atmosphere. See, e.g., Lemon v. Kurtzman, 403 U.S. 602, 618 (1971).

91. Nina H. Shokraii & Dorothy B. Hanks, *School Choice Programs 1997: What's Happening in the States,* HERITAGE FOUNDATION REPORTS iii (July 1997).

NOTES TO CHAPTER 6

1. Cantwell v. Connecticut, 310 U.S. 296, 303 (1940).

2. John T. Noonan, Jr., *The Language of Judging: The Relation of Words to Power,* 70 ST. JOHN'S L. REV. 13, 16 (1996). *Unveiled Mysteries* was written under the pen name Godfre Ray King. Id.

3. Id. See also JOHN T. NOONAN, JR., THE BELIEVER AND THE

POWERS THAT ARE: CASES, HISTORY, AND OTHER DATA BEAR-ING ON THE RELATION OF RELIGION AND GOVERNMENT 300 (1987).

4. John T. Noonan, Jr., *The Language of Judging: The Relation of Words to Power,* 70 ST. JOHN'S L. REV. 13, 16 (1996); JOHN T. NOO-NAN, JR., THE BELIEVER AND THE POWERS THAT ARE: CASES, HISTORY, AND OTHER DATA BEARING ON THE RELATION OF RE-LIGION AND GOVERNMENT 300 (1987); United States v. Ballard, 322 U.S. 78, 79–80 (1944).

5. United States v. Ballard, 322 U.S. 78, 86 (1944).

6. Id. at 86–87.

7. Id. at 87.

8. *Id.*

9. The Supreme Court left open the question of whether the jury could examine the good faith of the Ballards' representations. In other words, if the Ballards did not believe what they were saying, it is possible they could still be guilty of fraud. Ultimately, the Ballards' convictions were set aside on grounds unrelated to religious freedom, and they were not reindicted. See MICHAEL S. ARIENS & ROBERT A. DESTRO, RELIGIOUS LIB-ERTY IN A PLURALISTIC SOCIETY 959–960 (1996). For a thorough treatment of the Ballard litigation, see JOHN T. NOONAN, JR., THE LUSTRE OF OUR COUNTRY: THE AMERICAN EXPERIENCE OF RE-LIGIOUS FREEDOM 141–176 (1998).

10. Church of the Lukumi Babalu Aye, Inc., v. City of Hialeah, 113 S. Ct. 2217, 2222 (1993).

11. Id. at 2222–2223.

12. Id. at 2231.

13. Id.

14. Id.

15. Id. at 2224.

16. Id. at 2232–2233.

17. Id. at 2231.

18. JOHN T. NOONAN, JR., THE BELIEVER AND THE POWERS THAT ARE: CASES, HISTORY, AND OTHER DATA BEARING ON THE RELATION OF RELIGION AND GOVERNMENT 194 (1987).

19. Id. at 195.

20. Id.

21. Id. at 196.

22. Reynolds v. United States, 98 U.S. 145 (1879).

23. Id. at 164, 166.

24. Id. at 164.

25. Id. at 167.

26. Id. at 166.

27. MICHAEL S. ARIENS & ROBERT A. DESTRO, RELIGIOUS LIBERTY IN A PLURALISTIC SOCIETY 204–205 (1996).

28. 374 U.S. 398 (1963).

29. Id. at 399.

30. Id. at 401.

31. Id. at 404.

32. Id. at 406; see also id. at 403.

33. Id. at 406–407. The Court says that the state must show that "no alternative forms of regulation" would achieve its compelling interest, Id. at 407; this was phrased as the "least restrictive means" test in later decisions. See Thomas v. Review Board, 450 U.S. 707, 718 (1981).

34. One could justifiably wonder whether the justices who decided *Reynolds* would in fact protect a minority religion from a law aimed directly at it—after all, the antibigamy laws were rather directly aimed at the Mormons, although they were written in more general language. But as we will see in the later portions of this chapter, the *Smith* decision—the modern version of *Reynolds*—does retain protection for singled-out groups. Indeed, the Supreme Court decision protecting the Santeria church came after *Smith*.

35. Thomas v. Review Board, 450 U.S. 707 (1981).

36. Hobbie v. Unemployment Appeals Commission of Florida, 480 U.S. 136 (1987); Frazee v. Illinois Department of Employment Security, 489 U.S. 829 (1989).

37. Wisconsin v. Yoder, 406 U.S. 205 (1972).

38. Id. at 210–211.

39. Id. at 220–229.

40. Pierce v. Society of Sisters, 268 U.S. 510 (1925). *Pierce,* which found that parents had a constitutional right to send their children to private school, is discussed in chapter 5.

41. Wisconsin v. Yoder, 406 U.S. 205, 213 (1972).

42. See, e.g., United States v. Lee, 455 U.S. 252 (1982) (the Amish must pay social security taxes despite the burden on their religious beliefs).

43. Goldman v. Weinberger, 475 U.S. 503 (1986).

44. Id. at 506–507.
45. Michael W. McConnell, *Free Exercise Revisionism and the Smith Decision,* 57 U. CHI. L. REV. 1109 (1990).
46. Employment Division v. Smith, 494 U.S. 872 (1990).
47. The Supreme Court's 1990 decision in *Employment Division v. Smith* has a complex history. Alfred Smith and Galen Black were fired from their jobs because they used peyote in Native American ceremonies. When they were denied unemployment compensation because they had been discharged for misconduct, they brought suit. At first the Oregon courts declined to decide whether state law banned peyote use in religious rituals, believing that was irrelevant to the claim for unemployment benefits. But the U.S. Supreme Court ruled otherwise, and the case went back to the Oregon Supreme Court. After that body found that Oregon law did indeed ban peyote use in religious ceremonies, the case reached the U.S. Supreme Court again, and the Court then rendered its historic decision on the general scope of the free exercise clause. The procedural history is set forth in Employment Division v. Smith, 494 U.S. 872, 874–876 (1990).
48. Id. at 884.
49. Id. at 881.
50. Id. at 879 (quoting from *Reynolds*).
51. Id. at 886–887.
52. Id. at 890.
53. Id. at 891 (O'Connor, J., concurring in the judgment).
54. For a collection of articles reacting to *Smith,* see MICHAEL S. ARIENS & ROBERT A. DESTRO, RELIGIOUS LIBERTY IN A PLURALISTIC SOCIETY 253 (1996).
55. State constitutions can be interpreted differently from the federal Constitution just so long as the state interpretation does not violate federal constitutional law. For state cases that reject *Smith,* see id. at 253–254.
56. Peter Steinfels, *Clinton Signs Law Protecting Religious Practices,* N.Y. TIMES, Nov. 17, 1993, at A18.
57. See Marbury v. Madison, 1 Cranch (5 U.S.) 137 (1803).
58. U.S. CONSTITUTION, amend. 5.
59. See generally Boerne v. Flores, 117 S. Ct. 2157 (1997).
60. Id. at 2169.
61. The vote in the Senate was 97 to 3; in the House it passed by voice vote without objection. Peter Steinfels, *Clinton Signs Law Protecting Religious Practices,* N.Y. TIMES, Nov. 17, 1993, at A18.

62. Id. The Religious Freedom Restoration Act was codified at 42 U.S.C. §§2000bb–2000bb–4 (Supp V 1993).

63. Boerne v. Flores, 117 S. Ct. 2157 (1997). The case involved historic-preservation regulations in Texas that prevented the enlargement of a Catholic church.

64. Id. at 2176 (O'Connor, J., dissenting).

65. Id. at 2170.

66. Ecumenical Leaders' Statement, *Charles Colson, Richard Neuhaus and a Diverse Coalition Calling for Christians to Vigorously Respond to Supreme Court Rulings on Religion,* July 2, 1997, at 2. The statement is discussed in David Gibson, *Christian Group Criticizes Courts: Says They Usurp Democracy,* BERGEN RECORD, July 2, 1997, at A1.

67. *Religious Action Center Calls Supreme Court Ruling a Blow to Religious Liberty,* U.S. NEWSWIRE, June 25, 1997, at 1 (statement of Rabbi David Saperstein, director of the Religious Action Center of Reform Judaism).

68. Patricia Rice, *Court Decision Concerns Some St. Louis Church Officials,* ST. LOUIS POST-DISPATCH June 26, 1997, at A8 (statement of Rudy Pulido, president of the St. Louis chapter of Americans United for Separation of Church and State).

69. Boerne v. Flores, 117 S. Ct. 2157, 2176, 2185, 2186 (1997) (opinions of O'Connor, J., Souter, J., and Breyer, J.)

70. Employment Division v. Smith, 494 U.S. 872, 890 (1990).

71. Id.

72. Id. Further support for the Court's acceptance of legislative accommodation to religious freedom may be found in Corporation of the Presiding Bishop v. Amos, 483 U.S. 327 (1987). In *Amos* the Court rejected an establishment clause challenge to §702 of the Civil Rights Act of 1964. This section allows religious employers to discriminate on religious grounds in hiring decisions.

73. See, e.g., Texas v. Johnson, 491 U.S. 397 (1989) (flag desecration statute is inconsistent with the First Amendment).

74. Employment Division v. Smith, 494 U.S. 872, 891 (1990) (O'Connor, J., concurring in the judgment).

75. Id. at 905, 906.

76. Id.

77. See Or. Rev. Stat. §475.992(5) (1995). Other state and federal exemptions for religious use are collected in Employment Division v. Smith, 494, U.S. 872, 906 (1990) (O'Connor, J., concurring in the judgment).

78. See, e.g., United States v. Lee, 455 U.S. 252 (1982) (the Amish must pay social security taxes despite the burden on their religious beliefs); Gillette v. United States, 401 U.S. 437, 462 (1971) (substantial government interest supports disallowance of a conscientious objector claim based on religious opposition to all war).

79. Goldman v. Weinberger, 475 U.S. 503 (1986).

80. 10 U.S.C. §774 (1987).

81. The statute directed the Department of Defense to implement its terms. The implementing regulations, which have had the effect of permitting yarmulkes, may be found at Department of Defense Directive 1300.17, Accommodation of Religious Practices within the Military Services (Feb. 3, 1988). See in particular 1300.17(C)(3).

82. See, e.g., John T. Noonan, Jr., *The End of Free Exercise?* 42 DE-PAUL L. REV. 567 (1992) (criticizing *Smith*); Mark Tushnet, *The Rhetoric of Free Exercise Discourse,* 1993 B.Y.U. L. REV. 117 (1993) (supporting *Smith*). This point is made in MICHAEL S. ARIENS & ROBERT A. DE-STRO, RELIGIOUS LIBERTY IN A PLURALISTIC SOCIETY 253 (1996).

83. STEVEN D. SMITH, FOREORDAINED FAILURE: THE QUEST FOR A CONSTITUTIONAL PRINCIPLE OF RELIGIOUS FREEDOM 126 (1995), cited in MICHAEL S. ARIENS & ROBERT A. DESTRO, RE-LIGIOUS LIBERTY IN A PLURALISTIC SOCIETY 253 (1996).

84. Since the *Boerne* decision striking down the Religious Freedom Restoration Act turned on a lack of power in the U.S. Congress, it does not prohibit state legislatures from passing state-level laws imposing the *Sher-bert* test on all government actions. So not only can the federal and state governments protect specific activities, such as the use of peyote in Native American rituals, but the state governments can also protect religious liberty generally. For a thorough discussion of this and other ways to lessen the impact of *Boerne,* see Robert F. Drinan, S.J., *Reflections on the Demise of the Religious Freedom Restoration Act,* 86 GEO. L. J. 101, 116–120 (1997).

NOTES TO CHAPTER 7

1. See generally Steven Goldberg, *The Constitutional Status of American Science,* 1979 U. ILL. L. FOR. 1 (1979).

2. See, e.g., Miller v. California, 413 U.S. 15, 34 (1973) ("The First Amendment protects works, which taken as a whole, have serious . . . sci-

entific value, regardless of whether the government or a majority of the people approve of the ideas those works represent.")

3. Id. If an article poses an imminent danger to national security, it may not be eligible for First Amendment protection. See, e.g., United States v. Progressive, Inc., 467 F. Supp. 990 (W.D. Wisc. 1979), dismissed as moot, 610 F. 2d 819 (7th Cir. 1979).

4. See, e.g., John A. Robertson, *The Scientists' Right to Research: A Constitutional Analysis*, 51 S. CAL. L. REV. 1203, 1254–1256 (1978). See also 42 U.S.C. §2061(1) (1976) (prohibiting private research activities involving certain nuclear materials).

5. On the constitutional basis for the funding of scientific research, which stems from specific powers such as those relating to the military as well as from the general power to spend for the general welfare, see STEVEN GOLDBERG, CULTURE CLASH: LAW AND SCIENCE IN AMERICA 31–39 (1994). On how the ban on established religion restricts the direct funding of religious practices, see, e.g., Everson v. Board of Education, 330 U.S. 1, 16 ("No tax in any amount, large or small, can be levied to support any religious activities.")

6. STEVEN GOLDBERG, CULTURE CLASH: LAW AND SCIENCE IN AMERICA 39 (1994).

7. Id. at 52–53.

8. Id. at 85–86.

9. See, e.g., Grasetti v. Weinberger, 408 F. Supp. 142 (N.D. Cal. 1976).

10. Engel v. Vitale, 370 U.S. 421, 422–423 (1962).

11. Id. at 422.

12. Id. at 423.

13. Id. at 431.

14. Id.

15. Id. at 436.

16. Id. at 432.

17. 374 U.S. 203 (1963).

18. The challengers in the *Schempp* case were Unitarians. Id. at 206. In the companion case of Murray v. Curlett, 374 U.S. 203 (1963), the plaintiffs were Madalyn Murray and her son, William, who were avowed atheists. See LYNDA BECK FENWICK, SHOULD THE CHILDREN PRAY? A HISTORICAL, JUDICIAL, AND POLITICAL EXAMINATION OF PUBLIC SCHOOL PRAYER 138 (1989).

19. Abington School District v. Schempp, 374 U.S. 203, 225 (1963).

20. Id. at 209, 225.

21. Id. at 225.

22. See, e.g., LYNDA BECK FENWICK, SHOULD THE CHILDREN PRAY? A HISTORICAL, JUDICIAL, AND POLITICAL EXAMINATION OF PUBLIC SCHOOL PRAYER 140 (1989); ROBERT S. ALLEY, SCHOOL PRAYER: THE COURT, THE CONGRESS, AND THE FIRST AMENDMENT 107–124 (1994).

23. ROBERT S. ALLEY, SCHOOL PRAYER: THE COURT, THE CONGRESS, AND THE FIRST AMENDMENT 107 (1994).

24. See, e.g., LYNDA BECK FENWICK, SHOULD THE CHILDREN PRAY? A HISTORICAL, JUDICIAL, AND POLITICAL EXAMINATION OF PUBLIC SCHOOL PRAYER 186, n. 24 (1989).

25. Lee v. Weisman, 505 U.S. 577 (1992).

26. Id.

27. Id. at 587–588.

28. Id. at 593 (students would be pressured to "stand as a group or, at least, maintain respectful silence.")

29. Id. at 631 (Justice Scalia, with whom the Chief Justice [Rehnquist], Justice White, and Justice Thomas join, dissenting.)

30. See, e.g., Ingebretsen v. Jackson Public School District, 88 F. 3d 274 (5th Cir. 1996) (student-initiated nonsectarian prayer at graduation may be acceptable); American Civil Liberties Union v. Black Horse Pike Regional Board of Education, 84 F. 3d 1471 (3d Cir. 1996) (student-led prayer at graduation violates establishment clause).

31. Lee v. Weisman, 505 U.S. 577, 643 (1992).

32. ROBERT S. ALLEY, SCHOOL PRAYER: THE COURT, THE CONGRESS, AND THE FIRST AMENDMENT 212–213 (1994).

33. Donahoe v. Richards, 38 Me. 379 (1854).

34. MICHAEL S. ARIENS & ROBERT A. DESTRO, RELIGIOUS LIBERTY IN A PLURALISTIC SOCIETY 155 (1996).

35. Commonwealth v. Cooke, 7 Am. L. Reg. 417 (Police Court, Boston, Mass. 1859). For an extensive treatment of Bible-reading controversies in this era, see MICHAEL S. ARIENS & ROBERT A. DESTRO, RELIGIOUS LIBERTY IN A PLURALISTIC SOCIETY 148–165 (1996).

36. Commonwealth v. Cooke, 7 Am. L. Reg. 417 (Police Court, Boston, Mass., 1859).

37. Stone v. Graham, 449 U.S. 39 (1980).

38. Id.

39. In Deuteronomy, for example, the commandment to observe the

Sabbath day includes the language "and remember that you were a slave in the land of Egypt, and the Lord your God brought you out from there by a mighty hand and by an outstretched arm; therefore the Lord your God commanded you to keep the Sabbath day." Deut. 5:15 (King James Version). This language does not appear in the Ten Commandments as re-counted in Exodus. See Ex. 20:1–17 (King James Version).

40. JOHN T. NOONAN, JR., THE BELIEVER AND THE POWERS THAT ARE: CASES, HISTORY, AND OTHER DATA BEARING ON THE RELATION OF RELIGION AND GOVERNMENT 3–4 (1987).

41. Id.

42. Id.

43. Id. at 4. See also J. J. STAMM & M. E. ANDREW, THE TEN COMMANDMENTS IN RECENT RESEARCH 98 (1967) ("The sixth commandment . . . is familiar to us in the translation 'You shall not kill': but 'You shall not murder' is often preferred to this. Neither of them is completely beyond doubt.") The Stamm and Andrew text provides a de-tailed discussion of many issues involving the text of the Ten Command-ments.

44. Lee v. Weisman, 505 U.S. 577, 581, 582 (1992).

45. Id. at 581.

46. Id. at 589.

47. RALPH REED, POLITICALLY INCORRECT: THE EMERGING FAITH FACTOR IN AMERICAN POLITICS 44 (1994).

48. Lemon v. Kurtzman, 403 U.S. 602, 612–613 (1971), says there is an unconstitutional establishment of religion if government action lacks a sec-ular purpose or has the primary effect of advancing religion or excessively entangles church and state, but the Court has at times ignored this ap-proach; other approaches, such as analyzing whether the government ac-tion endorses or coerces religion, have at times been used by various jus-tices. See Michael J. Stick, *Educational Vouchers: A Constitutional Analy-sis,* 28 COLUM. J. L. & SOC. PROBS. 423 (1995). For a thoughtful discussion of the endorsement idea supported by Justice O'Connor, see JESSE H. CHOPER, SECURING RELIGIOUS LIBERTY: PRINCIPLES FOR JUDICIAL INTERPRETATION OF THE RELIGION CLAUSES 27–34 (1995).

49. Lynch v. Donnelly, 465 U.S. 668, 671 (1984).

50. Id. at 679.

51. Id. at 685.

52. Id. at 671.

53. Id.

54. Id.

55. American Civil Liberties Union v. Birmingham, 791 F. 2d 1581, 1569 (6th Cir. 1986) (Nelson, J., dissenting), cert. denied 479 U.S. 939 (1986).

56. American Jewish Congress v. City of Chicago, 827 F. 2d 120, 129 (7th Cir. 1987) (Easterbrook, J., dissenting).

57. Philip B. Kurland, *Commentary: The Religion Clauses and the Burger Court,* 34 CATH. U. L. REV. 1, 13, 14 (1984).

58. County of Allegheny v. American Civil Liberties Union, 492 U.S. 573 (1989).

59. Id. at 655 (Kennedy, J., concurring in the judgment in part and dissenting in part, joined by Rehnquist, C.J., White and Scalia, J.J.).

60. Id. at 637 (Brennan, J., concurring in part and dissenting in part, joined by Marshall and Stevens, J.J.).

61. Id. at 578 (Blackmun, J.); Id. at 623 (O'Connor, J.).

62. Id. at 598 (Blackmun, J.); see also id. at 626 (O'Connor, J.).

63. Id. at 613 (Blackmun, J.).

64. Id. at 616 (Blackmun, J.). Justice O'Connor offers the slightly different view that although the menorah is a religious symbol, placing it next to the Christmas tree and the sign saluting liberty "sends a message of pluralism and freedom" rather than a message of government endorsement of religion. Id. at 634 (O'Connor, J.).

65. David M. Cobin, *Essay: Crèches, Christmas Trees, and Menorahs: Weeds Growing in Roger Williams' Garden,* 1990 WIS. L. REV. 1597, 1608, 1610 (1990).

66. Cammack v. Waihee, 932 F. 2d 765 (9th Cir. 1991).

67. Id. at 778.

68. Id.

69. Granzeier v. Middleton, 955 F. Supp. 741, 744 (E.D. Ky. 1997).

70. Id. at 747.

71. Americans United for Separation of Church and State v. County of Kent, 97 Mich. App. 72, 78, 293 N.W. 2d 723, 726 (Ct. of Appeals of Michigan 1980).

72. Koenick v. Felton, 973 F. Supp. 522, 525 (D. Md. 1997) (noting that the schools were closed from the Friday before Easter to the Sunday after Easter).

73. Metzl v. Leininger, 57 F. 3d 618, 619 (7th Cir. 1995). See also Freedom from Religion Foundation v. Thompson, 920 F. Supp. 969 (W.D. Wis.

1996); Griswold Inn v. Connecticut, 441 A. 2d 16 (Sup. Ct. of Conn. 1981).

74. Under some more ambitious voucher plans, public schools would determine what their "tuition" would be and would compete with private schools for students, all of whom would be using vouchers. See Mai-lan E. Wong, *The Implications of School Choice for Children with Disabilities*, 103 YALE L. J. 827, 834 (1993).

75. Wisconsin enacted an early voucher plan in 1990. See Craig Gilbert, *School Choice Wars*, WEEKLY STANDARD, Mar. 31, 1997, at 17. An amended version of this plan, which included aid for religious schools, was upheld by the Wisconsin Supreme Court on June 10, 1998. Ethan Bronner, *Wisconsin Court Upholds Vouchers in Church Schools*, N.Y. TIMES, June 11, 1998 at A1.

76. For a thoughtful discussion of vouchers in the context of alternative proposals for school reform, see PAUL T. HILL, REINVENTING PUBLIC EDUCATION 73–87 (1995).

77. See, e.g., Cynthia Bright, *The Establishment Clause and School Vouchers: Private Choice and Proposition 174*, 31 CAL. W. L. REV. 193 (1995); Eric Nasstrom, *School Vouchers in Minnesota: Confronting the Walls Separating Church and State*, 22 WM. MITCHELL L. REV. 1065 (1997).

78. As we noted above, Lemon v. Kurtzman, 403 U.S. 602, 612–613 (1971), says there is an unconstitutional establishment of religion if government action lacks a secular purpose or has the primary effect of advancing religion or excessively entangles church and state, but the Court has at times ignored this approach; and other approaches, such as analyzing whether the government action endorses or coerces religion, have at times been used by various justices. See Michael J. Stick, *Educational Vouchers: A Constitutional Analysis*, 28 COLUM. J. L. & SOC. PROBS. 423 (1995).

79. See, e.g., Lemon v. Kurtzman, 403 U.S. 602 (1971); Zobrest v. Catalina Foothills School District, 509 U.S. 1 (1993).

80. See Board of Education v. Allen, 392 U.S. 236 (1968) (allowing the loan of textbooks to nonpublic schools); Wolman v. Walter, 433 U.S. 229, 249–250) (1977) (barring public expenditures for maps in nonpublic schools).

81. This observation has been attributed to Sen. Daniel P. Moynihan. See George F. Will, *The Court and Prayer in Nebraska*, WASHINGTON POST, July 12, 1983, at A17.

82. Agostini v. Felton, 117 S. Ct. 1997 (1997) (overruling Aguilar v. Felton, 473 U.S. 402 [1985]).

83. See, e.g., Daniel Wise, *Parochial School Teaching May Be Paid by Federal Funds*, N.Y. LAW JOURNAL, June 24, 1997, at 1 (quoting Mark E. Chopko as saying vouchers would be upheld); Peter Applebome, *Ruling May Open Doors to Parochial Vouchers*, PATRIOT LEDGER, June 26, 1997, at 13 (quoting Steven Shapiro as saying the constitutionality of vouchers remains in doubt).

84. See Michael J. Stick, *Educational Vouchers: A Constitutional Analysis*, 28 COLUM. J. L. & SOC. PROBS. 423 (1995).

85. Id. at 431, n. 47 (quoting Milton Friedman & Rose Friedman, FREE TO CHOOSE: A PERSONAL STATEMENT 164 [1980]).

86. Id.

87. David Futterman, *School Choice and the Religion Clauses: The Law and Politics of Public Aid to Private Parochial Schools*, 81 GEO. L. J. 711, 739 (1993).

88. CHARLES GLENN, CHOICE OF SCHOOLS IN SIX NATIONS 41–42, 189–190, 210–211 (1989), cited in Douglas Dewey, *Vouchers and Educational Freedom: A Debate*, CATO INSTITUTE POLICY ANALYSIS No. 269, Mar. 12, 1997, at 37.

89. Id.

90. Michael Heise, *Public Funds, Private Schools, and the Court: Legal Issues and Policy Consequences*, 25 TEX. TECH. L. REV. 137, 146 (1993).

NOTES TO CHAPTER 8

1. LAURENCE H. TRIBE, AMERICAN CONSTITUTIONAL LAW 1205 (2d ed. 1988).

2. John Hart Ely, *Legislative and Administrative Motivation in Constitutional Law*, 79 YALE L. J. 1205, 1326, n. 376 (1970).

3. Wallace v. Jaffree, 472 U.S. 38, 70 (1985) (O'Connor, J., concurring in the judgment).

4. LAURENCE H. TRIBE, AMERICAN CONSTITUTIONAL LAW 1204 (2d ed. 1988).

5. A. H. LEWIS, A CRITICAL HISTORY OF SUNDAY LEGISLATION FROM 321 TO 1888 A.D. 19 (1888).

6. Id.

7. Id. at 18–40.

8. McGowan v. Maryland, 366 U.S. 420, 470–471 (1961) (opinion of Frankfurter, J.).

9. Id. at 484–488.

10. Id. at 487.

11. Id. at 491–492.

12. For a spirited account of some of these battles from the perspective of an opponent of Sunday closing laws, see WARREN L. JOHNS, DATELINE SUNDAY, U.S.A. (1967).

13. Specht v. Commonwealth, 8 Pa. St. (Barr) 312, 323 (1848).

14. MICHAEL S. ARIENS & ROBERT A. DESTRO, RELIGIOUS LIBERTY IN A PLURALISTIC SOCIETY 123–129 (1996). The California decisions are Ex Parte Newman, 9 Cal. 502 (1858) and Ex Parte Andrews, 18 Cal. 678 (1861).

15. Soon Hing v. Crowley, 113 U.S. 703 (1885); Hennington v. Georgia, 163 U.S. 299 (1896); Petit v. Minnesota, 177 U.S. 164 (1900).

16. Soon Hing v. Crowley, 113 U.S. 703, 710 (1885).

17. McGowan v. Maryland, 366 U.S. 420, 422 (1961).

18. Id. at 422–424.

19. Id. at 422. *McGowan* was one of four cases the Supreme Court decided the same day. In these cases the Court rejected not only the establishment clause challenge to Sunday closing laws, but challenges based on the free exercise, equal protection, and due process clauses as well. See Braunfeld v. Brown, 366 U.S. 599 (1961); Two Guys from Harrison-Allentown, Inc., v. McGinley, 366 U.S. 582 (1961); and Gallagher v. Crown Kosher Super Market, Inc., 366 U.S. 617 (1961).

20. McGowan v. Maryland, 366 U.S. 420, 434–435 (1961).

21. Id. at 435, 445.

22. Id. at 450.

23. Id. at 442.

24. See, e.g., Martin E. Marty, *Where Do You Draw the Line? Negotiating with Modernity*, 114 CHRISTIAN CENTURY 38 (1997).

25. LAURENCE H. TRIBE, AMERICAN CONSTITUTIONAL LAW 1205 (2d ed. 1988).

26. Wallace v. Jaffree, 472 U.S. 38 (1985).

27. Id. at 40, n. 1. There were two other nonmaterial changes between the 1978 and 1981 statutes. Id. at 58–59.

28. Id. at 59.

29. Id.

30. Id. at 56–57.

31. Id. at 57.
32. Id. at 56–57 (emphasis in original).
33. Id. at 60.
34. Id. at 61.
35. Id. at 67 (O'Connor, J., concurring in the judgment).
36. Id.
37. Id. at 70.
38. Roe v. Wade, 410 U.S. 113 (1973).
39. Id. at 160–161.
40. Harris v. McRae, 448 U.S. 297, 301–303 (1980).
41. Id.
42. Id.
43. Id. at 319–320.
44. Id. at 319.
45. Id.
46. Id. at 319–320.
47. The only Supreme Court justice to offer a contrary view was Justice Stevens when he found in 1989 that portions of a Missouri statute embodied the Roman Catholic view of abortion and served no secular purpose. Webster v. Reproductive Health Services, 492 U.S. 490, 566–572 (1989) (opinion of Stevens, J.). Professor Laurence H. Tribe once took the position that any governmental resolution of the abortion issue constituted an establishment of religion, but he has abandoned that view and now believes that religion cannot be kept out of the political debate over abortion. LAURENCE H. TRIBE, ABORTION: THE CLASH OF ABSOLUTES 116, n. 3 (1992).
48. See, e.g., ELIZABETH ADELL COOK, TED G. JELEN, & CLYDE WILCOX, BETWEEN TWO ABSOLUTES: PUBLIC OPINION AND THE POLITICS OF ABORTION 93–130 (1992).
49. Id. at 119.
50. JOEL FEINBERG (ed.), THE PROBLEM OF ABORTION 3 (2d ed. 1984) (emphasis in original) (Professor Feinberg is the author of the introductory note from which this quotation is taken).
51. LAURENCE H. TRIBE, ABORTION: THE CLASH OF ABSOLUTES 117 (1992).
52. Frank H. Boehm, *When Life Begins? There Are Many Answers*, THE TENNESSEAN, Sept. 2, 1997, at 15A.
53. LAURENCE H. TRIBE, ABORTION: THE CLASH OF ABSOLUTES 117–118 (1992).

54. Frank H. Boehm, *When Life Begins? There Are Many Answers,* THE TENNESSEAN, Sept. 2, 1997, at 15A.

55. ROBERT J. SAWYER, THE TERMINAL EXPERIMENT 117–118 (1995).

56. Editorial, *The "Christian Nation" Controversy,* THE AMERICAN LAWYER, June 1989, at 70.

57. Id.

58. Id.

59. Id.

60. Id.

61. Id.

62. Allegheny County v. Greater Pittsburgh ACLU, 492 U.S. 573, 627 (1989) (opinion of O'Connor, J.).

63. Zorach v. Clauson, 343 U.S. 306 (1952).

64. Id. at 313.

65. Id.

66. McGowan v. Maryland, 366 U.S. 420, 563 (1961) (Douglas, J., dissenting).

67. Engel v. Vitale, 370 U.S. 421, 442–443 (1962) (Douglas, J., concurring).

68. McGowan v. Maryland, 366 U.S. 420, 461 (1961) (opinion of Frankfurter, J.).

69. Church of the Holy Trinity v. United States, 143 U.S. 457 (1892).

70. Id. at 464.

71. Id. at 465.

72. Id. at 471.

73. MICHAEL S. ARIENS & ROBERT A DESTRO, RELIGIOUS LIBERTY IN A PLURALISTIC SOCIETY 182 (1996). Ariens and Destro note that Chief Justice Earl Warren spoke of the great influence of Christianity on American institutions. Id.

74. Id.

75. Id.

76. Church of the Holy Trinity v. United States, 143 U.S. 457, 472 (1892).

NOTES TO CHAPTER 9

1. For a historical overview of the interaction of science and religion since the seventeenth century, see IAN G. BARBOUR, RELIGION AND

SCIENCE: HISTORICAL AND CONTEMPORARY ISSUES 3–74 (1997). I refer briefly to some aspects of this interaction in the next chapter.

2. This is hardly the first historical era in which that has been true. Christianity was vital to the rise of modern science. Id. at 90. See also MARGARET WERTHEIM, PYTHAGORAS' TROUSERS: GOD, PHYSICS, AND THE GENDER WARS 7 (1995) ("historians have shown, the idea of a long-standing war between science and religion is a historical fiction.")

3. Mic. 6:8 (New King James Version, 1982). On the centrality of humility in the Christian tradition, see GEORGE MALONEY, ON THE ROAD TO PERFECTION: CHRISTIAN HUMILITY IN MODERN SOCIETY (1995). Maloney writes that the image of Jesus "that rings truest to the gospels is that of Jesus, humble of heart." Id. at 15 (quoting Matt. 11:29).

4. See, e.g., Micha Odenhiemer, *False Positive: There's a Price to Be Paid for Wanting to Be Proven Right,* JERUSALEM REPORT, Oct. 16, 1997, at 59.

5. STEPHEN MITCHELL, THE BOOK OF JOB xix (1987).

6. LEON LEDERMAN, THE GOD PARTICLE: IF THE UNIVERSE IS THE ANSWER, WHAT IS THE QUESTION? (1993).

7. See the discussion of Stephen Hawking in MARGARET WERTHEIM, PYTHAGORAS' TROUSERS: GOD, PHYSICS, AND THE GENDER WARS 218 (1995).

8. Id. at 219 (discussion of George Smoot).

9. C.P. SNOW, THE TWO CULTURES: AND A SECOND LOOK 13–14 (1963).

10. On whether some form of theism is necessary for doing science, see IAN G. BARBOUR, RELIGION AND SCIENCE: HISTORICAL AND CONTEMPORARY ISSUES 90 (1997).

11. MARGARET WERTHEIM, PYTHAGORAS' TROUSERS: GOD, PHYSICS, AND THE GENDER WARS 203 (1995).

12. Id. at 221.

13. LEON LEDERMAN, THE GOD PARTICLE: IF THE UNIVERSE IS THE ANSWER, WHAT IS THE QUESTION? (1993).

14. Id. at 372.

15. MARGARET WERTHEIM, PYTHAGORAS' TROUSERS: GOD, PHYSICS, AND THE GENDER WARS 220–221 (1995).

16. Id. at 218.

17. Id. at 219.

18. Id. at 213.

19. STEVEN WEINBERG, DREAMS OF A FINAL THEORY 242 (1992).

20. See, e.g., Abraham Edel, *Attempts to Derive Definitive Moral Patterns from Biology,* and Elizabeth Allen, et al., *Against "Sociobiology,"* both in ARTHUR L. CAPLAN (ed.), THE SOCIOBIOLOGY DEBATE: READINGS ON ETHICAL AND SCIENTIFIC ISSUES 111, 259 (1978).

21. Edward O. Wilson, *For Sociobiology,* in ARTHUR L. CAPLAN (ED.), THE SOCIOBIOLOGY DEBATE: READINGS ON ETHICAL AND SCIENTIFIC ISSUES 267 (1978).

22. Id.

23. EDWARD O. WILSON, CONSILIENCE: THE UNITY OF KNOWLEDGE 256, 255, 251 (1998).

24. STEVEN PINKER, HOW THE MIND WORKS (1997).

25. Id. at 559.

26. Id. at 406.

27. Id. at 404.

28. Steve Jones, *The Set within the Skull,* N.Y. REV. BOOKS, Nov. 6, 1997, at 13, 15.

29. Ruth Mattern, *Altruism, Ethics, and Sociobiology,* in ARTHUR L. CAPLAN (ed.), THE SOCIOBIOLOGY DEBATE: READINGS ON ETHICAL AND SCIENTIFIC ISSUES 462, 470 (1978).

30. BERNARD WILLIAMS, ETHICS AND THE LIMITS OF PHILOSOPHY 44 (1985). Williams goes on to note that before sociobiology can make even this contribution, it would "have to be able to read the historical record of human culture much better than it does now." Id.

31. See, e.g., Lee Alexander, *An "Inclusivity" Church Opens in Greensboro,* GREENSBORO NEWS & RECORD, Aug. 9, 1997, at B6 (statement of pastor of St. Philip's Anglican Church); Lindsy Van Gelder, *The "Born That Way" Trap,* in ROBERT M. BAIRD & M. KATHERINE BAIRD (eds.), HOMOSEXUALITY: DEBATING THE ISSUES 80 (1995) (quoting the bishop of the Episcopal Diocese of Newark).

32. See, e.g., Lindsy Van Gelder, *The "Born That Way" Trap,* in ROBERT M. BAIRD & M. KATHERINE BAIRD (eds.), HOMOSEXUALITY: DEBATING THE ISSUES 81 (1995).

33. ROGER PENROSE, THE EMPEROR'S NEW MIND: CONCERNING COMPUTERS, MINDS, AND THE LAWS OF PHYSICS 280 (1989).

34. For example, Niels Bohr, a founder of quantum theory, disagreed

with Einstein about that theory's limits but accepted that human reason could go only so far in understanding the world. See IAN G. BARBOUR, RELIGION AND SCIENCE: HISTORICAL AND CONTEMPORARY IS-SUES 167–170 (1997).

35. RICHARD DAWKINS, THE SELFISH GENE 330 (1989).

36. For an introduction to the philosophy of science, see Alex C. Michalos, *Philosophy of Science: Historical, Social, and Value Aspects,* in PAUL T. DURBIN (ed.), A GUIDE TO THE CULTURE OF SCIENCE, TECHNOLOGY, AND MEDICINE 197 (1980). Particularly relevant for present purposes are pp. 225–232.

37. RICHARD DAWKINS, THE BLIND WATCHMAKER 272 (1986).

38. See Steven Goldberg, *The Changing Face of Death: Computers, Consciousness, and Nancy Cruzan,* 43 STANFORD L. REV. 659, 663–670 (1991).

39. Washington v. Glucksberg, 117 S. Ct. 2258 (1997); Vacco v. Quill, 117 S. Ct. 2293 (1997).

40. Washington v. Glucksberg, 117 S. Ct. 2258, 2303 (1997) (O'Connor, J., concurring).

41. Bill Broadway, *In a Caring Congregation, Great Comfort for the Dying,* WASHINGTON POST, June 28, 1997, at B1.

42. Id. at B6.

43. Id.

44. Committee on Medical Ethics, Episcopal Diocese of Washington, *Assisted Suicide and Euthanasia: Christian Moral Perspectives,* THE WASHINGTON REPORT 29 (1997).

45. Washington v. Glucksberg, 117 S. Ct. 2258, 2275 (1997).

46. For a tabular summary of the views of many religions on assisted suicide, see Bill Broadway, *In a Caring Congregation, Great Comfort for the Dying,* WASHINGTON POST, June 28, 1997, at B1, B6. For a thoughtful discussion of the intersection of religious belief and assisted suicide, see Matthew P. Previn, *Assisted Suicide and Religion: Conflicting Conceptions of the Sanctity of Human Life,* 84 GEO. L. J. 589 (1996). Although Previn is critical of the Supreme Court's establishment clause doctrine, he concedes that under that doctrine religious perspectives can play a role in formulating legislative responses to assisted suicide. Id. at 608.

47. See KENT GREENAWALT, PRIVATE CONSCIENCES AND PUBLIC REASONS (1995).

48. See JOHN RAWLS, POLITICAL LIBERALISM (1993).

49. MICHAEL J. PERRY, RELIGION IN POLITICS: CONSTITU-TIONAL AND MORAL PERSPECTIVES 61 (1997).

50. Id. at 6. Perry would allow religious arguments even in the absence of secular justifications when the subject is the morality of human conduct. For example, a solely religious argument could support the view that all human beings, rather than merely some, are sacred. Id.

51. Id. at 50–51. Perry here points out that some secular arguments by legislators could alienate constituents in much the same way that religious arguments might.

52. MICHAEL J. SANDEL, DEMOCRACY'S DISCONTENT: AMER-ICA IN SEARCH OF A PUBLIC PHILOSOPHY 23 (1996).

53. Id.

54. SAMUEL SCOLNIC, ECHOES FROM THE BIMAH (1988).

55. Id. at 74.

56. Id.

57. Id. at 76.

58. CHRISTOPHER P. TOUMEY, GOD'S OWN SCIENTISTS: CRE-ATIONISTS IN A SECULAR WORLD 259 (1994). I discuss creation science in chapter 3.

59. SAMUEL SCOLNIC, ECHOES FROM THE BIMAH 29–30 (1988).

60. Id. at 30.

61. Id.

NOTES TO CHAPTER 10

1. IAN G. BARBOUR, RELIGION AND SCIENCE: HISTORICAL AND CONTEMPORARY ISSUES 3–4 (1997).

2. JOHN HEDLEY BROOKS, SCIENCE AND RELIGION: SOME HISTORICAL PERSPECTIVES 321 (1991).

3. Id. at 19.

4. IAN G. BARBOUR, RELIGION AND SCIENCE: HISTORICAL AND CONTEMPORARY ISSUES 15 (1997).

5. Id. at 25.

6. Id. at 25–26.

7. DON K. PRICE, AMERICA'S UNWRITTEN CONSTITUTION: SCIENCE, RELIGION, AND POLITICAL RESPONSIBILITY 15 (1983).

8. EDWARD O. WILSON, CONSILIENCE: THE UNITY OF KNOWLEDGE 262 (1998).

9. Id. at 263.

10. See, e.g., PERVEZ HOODBHOY, ISLAM AND SCIENCE: RELIGIOUS ORTHODOXY AND THE BATTLE FOR RATIONALITY 85 (1991).

11. See generally Id. and NASIM BUTT, SCIENCE AND MUSLIM SOCIETIES (1991).

12. NOLAN PLINY JACOBSON, BUDDHISM AND THE CONTEMPORARY WORLD 143 (1983).

13. DAVID G. STERN, WITTGENSTEIN ON MIND AND LANGUAGE 8 (1995) (quoting from the Ogden translation of Wittgenstein's TRACTATUS, 6.54–57). In his later work Wittgenstein appeared to move away from these sentiments. Id. at 3.

14. OLIVER TODD, ALBERT CAMUS: A LIFE 145 (1997).

15. BERNARD WILLIAMS, ETHICS AND THE LIMITS OF PHILOSOPHY 136 (1985).

16. See generally PAUL R. GROSS & NORMAN LEVITT, HIGHER SUPERSTITION: THE ACADEMIC LEFT AND ITS QUARRELS WITH SCIENCE (1998).

17. Id. The Gross and Levitt book is a vigorous attack on the deconstructionist opponents of science. For an introduction to Feyerabend's work, see PAUL FEYERABEND, SCIENCE IN A FREE SOCIETY (1978).

18. PAUL R. GROSS & NORMAN LEVITT, HIGHER SUPERSTITION: THE ACADEMIC LEFT AND ITS QUARRELS WITH SCIENCE 49–50, 261, 313 (1998) (quoting from Feyerabend's article *Atoms and Consciousness*).

19. WENDY KAMINER, I'M DYSFUNCTIONAL, YOU'RE DYSFUNCTIONAL: THE RECOVERY MOVEMENT AND OTHER SELF-HELP FASHIONS 113–114 (1993).

20. MICHAEL DROSNIN, THE BIBLE CODE 13 (1997); JEFFREY SATINOVER, CRACKING THE BIBLE CODE 6 (1997).

21. JEFFREY SATINOVER, CRACKING THE BIBLE CODE 9 (1997).

22. MICHAEL DROSNIN, THE BIBLE CODE 11 (1997).

23. JOHN POLKINGHORNE, BEYOND SCIENCE: THE WIDER HUMAN CONTEXT 77 (1996).

24. See Baruch Sterman, *Science and Theology,* JERUSALEM POST, Aug. 1, 1996, at 3.

25. JOHN POLKINGHORNE, THE FAITH OF A PHYSICIST 1, 76 (1994).

26. Id. at 182, 183, 1. (In using the phrase, "turn the images of religion," Polkinghorne is quoting from K. Ward's IMAGES OF ETERNITY (1987).)

27. GERALD L. SCHROEDER, THE SCIENCE OF GOD: THE CONVERGENCE OF SCIENTIFIC AND BIBLICAL WISDOM 3 (1997).

28. Id. at 61.

29. Id. at 46. (This quotation is from Gen. 2:4; Schroeder also cites Gen. 5:1. In a related context he cites Ps. 90:4. Id. at 42.)

30. Id. at 68, 204–205.

31. Id. at 5.

32. John Noble Wilford, *Wary Astronomers Ponder an Accelerating Universe,* N.Y. TIMES, Mar. 3, 1998, at F1.

33. GERALD L. SCHROEDER, THE SCIENCE OF GOD: THE CONVERGENCE OF SCIENTIFIC AND BIBLICAL WISDOM 23 (1997).

34. GERALD L. SCHROEDER, GENESIS AND THE BIG BANG, THE DISCOVERY OF HARMONY BETWEEN MODERN SCIENCE AND THE BIBLE 82–83 (1990).

35. Id. at 83.

36. James Glanz, *Astronomers See a Cosmic Antigravity Force at Work,* 279 SCIENCE 1298 (1998), at 1298.

37. GERALD L. SCHROEDER, THE SCIENCE OF GOD: THE CONVERGENCE OF SCIENTIFIC AND BIBLICAL WISDOM 191 (1997).

38. Id. at 193.

39. Id. at 191.

40. PATRICK GLYNN, GOD: THE EVIDENCE: THE RECONCILIATION OF FAITH AND REASON IN A POSTSECULAR WORLD 11 (1997).

41. See, e.g., id. at 55, 166.

42. Id. at 29.

43. Id. at 22–23.

44. Id. at 29.

45. Id. at 48–53.

46. Id. at 18–20 (Glynn is referring here to discoveries not only in astronomy, but also in psychology, medicine, and related fields).

47. Id. at 19.

48. GERALD SCHROEDER, THE SCIENCE OF GOD: THE CONVERGENCE OF SCIENTIFIC AND BIBLICAL WISDOM 115–116 (1997).

49. JOHN POLKINGHORNE, BEYOND SCIENCE: THE WIDER HUMAN CONTEXT 75–77 (1996).

50. Id. at 76.

51. Id. at 77.

52. IAN G. BARBOUR, RELIGION AND SCIENCE: HISTORICAL AND CONTEMPORARY ISSUES 16 (1997).

53. See, e.g., PATRICK GLYNN, GOD: THE EVIDENCE: THE REC-ONCILIATION OF FAITH AND REASON IN A POSTSECULAR WORLD 89 (1997).

54. EDWARD O. WILSON, CONSILIENCE: THE UNITY OF KNOWLEDGE 261, 258 (1998).

55. PATRICK GLYNN, GOD: THE EVIDENCE: THE RECONCILI-ATION OF FAITH AND REASON IN A POSTSECULAR WORLD 80 (1997).

NOTES TO CHAPTER 11

1. Gary Burge, *Missing God at Church?* CHRISTIANITY TODAY, Oct. 6, 1997, at 20.

2. Id. at 22.

3. Id.

4. Id. at 27.

5. William Raspberry, *Spirituality: A Force for the Public Good,* WASHINGTON POST, Oct. 27, 1997, at A25.

6. Jeffrey Klein, *Editor's Note: Stepping on Sacred Ground,* MOTHER JONES, Dec. 1997, at 5.

7. Id. at 3, 5.

8. *God Decentralized,* N.Y. TIMES MAGAZINE, Dec. 7, 1997, at 55.

9. Robert Lee Hotz, *Response to Religion May Lie in Brain Makeup, Study Says,* AUSTIN AMERICAN-STATESMAN, Oct. 29, 1997, at A1.

10. Id.

11. *Brain Research Reveals Interesting Information on God and the Mind,* NBC NIGHTLY NEWS, Oct. 29, 1997 (From Lexis/Nexus database) (comment of Father Aidan Comerford).

12. Id. (comment of Kenneth Bonnell).

13. See, e.g., STEVEN GOLDBERG, CULTURE CLASH: LAW AND SCIENCE IN AMERICA 183 (1994).

Bibliography

BOOKS

ALLEY, ROBERT S., SCHOOL PRAYER: THE COURT, THE CONGRESS, AND THE FIRST AMENDMENT (1994).

ARIENS, MICHAEL S., & ROBERT A. DESTRO, RELIGIOUS LIBERTY IN A PLURALISTIC SOCIETY (1996).

BAIRD, ROBERT M., & M. KATHERINE BAIRD (eds.), HOMOSEXUALITY: DEBATING THE ISSUES (1995).

BARBOUR, IAN G., RELIGION AND SCIENCE: HISTORICAL AND CONTEMPORARY ISSUES (1997).

BENSON, HERBERT, TIMELESS HEALING: THE POWER AND BIOLOGY OF BELIEF (1996).

BROOKS, JOHN HEDLEY, SCIENCE AND RELIGION: SOME HISTORICAL PERSPECTIVES (1991).

BUTT, NASIM, SCIENCE AND MUSLIM SOCIETIES (1991).

CAPLAN, ARTHUR L. (ed.), THE SOCIOBIOLOGY DEBATE: READINGS ON ETHICAL AND SCIENTIFIC ISSUES (1978).

CARMELL, ARYEH, & CYRIL DOMB (eds.), CHALLENGE: TORAH VIEWS ON SCIENCE AND ITS PROBLEMS (1988).

CARTER, STEPHEN L., THE CULTURE OF DISBELIEF: HOW AMERICAN LAW AND POLITICS TRIVIALIZE RELIGIOUS DEVOTION (1993).

CARTER, STEPHEN L., THE DISSENT OF THE GOVERNED: A MEDITATION ON LAW, RELIGION, AND LOYALTY (1998).

CHALMERS, DAVID J., THE CONSCIOUS MIND: IN SEARCH OF A FUNDAMENTAL THEORY (1996).

CHOPER, JESSE H., SECURING RELIGIOUS LIBERTY: PRINCIPLES FOR JUDICIAL INTERPRETATION OF THE RELIGION CLAUSES (1995).

COOK, ELIZABETH ADELL, TED G. JELEN, & CLYDE WILCOX, BE-TWEEN TWO ABSOLUTES: PUBLIC OPINION AND THE POLI-TICS OF ABORTION (1992).

DAVIS, PERCIVAL, & DEAN H. KENYON, OF PANDAS AND PEOPLE: THE CENTRAL QUESTION OF BIOLOGICAL ORIGINS (2d ed. 1993).

DAWKINS, RICHARD, THE BLIND WATCHMAKER (1986).

DAWKINS, RICHARD, THE SELFISH GENE (1989).

DOSSEY, LARRY, BE CAREFUL WHAT YOUR PRAY FOR—YOU JUST MIGHT GET IT (1997).

DOSSEY, LARRY, HEALING WORDS: THE POWER OF PRAYER AND THE PRACTICE OF MEDICINE (1993).

DOSSEY, LARRY, PRAYER IS GOOD MEDICINE: HOW TO REAP THE HEALING BENEFITS OF PRAYER (1996).

DROSNIN, MICHAEL, THE BIBLE CODE (1997).

DRUCKMAN, DANIEL, & ROBERT A. BJORK (eds.), IN THE MIND'S EYE: ENHANCING HUMAN PERFORMANCE (1991).

DURBIN, PAUL T. (ed.), A GUIDE TO THE CULTURE OF SCIENCE, TECHNOLOGY, AND MEDICINE (1980).

EDDY, MARY BAKER, SCIENCE AND HEALTH WITH KEY TO THE SCRIPTURES (1934).

EVE, RAYMOND A., & FRANCIS B. HARROLD, THE CREATIONIST MOVEMENT IN MODERN AMERICA (1991).

FEINBERG, JOEL (ed.), THE PROBLEM OF ABORTION (2d ed. 1984).

FELDMAN, STEPHEN M., PLEASE DON'T WISH ME A MERRY CHRISTMAS: A CRITICAL HISTORY OF THE SEPARATION OF CHURCH AND STATE (1997).

FENWICK, LYNDA BECK, SHOULD THE CHILDREN PRAY? A HIS-TORICAL, JUDICIAL, AND POLITICAL EXAMINATION OF PUB-LIC SCHOOL PRAYER (1989).

FEYERABEND, PAUL, SCIENCE IN A FREE SOCIETY (1978).

FISHER, LOUIS, & NEAL DEVINS, POLITICAL DYNAMICS OF CON-STITUTIONAL LAW (1992).

FRIEDMAN, MILTON, & ROSE FRIEDMAN, FREE TO CHOOSE: A PERSONAL STATEMENT (1980).

FUTUYMA, DOUGLAS J., SCIENCE ON TRIAL: THE CASE FOR EVO-LUTION (1995).

GILBERT, JAMES, REDEEMING CULTURE: AMERICAN RELIGION IN AN AGE OF SCIENCE (1997).

GLENN, CHARLES, CHOICE OF SCHOOLS IN SIX NATIONS (1989).

GLYNN, PATRICK, GOD: THE EVIDENCE: THE RECONCILIATION OF FAITH AND REASON IN A POSTSECULAR WORLD (1997).

GOLDBERG, STEVEN, CULTURE CLASH: LAW AND SCIENCE IN AMERICA (1994).

GREENAWALT, KENT, PRIVATE CONSCIENCES AND PUBLIC REASONS (1995).

GROSS, PAUL R., & NORMAN LEVITT, HIGHER SUPERSTITION: THE ACADEMIC LEFT AND ITS QUARRELS WITH SCIENCE (1998).

GRUDEN, WAYNE A. (ed.), ARE MIRACULOUS GIFTS FOR TODAY? (1996).

HILL, PAUL T., REINVENTING PUBLIC EDUCATION (1995).

HOODBHOY, PERVEZ, ISLAM AND SCIENCE: RELIGIOUS ORTHODOXY AND THE BATTLE FOR RATIONALITY (1991).

JACOBSON, NOLAN PLINY, BUDDHISM AND THE CONTEMPORARY WORLD (1983).

JAMES, WILLIAM, THE VARIETIES OF RELIGIOUS EXPERIENCE (1990).

JOHNS, WARREN L., DATELINE SUNDAY, U.S.A. (1967).

JOHNSON, PHILLIP E., DARWIN ON TRIAL (1991).

JOHNSON, PHILLIP E., REASON IN THE BALANCE: THE CASE AGAINST NATURALISM IN SCIENCE, LAW, & EDUCATION (1995).

KAMINER, WENDY, I'M DYSFUNCTIONAL, YOU'RE DYSFUNCTIONAL: THE RECOVERY MOVEMENT AND OTHER SELF-HELP FASHIONS (1993).

KITCHER, PHILIP, ABUSING SCIENCE: THE CASE AGAINST CREATIONISM (1982).

KOENIG, HAROLD G., IS RELIGION GOOD FOR YOUR HEALTH? (1997).

KOHLER, KAUFMANN, JEWISH THEOLOGY SYSTEMATICALLY AND HISTORICALLY CONSIDERED (1968).

KRISTOL, IRVING (ed.), AMERICA'S CONTINUING REVOLUTION: AN ACT OF CONSERVATION (1975).

KUHN, THOMAS S., THE STRUCTURE OF SCIENTIFIC REVOLUTIONS (1962).

KUSHNER, HAROLD S., WHEN BAD THINGS HAPPEN TO GOOD PEOPLE (1983).

LARSON, EDWARD J., SUMMER OF THE GODS: THE SCOPES TRIAL AND AMERICA'S CONTINUING DEBATE OVER SCIENCE AND RELIGION (1997).

LARSON, EDWARD J., TRIAL AND ERROR: THE AMERICAN CONTROVERSY OVER CREATION AND EVOLUTION (1989).

LEDERMAN, LEON, THE GOD PARTICLE: IF THE UNIVERSE IS THE ANSWER, WHAT IS THE QUESTION? (1993).

LEWIS, A. H., A CRITICAL HISTORY OF SUNDAY LEGISLATION FROM 321 TO 1888 A.D. (1888).

MALONEY, GEORGE, ON THE ROAD TO PERFECTION: CHRISTIAN HUMILITY IN MODERN SOCIETY (1995).

MATTHEWS, DALE A., THE FAITH FACTOR: PROOF OF THE HEALING POWER OF PRAYER (1998).

MAZLISH, BRUCE, THE FOURTH DISCONTINUITY: THE CO-EVOLUTION OF HUMANS AND MACHINES (1993)

MCGINN, COLIN, THE PROBLEM OF CONSCIOUSNESS: ESSAYS TOWARDS A RESOLUTION (1991).

MERGES, ROBERT PATRICK, PATENT LAW AND POLICY: CASES AND MATERIALS (1992).

MITCHELL, STEPHEN, THE BOOK OF JOB (1987).

NAGEL, THOMAS, THE VIEW FROM NOWHERE (1986).

NATIONAL ACADEMY OF SCIENCES, SCIENCE AND CREATIONISM (1984).

NELKIN, DOROTHY, THE CREATION CONTROVERSY: SCIENCE OR SCRIPTURE IN THE SCHOOLS (1982).

NEUHAUS, RICHARD JOHN, THE NAKED PUBLIC SQUARE: RELIGION AND DEMOCRACY IN AMERICA (1984).

NOONAN, JOHN T., JR., THE BELIEVER AND THE POWERS THAT ARE: CASES, HISTORY, AND OTHER DATA BEARING ON THE RELATION OF RELIGION AND GOVERNMENT (1987).

NOONAN, JOHN T., JR., THE LUSTRE OF OUR COUNTRY: THE AMERICAN EXPERIENCE OF RELIGIOUS FREEDOM (1998).

NUMBERS, RONALD, L., THE CREATIONISTS: THE EVOLUTION OF SCIENTIFIC CREATIONISM (1992).

NUMBERS, RONALD L. (ed.), 1 CREATIONISM IN TWENTIETH-CENTURY AMERICA: A TEN VOLUME ANTHOLOGY OF DOCUMENTS, 1930–1961 (1995).

PENROSE, ROGER, THE EMPEROR'S NEW MIND: CONCERNING COMPUTERS, MINDS, AND THE LAWS OF PHYSICS (1989).

PERRY, MICHAEL J., RELIGION IN POLITICS: CONSTITUTIONAL AND MORAL PERSPECTIVES (1997).
PETUCHOWSKI, JAKOB J., UNDERSTANDING JEWISH PRAYER (1972).
PHILLIPS, D. Z., THE CONCEPT OF PRAYER (1965).
PINKER, STEVEN, HOW THE MIND WORKS (1997).
POLKINGHORNE, JOHN, BEYOND SCIENCE: THE WIDER HUMAN CONTEXT (1996).
POLKINGHORNE, JOHN, THE FAITH OF A PHYSICIST (1994).
POPPER, KARL, REALISM AND THE AIM OF SCIENCE (1992).
PRICE, DON K., AMERICA'S UNWRITTEN CONSTITUTION: SCIENCE, RELIGION, AND POLITICAL RESPONSIBILITY (1983).
RAHNER, KARL, THEOLOGICAL INVESTIGATIONS: VOLUME III, THE THEOLOGY OF THE SPIRITUAL LIFE (1967).
RAWLS, JOHN, POLITICAL LIBERALISM (1993).
REED, RALPH, AFTER THE REVOLUTION: HOW THE CHRISTIAN COALITION IS IMPACTING AMERICA (1994).
REED, RALPH, POLITICALLY INCORRECT: THE EMERGING FAITH FACTOR IN AMERICAN POLITICS (1994).
ROBERTS, JON H., DARWINISM AND THE DIVINE IN AMERICA: PROTESTANT INTELLECTUALS AND ORGANIC EVOLUTION, 1859–1900 (1988).
ROSS, WILLIAM G., FORGING NEW FREEDOMS: NATIVISM, EDUCATION, AND THE CONSTITUTION, 1917–1927 (1994).
SANDEL, MICHAEL J., DEMOCRACY'S DISCONTENT: AMERICA IN SEARCH OF A PUBLIC PHILOSOPHY (1996).
SATINOVER, JEFFREY, CRACKING THE BIBLE CODE (1997).
SAWYER, ROBERT J., THE TERMINAL EXPERIMENT (1995).
SCHROEDER, GERALD L., GENESIS AND THE BIG BANG, THE DISCOVERY OF HARMONY BETWEEN MODERN SCIENCE AND THE BIBLE (1990).
SCHROEDER, GERALD L., THE SCIENCE OF GOD: THE CONVERGENCE OF SCIENTIFIC AND BIBLICAL WISDOM (1997).
SCOLNIC, SAMUEL, ECHOES FROM THE BIMAH (1988).
SINGER, PETER, ANIMAL LIBERATION (2d ed. 1990).
SMITH, STEVEN D., FOREORDAINED FAILURE: THE QUEST FOR A CONSTITUTIONAL PRINCIPLE OF RELIGIOUS FREEDOM (1995).
SNOW, C. P., THE TWO CULTURES: AND A SECOND LOOK (1963).

STAMM, J. J. & M. E. ANDREW, THE TEN COMMANDMENTS IN
RECENT RESEARCH (1967).
STERN, DAVID G., WITTGENSTEIN ON MIND AND LANGUAGE
(1995).
TODD, OLIVER, ALBERT CAMUS: A LIFE (1997).
TOUMEY, CHRISTOPHER P., GOD'S OWN SCIENTISTS: CREATION-
ISTS IN A SECULAR WORLD (1994).
TRIBE, LAURENCE H., ABORTION: THE CLASH OF ABSOLUTES
(1992).
TRIBE, LAURENCE H., AMERICAN CONSTITUTIONAL LAW (2d ed.
1988).
TURNER, JAMES, WITHOUT GOD, WITHOUT CREED: THE ORI-
GINS OF UNBELIEF IN AMERICA (1985).
VAN ALSTYNE, WILLIAM W., FIRST AMENDMENT: CASES AND
MATERIALS (2d ed. 1995).
WARREN, EARL, A REPUBLIC IF YOU CAN KEEP IT (1972).
WEBBER, DAVID J. (ed.), BIOTECHNOLOGY: ASSESSING SOCIAL
IMPACTS AND POLICY IMPLICATIONS (1990).
WEINBERG, STEVEN, DREAMS OF A FINAL THEORY (1992).
WERTHEIM, MARGARET, PYTHAGORAS' TROUSERS: GOD,
PHYSICS, AND THE GENDER WARS (1995).
WHITCOMB, JOHN C., JR., & HENRY M. MORRIS, THE GENESIS
FLOOD: THE BIBLICAL RECORD AND ITS SCIENTIFIC IMPLICA-
TIONS (1961).
WILLIAMS, BERNARD, ETHICS AND THE LIMITS OF PHILOSOPHY
(1985).
WILSON, EDWARD O., CONSILIENCE: THE UNITY OF KNOWL-
EDGE (1998).
WOOD, JAMES E., JR., & DEREK DAVIS (eds.), THE ROLE OF RELI-
GION IN THE MAKING OF PUBLIC POLICY (1991).

ARTICLES

Adams, Mark L., *Fear of Foreigners: Nativism and Workplace Language
Restrictions,* 74 OR. L. REV. 849 (1995).
Adler, Reid G., *Biotechnology as an Intellectual Property,* 224 SCIENCE
357 (1984).
Alexander, Lee, *An "Inclusivity" Church Opens in Greensboro,* GREENS-
BORO NEWS & RECORD (Aug. 9, 1997).

Allen, Elizabeth, et al., *Against "Sociobiology,"* THE SOCIOBIOLOGY DEBATE: READINGS ON ETHICAL AND SCIENTIFIC ISSUES 259 (Caplan, ed., 1978).

Amar, Akhil R., *The Bill of Rights as a Constitution,* 100 YALE L. J. 1131 (1991).

Andrews, Edmund L., *Religious Leaders Prepare to Fight Patents on Genes,* N.Y. TIMES (May 13, 1995).

Applebome, Peter, *Ruling May Open Doors to Parochial Vouchers,* PATRIOT LEDGER (June 26, 1997).

Bearden, Michelle, *Prescription for Prayer: Doctors Examine the Role of Faith in Healing,* TAMPA TRIBUNE (May 19, 1996).

Berger, Peter L., *Religion in a Revolutionary Society,* AMERICA'S CONTINUING REVOLUTION: AN ACT OF CONSERVATION (Kristol, ed., 1975).

Boehm, Frank H., *When Life Begins? There Are Many Answers,* THE TENNESSEAN (Sept. 2, 1997).

Bowman, Lee, *Does Prayer Aid Healing? Researchers Are Considering Scientific Study of Whether and How Spirituality in Patients Affects Their Chances of Recovery and Long Life,* PITTSBURGH POST-GAZETTE (July 29, 1996).

Bright, Cynthia, *The Establishment Clause and School Vouchers: Private Choice and Proposition 174,* 31 CAL. W. L. REV. 193 (1995).

Broadway, Bill, *In a Caring Congregation, Great Comfort for the Dying,* WASHINGTON POST (June 28, 1997).

Broadway, Bill, *Researchers Explore Healing's Spiritual Side: Study Challenges Common Ideas on the Power of Prayer,* WASHINGTON POST (Apr. 27, 1996).

Bronner, Ethan, *Wisconsin Court Upholds Vouchers in Church Schools,* N.Y. TIMES (June 11, 1998).

Burge, Gary, *Missing God at Church?* CHRISTIANITY TODAY (Oct. 6, 1997).

Cobin, David M., *Essay: Crèches, Christmas Trees, and Menorahs: Weeds Growing in Roger Williams' Garden,* 1990 WIS. L. REV. 1597 (1990).

Cole-Turner, Ronald, *Religion and Gene Patenting,* 270 SCIENCE 52 (1995).

Cookson, Peter W., *New Kid on the Block? A Close Look at America's Private Schools,* 15 BROOKINGS REVIEW 22 (1997).

Cronin, Mary Elizabeth, *Healing Hands—Therapeutic Touch Helps Re-*

duce Pain and Anxiety and Speeds Healing, SEATTLE TIMES (Jan. 1, 1997).

Cubert, Jeremy, U.S. Patent Policy and Biotechnology: Growing Pains on the Cutting Edge, 77 J. PAT. & TRADEMARK OFF. SOC'Y 151 (1995).

Dart, John, & Lee Romney, High Court's Ruling May Give Proposed Amendment a Boost, L.A. TIMES (June 28, 1997).

Dawson, Jim, Evolution Fight Has New Form, but Emotions Have Endured, MINNEAPOLIS STAR TRIBUNE (June 22, 1992).

Devins, Neal, Fundamentalist Christian Educators v. State: An Inevitable Compromise, 60 GEO. WASH. L. REV. 818 (1992).

Dewey, Douglas, Vouchers and Educational Freedom: A Debate, CATO INSTITUTE POLICY ANALYSIS No. 269 (Mar. 12, 1997).

Dossey, Larry, & Caren Goldman, Toxic Prayer, NEW AGE JOURNAL (Dec. 1997).

Dresser, Rebecca, Ethical and Legal Issues in Patenting New Animal Life, 28 JURIMETRICS J. 399 (1988).

Dreyfuss, Rochelle Cooper, & Dorothy Nelkin, The Jurisprudence of Genetics, 45 VAND. L. REV. 313 (1992).

Drinan, Robert F., S.J., Reflections on the Demise of the Religious Freedom Restoration Act, 86 GEO. L. J. 101 (1997).

Edel, Abraham, Attempts to Derive Definitive Moral Patterns from Biology, THE SOCIOBIOLOGY DEBATE: READINGS ON ETHICAL AND SCIENTIFIC ISSUES 111 (Caplan, ed., 1978).

Editorial, The "Christian Nation" Controversy, THE AMERICAN LAWYER (June 1989).

Eisenberg, Rebecca S., Genes, Patents, and Product Development, 257 SCIENCE 903 (1992).

Eisenberg, Rebecca S., Patenting The Human Genome, 39 EMORY L. J. 721 (1990).

Ely, John Hart, Legislative and Administrative Motivation in Constitutional Law, 79 YALE L. J. 1205 (1970).

Enda, Jodi, Clinton: No Cloning of Humans, but Experiments on Cells Are OK, DES MOINES REGISTER (June 10, 1997).

Flam, Faye, Therapeutic Touch Pinches Mainstream Doctors: They, Physicists Claim It's Fake, NEW ORLEANS TIMES-PICAYUNE (Jan. 26, 1997).

Fountain, Monica, Care for Body and Soul: Chaplains Play Larger Role in Patients' Well-Being, CHICAGO TRIBUNE (Nov. 27, 1994).

Frame, Randy, *Pope Says Evolution "More Than a Hypothesis,"* CHRISTIANITY TODAY (Dec. 9, 1996).

Freedberg, Louis, *80 Church Groups Ask for Ban on Gene Patents,* SAN FRANCISCO CHRONICLE (May 19, 1995).

Futterman, David, *School Choice and the Religion Clauses: The Law and Politics of Public Aid to Private Parochial Schools,* 81 GEO. L. J. 711 (1993).

Gibson, David, *Christian Group Criticizes Courts: Says They Usurp Democracy,* BERGEN RECORD (July 2, 1997).

Gilbert, Craig, *School Choice Wars,* WEEKLY STANDARD (Mar. 31, 1997).

Glanz, James, *Astronomers See a Cosmic Antigravity Force at Work,* 279 SCIENCE 1298 (1998).

Goldberg, Steven, *The Changing Face of Death: Computers, Consciousness, and Nancy Cruzan,* 43 STAN. L. REV. 659 (1991).

Goldberg, Steven, *The Constitutional Status of American Science,* 1979 U. ILL. L. FOR. 1 (1979).

Goldberg, Steven, *Gene Patents and the Death of Dualism,* 5 S. CAL. INTERDISC. L. J. 25 (1996).

Gould, Stephen Jay, *Impeaching a Self-Appointed Judge,* SCIENTIFIC AMERICAN (July 1992).

Green, Stephen, *Case for Halt to Patenting Human Genes Spelled Out,* SAN DIEGO UNION-TRIBUNE (May 19, 1995).

Greenhouse, Linda, *Laws Are Urged to Protect Religion,* N.Y. TIMES (July 15, 1997).

Hall, Carl T., *Theologians Split over Gene Rights,* SAN FRANCISCO CHRONICLE (May 20, 1995).

Hanson, Mark J., *Religious Voices in Biotechnology: The Case of Gene Patenting,* HASTINGS CENTER REPORT (Nov.–Dec. 1997).

Heise, Michael, *Public Funds, Private Schools, and the Court: Legal Issues and Policy Consequences,* 25 TEX. TECH. L. REV. 137 (1993).

Hendrick, Bill, *Duke University Researchers Say Studies Confirm the Effectiveness of Unorthodox Treatments Such as Prayer and Therapeutic Touch,* ATLANTA JOURNAL AND CONSTITUTION (Nov. 18, 1995).

Herald, Kim, *Prayer as Good Medicine: Although Skeptics Abound, Some Doctors and Researchers Say Spirituality Is Good for Your Health,* ORLANDO SENTINEL (Aug. 14, 1996).

Herbert, Wray, Jeffery L. Sheler, & Traci Watson, *The World after Cloning*, U.S. NEWS & WORLD REPORT (Mar. 10, 1997).

Hettinger, Ned, *Patenting Life: Biotechnology, Intellectual Property, and Environmental Ethics*, 22 B.C. ENVTL. AFF. L. REV. 267 (1995).

Hing, Bill Ong, *Beyond the Rhetoric of Assimilation and Cultural Pluralism: Addressing the Tension of Separatism and Conflict in an Immigration-Driven Multiracial Society*, 81 CALIF. L. REV. 863 (1993).

Holmer, Paul L., *Evolution and Being Faithful*, 84 CHRISTIAN CENTURY 1491 (1967).

Horgan, John, *Can Science Explain Consciousness*, SCIENTIFIC AMERICAN (July 1994).

Hotz, Robert Lee, *Response to Religion May Lie in Brain Makeup, Study Says*, AUSTIN AMERICAN-STATESMAN (Oct. 29, 1997).

Jones, Steve, *The Set within the Skull*, N.Y. REV. BOOKS (Nov. 6, 1997).

Karjala, Dennis S., *A Legal Research Agenda for the Human Genome Initiative*, 32 JURIMETRICS J. 121 (1992).

Kass, Leon R., *The Wisdom of Repugnance*, THE NEW REPUBLIC (June 2, 1997).

Kelly, Kevin, *The Elimination of Process: Will the Biotechnology Patent Protection Act Revive Process Patents?* 24 J. MARSHALL L. REV. 263 (1990).

Klein, Jeffrey, *Editor's Note: Stepping on Sacred Ground*, MOTHER JONES (Dec. 1997).

Kloehn, Steve, & Paul Salopek, *Humanity Still at Heart, Soul of Cloning Issue: Scientists and Theologians Agree We Are Our Own Person*, CHICAGO TRIBUNE (Mar. 2, 1997).

Kloehn, Steve, & Paul Salopek, *A Matter of Identity: Most Maintain Clone Would Be Its Own Person*, DALLAS MORNING NEWS (Mar. 9, 1997).

Kolata, Gina, *With Cloning of a Sheep, the Ethical Ground Shifts*, N.Y. TIMES (Feb. 24, 1997).

Kurland, Philip B., *Commentary: The Religion Clauses and the Burger Court*, 34 CATH. U. L. REV. 1 (1984).

Larson, Erik, *Darwinian Struggle: Instead of Evolution, a Textbook Proposes "Intelligent Design,"* WALL ST. JOURNAL (Nov. 14, 1994).

Lauroesch, Mark W., *Note: Genetic Engineering: Innovation and Risk Minimization*, 57 GEO. WASH. L. REV. 100 (1988).

Lupu, Ira C., *Home Education, Religious Liberty, and the Separation of Powers*, 67 B.U. L. REV. 971 (1987).

MacMullan, Jack, *The Constitutionality of State Home Schooling Statutes,* 29 VILL. L. REV. 1309 (1994).

MacMullan, Jack, *Increase in Home Schooling Opens Market for Materials,* TULSA WORLD (Aug. 30, 1996).

Marty, Martin E., *Where Do You Draw the Line? Negotiating with Modernity,* 114 CHRISTIAN CENTURY 38 (1997).

Mattern, Ruth, *Altruism, Ethics, and Sociobiology,* THE SOCIOBIOLOGY DEBATE: READINGS ON ETHICAL AND SCIENTIFIC ISSUES 462 (Caplan, ed., 1978).

McConnell, Michael W., *Free Exercise Revisionism and the Smith Decision,* 57 U. CHI. L. REV. 1109 (1990).

McGraw, Carol, and Susan Kelleher, *Can Cloning Also Give Life to a Soul? Religious Leaders and Scientists Wrestle with the Moral Issues Raised by the Technology,* ORANGE COUNTY REGISTER (Feb. 25, 1997).

McKay, Daniel L., *Comment: Patent Law and Human Genome Research at the Crossroads: The Need for Congressional Action,* 10 COMPUTER & HIGH TECH. L. J. 465 (1994).

Merges, Robert Patrick, *Intellectual Property in Higher Life Forms: The Patent System and Controversial Technologies,* 47 MD. L. REV. 1051 (1988).

Michalos, Alex C., *Philosophy of Science: Historical, Social, and Value Aspects,* A GUIDE TO THE CULTURE OF SCIENCE, TECHNOLOGY, AND MEDICINE 197 (Durbin, ed., 1980).

Miller, Susan Katz, *Activists Join Forces against Animal Patents,* 137 NEW SCIENTIST 8 (1993).

Nasstrom, Eric, *School Vouchers in Minnesota: Confronting the Walls Separating Church and State,* 22 WM. MITCHELL L. REV. 1065 (1997).

Nelson, J. Robert, *What Is Life?* 4 CHRISTIAN SOCIAL ACTION 4 (Jan. 1991).

Neuhaus, Richard John, *Who Needs God,* NAT'L REV. (Nov. 10, 1989).

Niebuhr, Gustav, *Clinton Talks about Religion as His Anchor,* N.Y. TIMES (Oct. 4, 1994).

Noonan, John T., Jr., *The End of Free Exercise?* 42 DEPAUL L. REV. 567 (1992).

Noonan, John T., Jr., *The Language of Judging: The Relation of Words to Power,* 70 ST. JOHN'S L. REV. 13 (1996).

Novak, Michael, *Think Tank: Is America Becoming Anti-Religious?* Television Broadcast (May 20, 1994).

O'Connor, Sean, *The Supreme Court's Philosophy of Science: Will the Real Karl Popper Please Stand Up?* 35 JURIMETRICS J. 263 (1995).

Odenhiemer, Micha, *False Positive: There's a Price to Be Paid for Wanting to Be Proven Right,* JERUSALEM REPORT (Oct. 16, 1997).

Paulsen, Michael Stokes, *A Funny Thing Happened on the Way to the Limited Public Forum: Unconstitutional Conditions on "Equal Access" for Religious Speakers and Groups,* 29 U.C. DAVIS L. REV. 653 (1996).

Previn, Matthew P., *Assisted Suicide and Religion: Conflicting Conceptions of the Sanctity of Human Life,* 84 GEO. L. J. 589 (1996).

Radforce, Tim, *Newsbites,* THE GUARDIAN [London] (May 25, 1995).

Randall, E. Vance, *Private Schools and State Regulation,* 24 URBAN LAWYER 341 (1992).

Raspberry, William, *Spirituality: A Force for the Public Good,* WASHINGTON POST (Oct. 27, 1997).

Rhein, Reginald, *Gene Patent Crusade Moving from Church to Court,* BIOTECHNOLOGY NEWSWATCH (June 5, 1995).

Rice, Patricia, *Court Decision Concerns Some St. Louis Church Officials,* ST. LOUIS POST-DISPATCH (June 26, 1997).

Robertson, John A., *Liberty, Identity and Human Cloning,* 76 TEXAS L. REV. 1371 (1998).

Robertson, John A., *The Scientists' Right to Research: A Constitutional Analysis,* 51 S. CAL. L. REV. 1203 (1978).

Sacks, Oliver, *Neurology and the Soul,* N.Y. REV. BOOKS (Nov. 22, 1990).

Sander, William, & Anthony C. Krautmann, *Catholic Schools, Dropout Rates, and Educational Attainment,* 33 ECON. INQ. 217 (1995).

Scanlon, Leslie, *Cloning Technology Spawns Moral Dilemma, Words of Caution,* LOUISVILLE COURIER-JOURNAL (Apr. 7, 1997).

Searle, John R., *Consciousness and the Philosophers,* N.Y. REV. BOOKS (Mar. 6, 1997).

Shokraii, Nina H., & Dorothy B. Hanks, *School Choice Programs 1997: What's Happening in the States,* HERITAGE FOUNDATION REPORTS iii (July 1997).

Smith, George P., II, *Pathways to Immortality in the New Millennium: Human Responsibility, Theological Direction, or Legal Mandate,* 15 ST. LOUIS U. PUB. L. REV. 447 (1996).

Smolin, David M., *Essay: The Jurisprudence of Privacy in a Splintered Supreme Court,* 75 MARQ. L. REV. 975 (1992).

Steinfels, Peter, *Clinton Signs Law Protecting Religious Practices*, N.Y. TIMES (Nov. 17, 1993).

Sterman, Baruch, *Science and Theology*, JERUSALEM POST (Aug. 1, 1996).

Stick, Michael J., *Educational Vouchers: A Constitutional Analysis*, 28 COLUM. J. L. & SOC. PROBS. 423 (1995).

Tessman, Irwin, & Jack Tessman, *Mind and Body*, 276 SCIENCE 369 (1997).

Thaler, Stephen L., *Death of a Gedanken Creature*, 13 JOURNAL OF NEAR-DEATH STUDIES 149 (1995).

Thomas, Gary, *Doctors Who Pray: How the Medical Community Is Discovering the Power of Prayer*, CHRISTIANITY TODAY (Jan. 6. 1997).

Thompson, Ginger, *Prescription for Prayer*, BALTIMORE SUN (Feb. 13, 1997).

Tushnet, Mark, *The Rhetoric of Free Exercise Discourse*, 1993 B.Y.U. L. REV. 117 (1993).

United Methodist Church Genetic Science Task Force, *Draft Report to Annual and Central Conferences*, 4 CHRISTIAN SOCIAL ACTION 17 (Jan. 1991).

Wallis, Claudia, *Faith and Healing: Can Prayer, Faith, and Spirituality Really Improve Your Physical Health? A Growing and Surprising Body of Scientific Evidence Says They Can*, TIME (June 24, 1996).

Weiss, Rick, *New Lines of Research: Scientists Take a Look at Unorthodox Healing Arts*, WASHINGTON POST (Nov. 9, 1993).

Weiss, Rick, *What Is Patently Offensive? Policy on "Immoral" Inventions Troubles Legal, Medical Professionals*, WASHINGTON POST (May 11, 1998).

Wexler, Jay D., *Of Pandas, People, and the First Amendment: The Constitutionality of Teaching Intelligent Design in the Public Schools*, 49 STAN. L. REV. 439 (1997).

Wiegele, Thomas C., *Organized Religion and Biotechnology: Social Responsibility and the Role of Government*, BIOTECHNOLOGY: ASSESSING SOCIAL IMPACTS AND POLICY IMPLICATIONS 17 (Webber, ed., 1990).

Wilford, John Noble, *Wary Astronomers Ponder an Accelerating Universe*, N.Y. TIMES (Mar. 3, 1998).

Will, George F., *The Court and Prayer in Nebraska*, WASHINGTON POST (July 12, 1983).

Wilson, Edward O., *For Sociobiology*, THE SOCIOBIOLOGY DEBATE:

READINGS ON ETHICAL AND SCIENTIFIC ISSUES 267 (Caplan, ed., 1978).

Winston, Diane, *Hands-On Healing: Mainline Protestants Are Discovering Powerful New Spiritual Tool,* DALLAS MORNING NEWS (Mar. 1, 1997).

Wise, Daniel, *Parochial School Teaching May Be Paid by Federal Funds,* N.Y. L. J. (June 24, 1997).

Wong, Mai-lan E., *The Implications of School Choice for Children with Disabilities,* 103 YALE L. J. 827 (1993).

Woodhouse, Barbara Bennett, *"Who Owns the Child?": Meyer and Pierce and the Child as Property,* 33 WM & MARY L. REV. 995 (1992).

Woodward, Kenneth L., *Is God Listening?* NEWSWEEK (Mar. 31, 1997).

Yam, Philip, *As They Lay Dying,* SCIENTIFIC AMERICAN (May 1995).

CASES

Abington School District v. Schempp, 374 U.S. 203 (1963).

Agostini v. Felton, 117 S. Ct. 1997 (1997).

Allegheny County v. Greater Pittsburgh ACLU, 492 U.S. 573 (1989).

Allgeyer v. Louisiana, 165 U.S. 578 (1897).

American Civil Liberties Union v. Birmingham, 791 F. 2d 1581 (6th Cir. 1986).

American Civil Liberties Union v. Black Horse Pike Regional Board of Education, 84 F. 3d 1471 (3d Cir. 1996).

American Jewish Congress v. City of Chicago, 827 F. 2d 120 (7th Cir. 1987).

Americans United for Separation of Church and State v. County of Kent, 97 Mich. App. 72 (Ct. of Appeals of Michigan) (1980).

Barron v. Baltimore, 32 U.S. (7 Pet.) 243 (1833).

Bartels v. State of Iowa, 262 U.S. 404 (1923).

Board of Education v. Allen, 392 U.S. 236 (1968).

Boerne v. Flores, 117 S. Ct. 2157 (1997).

Braunfeld v. Brown, 366 U.S. 599 (1961).

Cammack v. Waihee, 932 F. 2d 765 (9th Cir. 1991).

Cantwell v. Connecticut, 310 U.S. 296 (1940).

Capitol Square Review and Advisory Board v. Pinette, 115 S. Ct. 2440 (1995).

Church of the Holy Trinity v. United States, 143 U.S. 457 (1892).

Church of the Lukumi Babalu Aye, Inc., v. City of Hialeah, 113 S. Ct. 2217 (1993).

Commonwealth v. Cooke, 7 Am. L. Reg. 417 (Police Court, Boston, Mass. 1859).

County of Allegheny v. American Civil Liberties Union, 492 U.S. 573 (1989).

Diamond v. Chakrabarty, 447 U.S. 303 (1980).

Dred Scott v. Sandford, 60 U.S. (19 How.) 393 (1857).

Edwards v. Aguillard, 482 U.S. 578 (1987).

Employment Division v. Smith, 494 U.S. 872 (1990).

Engel v. Vitale, 370 U.S. 421 (1962).

Epperson v. Arkansas, 393 U.S. 97 (1968).

Everson v. Board of Education, 330 U.S. 1 (1947).

Frazee v. Illinois Department of Employment Security, 489 U.S. 829 (1989).

Freedom from Religion Foundation v. Thompson, 920 F. Supp. 969 (W.D. Wis. 1996).

Funk Bros. Seed Co. v. Kalo Inoculant Co., 333 U.S. 127 (1948).

Gallagher v. Crown Kosher Super Market, Inc., 366 U.S. 617 (1961).

Gillette v. United States, 401 U.S. 437 (1971).

Goldman v. Weinberger, 475 U.S. 503 (1986).

Granzeier v. Middleton, 955 F. Supp. 741 (E.D. Ky. 1997).

Grasetti v. Weinberger, 408 F. Supp. 142 (N.D. Cal. 1976).

Griswold Inn v. Connecticut, 441 A. 2d 16 (Sup. Ct. of Conn. 1981).

Harris v. McRae, 448 U.S. 297 (1980).

Healy v. James, 408 U.S. 169 (1972).

Hennington v. Georgia, 163 U.S. 299 (1896).

Hobbie v. Unemployment Appeals Commission of Florida, 480 U.S. 136 (1987).

Ingebretsen v. Jackson Public School District, 88 F. 3d 274 (5th Cir. 1996).

Katcoff v. Marsh, 755 F. 2d 223 (2d Cir. 1985).

Kewanee Oil Co. v. Bicron Corp., 416 U.S. 470 (1974).

Koenick v. Felton, 973 F. Supp. 522 (D. Md. 1997).

Lamb's Chapel v. Center Moriches Union Free School District, 113 S. Ct. 2141 (1993).

Lee v. Weisman, 505 U.S. 577 (1992).

Lemon v. Kurtzman, 403 U.S. 602 (1971).

Lochner v. New York, 198 U.S. 45 (1905).

Lynch v. Donnelly, 465 U.S. 668 (1984).

Marbury v. Madison, 1 Cranch (5 U.S.) 137 (1803).

McDaniel v. Paty, 435 U.S. 618 (1978)

McGowan v. Maryland, 366 U.S. 420 (1961).

McLean v. Arkansas Board of Education, 529 F. Supp. 1255 (E.D. Ark. 1982).

Metzl v. Leininger, 57 F. 3d 618 (7th Cir. 1995).

Meyer v. Nebraska, 262 U.S. 390 (1923).

Miller v. California, 413 U.S. 15 (1973).

Mozert v. Hawkins County Board of Education, 827 F. 2d 1058 (6th Cir. 1987).

Murray v. Curlett, 374 U.S. 203 (1963).

New York Times Co. v. Sullivan, 376 U.S. 254 (1964).

Parke-Davis & Co. v. H. K. Mullford & Co., 189 F. 95 103 (S.D.N.Y. 1911).

Petit v. Minnesota, 177 U.S. 164 (1900).

Pierce v. Society of Sisters, 268 U.S. 510 (1925).

Reynolds v. United States, 98 U.S. 145 (1879).

Roe v. Wade, 410 U.S. 113 (1973).

Rosenberger v. Rector, 115 S. Ct. 2510 (1995).

School District of Abington Township v. Schempp, 374 U.S. 203 (1963).

Sherbet v. Verner, 374 U.S. 398 (1963).

Soon Hing v. Crowley, 113 U.S. 703 (1885).

Specht v. Commonwealth, 8 Pa. St. (Barr) 312 (1848).

State v. Cantwell, 8 A. 2d 533 (Conn. 1939).

Stone v. Graham, 449 U.S. 39 (1980).

Texas v. Johnson, 491 U.S. 397 (1989).

Thomas v. Review Board, 450 U.S. 707 (1981).

Tilghman v. Proctor, 102 U.S. 707 (1880)

Two Guys from Harrison-Allentown, Inc., v. McGinley, 366 U.S. 582 (1961).

United States v. Ballard, 322 U.S. 78 (1944).

United States v. Lee, 455 U.S. 252 (1982).

United States v. Progressive, Inc., 467 F. Supp. 990 (W.D. Wisc. 1979), 610 F. 2d 819 (7th Cir. 1979).

Vacco v. Quill, 117 S. Ct. 2293 (1997).

Wallace v. Jaffree, 472 U.S. 38 (1985).

Washington v. Glucksberg, 117 S. Ct. 2258 (1997).

West Coast Hotel Co. v. Parrish, 300 U.S. 379 (1937).

Widmar v. Vincent, 454 U.S. 263 (1981).

Wisconsin v. Yoder, 406 U.S. 205 (1972).
Wolman v. Walter, 433 U.S. 229 (1977).
Zinermon v. Burch, 494 U.S. 113 (1990).
Zobrest v. Catalina Foothills School District, 509 U.S. 1 (1993).
Zorach v. Clauson, 343 U.S. 306 (1952).

Index

About the Author

Steven Goldberg was born in Washington, D.C., and grew up in the nearby Maryland suburbs. After graduation from Harvard College and Yale Law School, he served as a law clerk to Justice William J. Brennan, Jr., on the U.S. Supreme Court. Goldberg then worked as an attorney with the U.S. Nuclear Regulatory Commission before joining the faculty of the Georgetown University Law Center.

At Georgetown, Professor Goldberg has taught and published extensively in the area of law, science, and values. He is the author of *Culture Clash: Law and Science in America*, winner of the Alpha Sigma Nu Book Award, and is coauthor of the widely used text *Law, Science, and Medicine*. Professor Goldberg and his wife Miriam live in Chevy Chase, Maryland. They have two children, Joseph and Rebecca.